Indiscreet Letters From Peking

The Tartar Wall, Peking

Indiscreet Letters From Peking
Letters Written by One of the Besieged From the Boxer Uprising to the Sack of the City

Bertram Lenox Putnam Weale

Indiscreet Letters From Peking
*Letters Written by One of the Besieged
From the Boxer Uprising to the Sack of the City*

by Bertram Lenox Putnam Weale

First published under the title
Indiscreet Letters From Peking

Leonaur is an imprint
of Oakpast Ltd

Copyright in this form © 2010 Oakpast Ltd

ISBN: 978-0-85706-320-5 (hardcover)
ISBN: 978-0-85706-319-9 (softcover)

http://www.leonaur.com

Publisher's Notes

The opinions of the authors represent a view of events in which he was a participant related from his own perspective, as such the text is relevant as an historical document.

The views expressed in this book are not necessarily those of the publisher.

Contents

Foreword	7

PART 1—THE WARNING

Fragments	11
Mutterings	15
Overcast Skies	18
Our Guards Arrive	22
The Plot Thickens	25
The Licking Flames Approach	29
The City of Peking and All Its Glories	33
Some Incidents and the One Man	39
The Coming of the Boxers	44
Barricades and Reliefs	52
Some Men and Things	59
Hell Hounds	62
A Few Crumbs	66
The Ultimatum	69
The Debacle Begins	74

PART 2—THE SIEGE

Chaos	83
The Retreat and the Return	91
Fires and Food	103
The Bonds Tighten	109
The Mysterious Board of Truce	116
Shells and Sorties	121
The Hospital and the Graveyard	132
The Failure	135
An Interlude	140
The Guns	143
Sniping	146
The Gallant French	153

The British Legation Base	157
The Ever-Growing Casualty List	161
The Armistice	166
The Resumption of a Semi-Diplomatic Life	171
Diplomacy Continues	176
The Unrest Grows and Diplomacy Continues	178
The First Real News	181
The Third Phase Continues	183
More Diplomacy	185
The World Beyond Our Bricks	187
Trifles	189
Diplomatic Confidences	193
The Plot Again Thickens	196
More Messengers	199
The Attacks Resumed	201
The Thirteenth	204
The Night of the Thirteenth	206
How I Saw the Relief	210

PART 3—THE SACK

The Palace	225
The Sack	239
The Sack Continues	258
Chaos	269
Settling Down	272
The Forbidden Fruit	274
The Few Remains	288
The Palsy Remains	298
Drifting	304
Picking Up Threads	307
The Impossible	310
Suspense	314
Still Drifting	316
Punitive Expeditions	318
The Climax	320
The End	322

Foreword

The publication of these letters, dealing with the startling events which took place in Peking during the summer and autumn of 1900, at this late date may be justified on a number of counts. In the first place, there can be but little doubt that an exact narrative from the pen of an eye-witness who saw everything, and knew exactly what was going on from day to day, and even from hour to hour, in the diplomatic world of the Chinese capital during the deplorable times when the dread Boxer movement overcast everything so much that even in England the South African War was temporarily forgotten, is of intense human interest, showing most clearly as it does, perhaps for the first time in realistic fashion, the extraordinary *bouleversement* which overcame everyone; the unpreparedness and the panic when there was really ample warning; the rivalry of the warring Legations even when they were almost *in extremis*, and the curious course of the whole siege itself owing to the division of counsels among the Chinese—this last a state of affairs which alone saved everyone from a shameful death.

In the second place, this account may dispel many false ideas which still obtain in Europe and America regarding the position of various Powers in China—ideas based on data which have long been declared of no value by those competent to judge. In the third place, the vivid and terrible description of the sack of Peking by the soldiery of Europe, showing the demoralisation into which all troops fall as soon as the iron hand of discipline is relaxed, may set finally at rest the mutual recriminations which have since been levelled publicly and privately. Everybody was tarred with the same brush.

Those armchair critics who have been too prone to state that brutalities no longer mark the course of war may reconsider their words, and remember that sacking, with all the accompanying excesses, is still regarded as the divine right of soldiery unless the provost-marshal's gallows stand ready. In the fourth place, those who still believe that the representatives assigned to Eastern countries need only be second-rate men—reserving for Europe the master-minds—may begin to ask themselves seriously whether the time has not come when only the most capable and brilliant diplomatic officials—men whose intelligence will help to shape events and not be led by them, and who will act with iron firmness when the time for such action comes—should be assigned to such a difficult post as Peking.

In the fifth place, the strange idea, which refuses to be eradicated, that the Chinese showed themselves in this Peking siege once and for all incompetent to carry to fruition any military plan, may be somewhat corrected by the plain and convincing terms in which the eye-witness describes the manner in which they stayed their hand whenever it could have slain, and the silent struggle which the Moderates of Chinese politics must have waged to avert the catastrophe by merely gaining time and allowing the Desperates to dash themselves to pieces when the inevitable swing of the pendulum took place. Finally, it will not escape notice that many remarks borne out all through the narrative tend to show that British diplomacy in the Far East was at one time at a low ebb.

Of course the Peking siege has already been amply described in many volumes and much magazine literature. Dr. Morrison, the famous Peking correspondent of the *Times*, informs me that he has in his library no less than forty-three accounts in English alone. The majority of these, however, are not as complete or enlightening as they might be; nor has the extraordinarily dramatic nature of the Warning, the Siege, and the Sack been shown. Thus few people, outside of a small circle in the Far East, have been able to understand from such accounts what actually occurred in Peking, or to realise the nature of the fighting which took place.

The two best accounts, Dr. Morrison's own statement and the French Minister's graphic report to his government, were both written rather to fix the principal events immediately after they had occurred than to attempt to probe beneath the surface, or to deal with the strictly personal or private side. Nor did they embrace that most remarkable portion of the Boxer year, the entire sack of Peking and the extraordinary scenes which marked this latter-day Vandalism. A veil has been habitually drawn over these little-known events, but in the narrative which follows it is boldly lifted for the first time.

The eye-witness whose account follows was careful to establish with as much lucidity as possible each phase of existence during five months of extraordinary interest. Much in these notes has had to be suppressed for many reasons, and much that remains may create some astonishment. Yet it is well to remember that "one eye-witness, however dull and prejudiced, is worth a wilderness of sentimental historians." The historians are already beginning to arise; these pages may serve as a corrective to many erroneous ideas.

Perhaps some also will allow that this curious tragedy, swept into Peking and playing madly round the entrenched European Legations, has intense human interest still. The vague terror which oppressed everyone before the storm actually burst; the manner in which the feeble chain of fighting men were locked round the European lines, and suffered grievously but were providentially saved from annihilation; the curious way in which diplomacy made itself felt from time to time only to disappear as the rude shock of events taking place near Tientsin and the sea were reflected in Peking; the final coming of the strange relief—all these points and many others are made in such a manner that everyone should be able to understand and to believe. The description of the last act of the upheaval—the complete sack of Peking—shows clearly how the lust for loot gains all men, and hand in hand invites such terrible things as wholesale rape and murder.

The eye-witness attempts to account for all that happened; to make real and living the hoarse roll of musketry, the savage cries of *desperadoes* stripped to the waist and glistening in their sweat; to give echo to the blood-curdling notes of Chinese trumpets; to limn the tall mountains of flames licking sky high. If there is failure in these efforts, it is due to the editing.

The summer of 1900 in Peking will ever remain as famous in the annals of the world's history as the Indian Mutiny; it was something unique and unparalleled. With the curious movements now at work in the Far East, it may not be unwise to study the story again. And after Port Arthur these pages may show something about which little has been written—the psychology of the siege. The siege is still the rudest test in the world. It is well to know it.

B. L. Putnam Weale.

China, June, 1906.

Part 1—The Warning

1

Fragments

12th May, 1900.

The weather is becoming hot, even here in latitude 40 and in the month of May. The Peking dust, distinguished among all the dusts of the earth for its blackness, its disagreeable insistence in sticking to one's clothes, one's hair, one's very eyebrows, until a grey-brown coating its visible to every eye, is rising in heavier clouds than ever. In the market-places, and near the great gates of the city, where Peking carts and camels from beyond the passes—*k'ou wai*, to use the correct vernacular—jostle one another, the dust has become damnable beyond words, and there can be no health possibly in us.

The Peking dust rises, therefore, in clouds and obscures the very sun at times; for the sun always shines here in our Northern China, except during a brief summer rainy season, and a few other days you can count on your fingers. The dust is without significance, you will say, since it is always there more or less. It is in any case—healthy; it chokes you, but is reputed also to choke germs; therefore it is good. All of which is true, only this year there is more of it than ever, meaning very dry weather indeed for this city, hanging near the gates of Mongolian deserts—a dry weather spelling the devil for the Northern farmer.

Meanwhile, is there anything special for me to chronicle? Not much, although there is a cloud no bigger than your hand in Shantung not a thousand miles from Weihaiwei, and the German Legation is consequently somewhat irate. It was noticed at our club, for instance, which, by the way, is a humble affair, that the German military *attaché*, a gentleman who wears bracelets, is somewhat effeminate, and plays vile tennis and worse billiards, had a "hostile attitude" towards the British Legation—that is, such of the British Legation as gather together each day at the "ice-shed"—which happens to be the club's peculiar Chinese name.

The military *attaché* is somewhat irate, because the spectacle of the Weihaiwei regiment, six hundred yellow men under twelve white Englishmen, chasing malcontents in Shantung, is derogatory to Teutonic aspirations. Germany has earmarked Shantung, and it is just like English bluntness to remind the would-be dominant Power that there is a British sphere and a British colony in the Chinese province, as well as a German sphere and a German colony. But the German Minister, a *beau garçon* with blue eyes and a handsome moustache, says nothing, and is quite calm.

Meanwhile the cloud no bigger than your hand is quite unremarked by the rank and file of Legation Street—that I will swear. Chinese malcontents—"the Society of Harmonious Fists," particular habitat Shantung province—are casually mentioned; but it is remembered that the provincial governor of Shantung is a strong Chinaman, one Yuan Shih-kai, who has some knowledge of military matters, and, better still, ten thousand foreign-drilled troops. Shantung is all right, never fear—such is the comment of the day.

But the political situation—the *situation politique* as we call it in our several conversations, which always have a diplomatic turn—although not grave, is unhappy; everybody at least acknowledges that. Peking has never been what it was before the Japanese war. In the old days we were all something of a happy family. There were merely the eleven Legations, the Inspectorate of Chinese Customs, with the aged Sir R—— H—— at its head, and perhaps a few favoured globe-trotters or nondescripts looking for rich concessions. Picnics and dinners, races and excursions, were the order of the day, and politics and political situations were not burning. Ministers plenipotentiary and envoys extraordinary wore Terai hats, very old clothes, and had an affable air—something like what Teheran must still be.

Then came the Japanese war, and the eternal political situation. Russia started the ball rolling and the others kicked it along. The Russo-Chinese Bank, appeared on the scenes led by the great P——, a man with an ominous black portfolio continually under his arm, as he hurried along Legation Street, and an intriguing expression always on his dark face—a veritable master of men and moneys, they say. This intriguing soon found Expression in the Cassini Convention, denounced as untrue, and followed by a perfectly open and frank Manchurian railway convention, a convention which, in spite of its frankness, had future trouble written unmistakably on the face of it. Besides these things there were always ominous reports of other things—of great things being done secretly.

After the Russo-Chinese Bank and the Manchurian railway business, there was the Kiaochow affair, then the Port Arthur affair, the Weihaiwei and Kwangchowwan affairs, nothing but "affairs" all tending in the same direction—the making of a very grave political situation. The juniors today make fun of it, it is true, and greet each other daily with the salutation, "*La situation politique est très grave*," and laugh at the good words. But it is grave notwithstanding the laughter.

Once in 1899, after the Empress Dowager's *coup d'état* and the virtual imprisonment of the Emperor, Legation Guards had to be sent for, a few files for each of the Legations that possess squadrons in the Far East, and, what is more, these guards had to stay for a good many months. The guards are now no more, but it is curious that the men they came mainly to protect us against—Tung Fu-hsiang's Mohammedan braves from the savage back province of Kansu who love the reactionary Empress Dowager—are still encamped near the Northern capital.

The old Peking society has therefore vanished, and in its place are highly suspicious and hostile Legations—Legations petty in their conceptions of men and things—Legations bitterly disliking one another—in fact, Legations richly deserving all they get, some of the cynics say.

The Peking air, as I have already said, is highly electrical and unpleasant in these hot spring days with the dust rising in heavy clouds. Squabbling and cantankerous, rather absurd and petty, the Legations are spinning their little threads, each one hedged in by high walls in its own compound and by the debatable question of the *situation politique*.

Outside and around us roars the noise of the Tartar city. At night the noise ceases, for the inner and outer cities are closed to one another by great gates; but at midnight the gates are opened by sleepy Manchu guards for a brief ten minutes, so that gorgeous red and blue-trapped carts, drawn by sleek mules, may speed into the Imperial City for the Daybreak Audience with the Throne. These conveyances contain the high officials of the Empire.

It has been noticed by a Legation stroller on the Wall—the Tartar Wall—that the number of carts passing in at midnight is far greater than usual; that the guards of the city gates now and again stop and question a driver. It is nothing.

Meanwhile the dust rises in clouds. It is very dry this year—that is all.

2

Mutterings

24th May, 1900.

We are beginning to call them Boxers—grudgingly and sometimes harking back and giving them their full name, "Society of Harmonious Fists," or the "Righteous Harmony Fist Society"; but still a beginning has been made, and they are becoming Boxers by the inevitable process of shortening which distinguishes speech.

We have been talking about them a good deal today, these Boxers, since it has been the birthday of her most excellent Majesty Queen Victoria, and the British Legation has been *en fête*. Her Majesty's Minister, in fine, has been entertaining us in the vast and princely gardens of the British Legation at his own expense. Weird Chinese lanterns have been lighted in the evening and slung around the grounds; champagne has been flowing with what effervescence it could muster; the eleven Legations and the nondescripts have forgotten their cares for a brief space and have been enjoying the evening air and the music of Sir R—— H——'s Chinese band.

Looking at lighted lanterns, drinking champagne cup, listening to a Chinese band—where the devil is the protocol and the political situation, you will say? Not quite forgotten, since the French Minister attracted the attention of many all the evening by his vehement manner. I pushed up once, too, and with a polite bow listened to what he was saying. Ah, the old words, the eternal words, the political situation, or the *situation politique*, whichever way you like to use them. But still you listen a bit, for it is droll to hear the yet unaccustomed word Boxers in French. "*Les Boxeurs*," he says; and what the French Minister says is always worth listening to, since he has the best Intelligence corps in the world—the Catholic priests of China—at his disposal.

Curiously enough, he was speaking of the arch-priest of priests, renowned above all others in this Peking world, Monseigneur F——, Vicar Apostolic of the Manchu capital—almost Vicar of God to countless thousands of dark-yellow converts. It is Monseigneur F——'s letter of the 19th May, written but five days ago, and already locally famous through leakage, which was the subject-matter of his impromptu oration. Monseigneur F—— wrote and demanded a guard of marines for his cathedral, his people and his chattels—*quarante ou cinquante marins pour protéger nos personnes et nos biens*, were his exact words, and his request has been cruelly refused by the Council of Ministers on the ground that it is absurd. The Vicar Apostolic, however, gave his grounds for making such a demand calmly and logically—depicted the damage already done by an anti-foreign and revolutionary movement in the districts not a thousand miles from Peking, and solemnly forecasted what was soon to happen....

The French Minister was irate and raised his fat hands above his fat person, took a discreet look around him, and then hinted that it was this Legation, the British Legation, which stopped the marines from coming.

The French Minister was quite irate, and after his discourse was ended he slipped quietly away—possibly to send some more telegrams. The crumbs of his conversation were soon gathered up and distributed and the conviviality somewhat damped. As yet, however, the Boxers are only laughed at and are not taken quite seriously. They have killed native Christians, it is true, and it has been proved conclusively now that it was they who murdered Brooks, the English missionary in Shantung. But Englishmen are cheap, since there is a glut in the home market, and their government merely gets angry with them when they get into trouble and are killed. So many are always getting killed in China.

So the Boxers, with half the governments of Europe, led by England, as we know by our telegrams, seeking to minimise their importance—in fact, trying to stifle the movement by ignoring it or lavishing on it their supreme contempt—have already moved from their particular habitat, which is Shantung, into the metropolitan province of Chihli. Already they are in some force at Chochou, only seventy miles to the southeast of Peking—always massacring, always advancing, and driving in bodies of native Christians before them on their march. Nobody cares very much, however, except a vicar apostolic, who urgently requests forty or fifty marines or sailors "to protect our persons and our chattels." Foolish bishop he is, is he not, when Christians have been expressly born to be massacred? Does he not know his history?

Lead on, blind ministers plenipotentiary and envoys extraordinary; lead on, with your eternal political situations in embryo, your eternal political situations that have not yet hatched out; while one that is more pregnant than any you have ever conceived is already born under your very noses and is being sniffed at by you. But no matter what happens outside, Peking is safe, that is your *dictum*, and the *dictum* of the day. So, yawning and somewhat tired of the evening's convivialities, we go our several ways home, in our Peking carts and our official chairs, and are soon lost in sleep—dreaming, perhaps, that we have been too long in this dry Northern climate, and that it is really affecting one's nerves.

3

Overcast Skies

28th May, 1900.

It is only four days since we discussed the Vicar Apostolic's letter, and laughed somewhat at French excitability; but in four days what a change! The cloud no bigger than your hand is now bigger than your whole body, bigger, indeed, than the combined bodies of all your neighbours, supposing you could spread them fantastically in great layers across the skies. What, then, has happened?

It is that the Boxers, christened by us, as you will remember, but two or three short weeks ago, have blossomed forth with such fierce growth that they have become the men of the hour to the exclusion of everything else, and were one to believe one tithe of the talk babbling all around, the whole earth is shaking with them. Yet it is a very local affair—a thing concerning only a tiny portion of a half-known corner of the world. But for us it is sufficiently grave. The Peking-Paotingfu railway is being rapidly destroyed; Fentai station, but six miles from Peking—think of it, only six miles from this Manchu holy of holies—has gone up in flames; a great steel bridge has succumbed to the destroying energy of dynamite.

All the European engineers have fled into Peking; and, worst of all, the Boxer banners have been unfurled; and lo and behold, as they floated in the breeze, the four dread characters, "*Pao Ch'ing Mien Yang*," have been read on blood-red bunting—"Death and destruction to the foreigner and all his works and loyal support to the great Ching dynasty."

Is that sufficiently enthralling, or should I add that the invulnerability of the Boxer has been officially and indisputably tested by the Manchus, according to the gossip of the day? Proceeding to the Boxer camp at Chochou, duly authorised officers of the Crown have seen recruits, who have performed all the dread rites, and are initiated, stand fearlessly in front of a full-fledged Boxer; have seen that Boxer load up his blunderbuss with powder, ramming down a wad on top; have witnessed a handful of iron buckshot added, but with no wad to hold the charge in place; have noticed that the master Boxer gesticulated with his lethal weapon the better to impress his audience before he fired, but have not noticed that the iron buckshot tripped merrily out of the rusty barrel since no wad held it in place; and finally, when the fire-piece belched forth flames and ear-breaking noise at a distance of a man's body from the recruit's person, they have seen, and with them thousands of others, that no harm came. It is astounding, miraculous, but it is true; henceforth, the Boxer is officially invulnerable and must remain so as long as the ground is parched. That is what our Chinese reports say.

There are myriads of men already in camp and myriads more speeding on their way to this Chochou camp of camps, while in village and hamlet local committees of public safety against the accursed foreigner and all his works are being quite naturally evolved, and red cloth—that sign manual of revolt—is already at a premium. The whole-province of Chihli is shaking; North China will soon be in flames; any one with half a nose can smell rebellion in the air....

This is one side of the picture, the side which friendly Chinese are painting for us. Yet when you glance at the eleven Legations, placidly living their own little lives, you will see them cynically listening to these old women's tales, while at heart they secretly wonder what political capital each of them can separately make out of the whole business, so that their governments may know that Peking has clever diplomats. Clever diplomats! There have been no clever diplomats in Peking since G—— of the French Legation took his departure, and that purring Slav P—— went to Seoul.

Of course Peking is safe, that goes without saying; but merely because there are foolish women and children, some nondescripts, and a good many missionaries, we will order a few guards. This, at least, has just been decided by the Council of Ministers—a rather foolish council, without backbone, excepting one man. All the afternoon everybody was occupied in telegraphing the orders and reports of the day, and these actions are now beyond recall.

Guards have been ordered from the ships lying out at the Taku bar. The guards will soon be here, and when they have come the movement will cease. Thus have the eleven Legations spoken, each telegraphing a different tale to its government, and each more than annoyed by this joint action. Incidentally each one is secretly wondering what is going to happen, and whether there is really any danger.

It has been directly telegraphed from London by Her Majesty's Secretary of Foreign Affairs, Lord Salisbury, so gossip says, that as quite enough has been heard of this Boxer business it must cease at once. Is not the South African War still proceeding, and has England not enough troubles without this additional one? It is almost pathetic, this peremptory order from a vacillating Foreign Office that never knows its own mind—this Canute-like bidding of the angry waves of human men to stand still at once and be no more heard of. People in Europe will never quite understand the East, for the East is ruled by things which are impossible in a temperate climate.

Meanwhile, in the Palace, whose pink walls we see blinking at us in the sun just beyond Legation Street, all is also topsy-turvy, the Chinese reports say. The Empress Dowager, shrewdly listening to this person and that, must feel in her own bones that it is a bad business, and that it will not end well, for she understands dynastic disasters uncommonly well. She has sent again and again for P'i Hsiao-li, "Cobbler's-wax" Li, as he is called, the reputed false eunuch who is master of her inner counsels, if Chinese small talk is to be believed. The eunuch Li has been told earnestly to find out the truth and nothing but the truth. A passionate old woman, this Empress Dowager of China, a veritable Catherine of Russia in her younger days they say, with her hot Manchu blood and her lust for ruling men.

"Cobbler's-wax" Li, son of a cobbler and falsely emasculated, they say, so that he might become an eunuch of the Palace, from which lowly estate he has blossomed into the real power behind the Throne, hastens off once more to the palace of Prince Tuan, the father of the titular heir-apparent. As Prince Tuan's discretion has long since been cast to the winds, and Lao t'uan-yeh, or spiritual Boxer chiefs, now sit at the princely banqueting tables discussing the terms on which they will rush the Tartar city with their flags unfurled and their yelling forces behind them, a foolish and irresolute government, made up of the most diverse elements, and a rouge-smirched Empress Dowager, will then have to side with them or be begulfed too.

Anxiously listening, "Cobbler's-wax" Li weights the odds, for no fool is this false eunuch, who through his manly charms leads an Empress who in turn leads an empire. Half suspicious and wholly unconvinced, he questions and demands the exact number of invulnerables that can be placed in line; and is forthwith assured, with braggart Chinese choruses, that they are as locusts, that the whole earth swarms with them, that the movement is unconquerable. Still unconvinced, the false eunuch takes his departure, and then the Throne decrees and counter decrees in agonised Edicts.

It is noticed, too, that the distributors of the official organ, the *Peking Gazette*, no longer staidly walk their rounds, pausing to gossip with their friends, but run with their wooden-block printed Edicts wet from the presses, and shout indiscreetly to the passers-by, "Aside, our business is important." In all faith there is something in this movement. It is also noticed that roughness and rudeness are growing in the streets; little things that are always the precursors of the coming storm in the East are freely indulged in, and "foreign devil" is now almost a chorus. The atmosphere is obviously unwholesome, but guards have been ordered and it will soon be well. All these other things of which I speak are merely native reports. . . .

Meanwhile each Legation does not forget its dignity, but walks stolidly alone. Alone in front of the French Legation is there some commotion almost hourly. It is, however, only the arrival and departure of Catholic priests posting to and from the Pei-t'ang about that little business of forty or fifty marines *pour protéger nos personnes et nos biens*, that is all. A singularly importunate fellow this Monseigneur F——, our most reverend Vicar Apostolic of the Manchu capital.

4
Our Guards Arrive

31st May, 1900.

We had been dining out, a number of us, this evening, with result that the good wine and the good fare, for the Peking markets are admirable, left us reasonably content and in quite a valorous spirit. The party I was at was neither very large nor very small; we were eighteen, to be exact, and the political situation was represented in all its gravity by the presence of a minister and his spouse. The former has always been pessimistic, and so we had Boxers for soup, Boxers with the *entrées*, and Boxers to the end.

In fact, if the truth be told, the Boxers surrounded us in a constant vapour of words so formidable that one might well have reason to be alarmed. P——, the Minister, was, indeed, very talkative and gesticulative; his wife was sad and sighed constantly—*elle poussait des soupirs tristes*—at the lurid spectacle her husband's words conjured up. According to him, anything was possible. There might be sudden massacres in Peking itself—the Chinese Government had gone mad. Rendered more and more talkative by the wine and the good fare, he became alarming, menacing in the end. But we became more and more valiant as we ate and drank. That is always so.

It was all the guards' fault. Telegrams despatched in the morning from Tientsin distinctly told us that the guards were entraining; later news said the guards had actually started; and yet when we were almost through dinner, and it was nearly ten o'clock, there was not a sign of them. That was the distressing point, and in the end, as it thrust itself more and more on people's attention, the first great valour began to ooze. For although the Guardian of the Nine Gates—a species of Manchu warden or grand constable of Peking—has been officially warned that foreign guards, whose arrival has been duly authorised by the Tsung-li Yamen, may be a little late and that consequently the Ch'ien Men, or the Middle Gate, should be kept open a couple of hours longer, the chief guardian may become nervous and irate and incontinently shut the gates. This alone might provoke an outbreak.

This train of thought once started, we busily followed it up, and soon all the wives were sighing in unison more heavily than ever. I shall always remember what happened at that psychological moment. A strip of red-lined native writing-paper was placed in somebody's hands with a long list of the different detachments which had just passed in through the Main Gate. At last the guards had arrived. Speedily we became very valorous again. P—— afterwards said that he knew something which he had not dared to tell anyone—not even his secretaries.

From this little list, it was soon clear that the British, French, Russian, American, Italian, and Japanese detachments had arrived. The Germans and the Austrians were missing, but we concluded that they would arrive by another train within very few hours. The important point was that men had been allowed to come through—that the Chinese Government, in spite of its enormous capacity for mischief, could not yet have made up its mind how to act. That consoled us.

After this, a faint-hearted attempt was made to continue our talk. But it was no good. We soon discovered that each one of us had been simulating a false interest in our never-ending discussion. We really wished to see with our own eyes these Legation Guards who might still save the situation.

Strolling out in the warm night, just as we were, we first came on them in the French Legation. The French detachment were merely sailors belonging to what they call their *Compagnies de débarquement*, and they were all brushing each other down and cursing the *sacrée poussière*. Such a leading *motif* has this Peking dust become that the very sailors notice it. Also we found two priests from Monseigneur F——'s Cathedral, sitting in the garden and patiently waiting for the Minister's return. I heard afterwards that they would not move until P—— decided that twenty-five sailors should march the next day to the Cathedral—in fact at daylight.

In all the Legations I found it was much the same thing—the men of the various detachments were brushing each other down and exchanging congratulations that they had been picked for Peking service. It was, perhaps, only because they were so glad to be allotted shore-duty after interminable service afloat off China's muddy coasts that they congratulated one another; but it might be also because they had heard tell throughout the fleets that the men who had come in '98, after the *coup d'état*, had had the finest time which could be imagined—all loafing and no duties. They did not seem to understand or suspect....

I found later in the night that there had actually been a little trouble at the Tientsin station. The British had tried to get through a hundred marines instead of the maximum of seventy-five which had been agreed on. The Chinese authorities had then refused to let the train go, and although an English ship's captain had threatened to hang the station-master, in the end the point was won by the Chinese. By one or two in the morning everybody was very gay, walking about and having drinks with one another, and saying that it was all right now. Then it was that I remembered that it was already June—the historic month which has seen more crises than any other—and I became a little gloomy again. It was so terribly sultry and dry that it seemed as if anything could happen. I felt convinced that the guards were too few.

5

The Plot Thickens

4th June, 1900.

No matter in what light you look at it, you realise that somehow—in some wonderful, inexplicable manner—normal conditions have ceased long ago—in the month of May, I believe. The days, which a couple of weeks ago had but twenty-four hours, have now at least forty-two. You cannot exactly say why this strange state of affairs obtains, for as yet there is nothing very definite to fix upon, and you have absolutely no physical sensation of fear; but the mercury of both the barometer and the thermometer has been somehow badly shaken, and the mainsprings of all watches and clocks, although still much as the mainsprings of clocks and watches in other parts of the world—bringing your mind to bear on it you know they are exactly the same—are merely mechanism, and allow the day to have at least forty-two hours. It is strange, is it not, and you begin to understand vaguely some of the quite impossible Indian metaphysics which tell you gravely that what is, is not, and that what is not can still be.... In the crushing heat you can understand that.

Perhaps it is all because the hours are now split into ten separate and different parts by the fierce rumours which rage for a few minutes and then, dissipating their strength through their very violence, die away as suddenly as they came. The air is charged with electricity of human passions until it throbs painfully, and then....You are merrily eating your *tiffin* or your dinner, and quite calmly cursing your *"boy"* because something is not properly iced. Your *"boy,"* who is a Bannerman or Manchu and of Roman Catholic family, as are all servants of polite Peking society, does not move a muscle nor show any passing indignation, as he would were the ordinary rules and regulations of life still in existence. He, like everyone of the hundreds of thousands of Peking and the millions of North China, is waiting—waiting more patiently than impatient Westerners, but waiting just as anxiously; waiting with ear wide open to every rumour; waiting with an eye on every shadow—to know whether the storm is going to break or blow away.

There is something disconcerting, startling, unseemly in being waited on by those who you know are in turn waiting on battle, murder, and sudden death. You feel that something may come suddenly at any moment, and though you do not dare to speak your thoughts to your neighbour, these thoughts are talking busily to you without a second's interruption. For if this storm truly comes, it must sweep everything before it and blot us all out in a horrible way. Our servants tell us so.

These servants of polite Peking society are favoured mortals, for they one and all are of the Eight Banners, direct descendants of the Manchu conquerors of China. And, strangely enough, although they are thus directly tied to the Manchu dynasty, and that some of them may be even Red Girdles or lineal descendants of collateral branches of the Imperial house, they are still more tightly tied to the foreigner because they are Roman Catholic dating from the early days of Verbiest and Schall, when the Jesuits were all supreme. On Sundays and feast days they all proceed to the Vicar Apostolic's own northern cathedral, and witness the Elevation of the Host to the discordant and strange sound of Chinese firecrackers, a curious accompaniment, indeed, permitted only by Catholic complacency. This they love more than the Throne.

Your Bannerman servant is now the medium of bringing in countless rumours which he barefacedly alleges are facts, and in impressing on you that everyone must certainly die unless we quickly act. The three Roman Catholic Cathedrals of Peking, placed at three points of the compass, are almost strategic centres surrounded by whole lanes and districts of Catholics captured to the tenets of Christ, or that portion deemed sufficient for yellow men, in ages gone by. Every household of these people during the past few weeks has seen fellow-religionists from the country places running in sorely distressed in body and mind, and but ill-equipped in money and means for this impromptu escape to the capital which everyone vainly hopes generally is to be a sanctuary.

The refugees, it is true, do not receive all the sympathy they expect, for the Peking Catholic being the oldest and most mature in the eighteen provinces of China, holds his head very high, and "new people"—that is, those whose families have only been baptized, let us say, during the nineteenth century—are somewhat disdained. In a word, the Peking cathedrals and their Manchu and other adherents are the Blacks; and not even in papal Rome could this aristocracy in religion be excelled. But although the newcomers are disdained, their news is not. Everything they say is believed. The servants, therefore, browsing rumours wherever they go, bring back a curious hotchpotch after each separate excursion.

Sometimes the balance swings this way, sometimes that; sometimes it is ominously black, sometimes only cloudy. You never know what it will be ten minutes hence, and you must content yourself as best you can. Your body-servant being a Bannerman (my particular one is a Manchu), and being reasonably young, is also a reservist of the Peking Field Force, and consorts with other Bannermen who may be actually on guard at one of the Palace gates. Who passes in and who passes out of the Palace now spreads like wildfire round the whole city, for the success of the Boxers will depend upon the support the Peking Government intends to give them when the worst comes to the worst. And the Peking Government is still fencing, because the Palace cannot make up its mind whether the time has really come when it must act. This lack of decision is fatal.

Late in the afternoon it transpired that the Empress Dowager was not in the Imperial city at all, but out at the Summer Palace on the Wan-shou-shan—the hills of ten thousand ages, as these are poetically called. Tung Fu-hsiang, whose ruffianly Kansu braves were marched out of the Chinese city—that is the outer ring of Peking—two nights before the Legation Guards came in, is also with the Empress, for his cavalry banners, made of black and blue velvet, with blood-red characters splashed splendidly across them, have been seen planted at the foot of the hills. Tung Fu-hsiang is an invincible one, who stamped out the Kansu rebellion a few years ago with such fierceness that his name strikes terror today into every Chinese heart.

As for P'i Hsiao-li—the false eunuch—he is everywhere, they say, sometimes here, sometimes there, and quite defying search. The eunuch has a mighty fortune at stake, and all natives believe that he will betray himself. Half the pawnshops and banks of Peking belong to him, and he will not sacrifice his thirty million *taels* until he is convinced that his head is at stake. The Summer Palace lies but a dozen miles beyond Peking's embattled walls, and from the top, straining your eyes to the west, you can vaguely see the Empress's *plaisaunce*. A journey in and out is nothing by cart, and this favoured eunuch has the best mules in the Empire—black *jennets* fifteen hands high—and is using them night and day. And so everyone is asking again and again whether the Empress has arranged with Prince Tuan, since that is the burning question; and did this eunuch of eunuchs have his fateful confidential interview with the secret Boxer leaders, which was to decide finally on extermination.

The families of other palace eunuchs say yes, and the wife of one eunuch, living near the South Cathedral, is quite positive, my servants inform me. Wife of a eunuch, did I say? You will think me mad, but it is nevertheless true, for Chinese eunuchs have wives. Why have they wives, you will ask, since they are only half men, and cannot perform the duties of the male? Well, I can only answer as did my teacher once when I asked him years ago.

"Eunuchs are still men," he said, smiling doubtfully, "insomuch as they like homes of their own beyond the palace walls and desire children to play with. Since their wives can bear no children they buy children from poor people, and these duly become their own. Thus when the eunuch dies he has children to worship at his grave."

In this land of mystery even eunuchs can correctly become ancestors. Yet this is a trivial detail which I should not speak of.

So the eunuch's wife living near the South Cathedral, who gossips with her Black Catholic neighbours, and whose gossip gives me news many times a day, avers most positively that the chief eunuch has been in town—that the whole matter has been decided—and that every foreigner will die. And very late in the evening my Manchu servant rushed in on me with his eyes sparkling strangely, and his voice so hoarse with excitement that he did not speak, but shout. "Master," he cried, "I have seen myself this time; three long carts full of swords and spears have passed in from the outer city through the Ha-ta Gate. The city guards stopped and questioned the drivers—then let them go. They had a pass from the Governor of Peking, and the people all say it is now coming." Now do you wonder about our clocks and our watches, and our time? Nothing can ever be normal again until this terrible question is solved.

6

The Licking Flames Approach

9th June 1900.

It is getting desperate, of that there is now no shadow of doubt. The Tientsin trains that have been lately running more and more slowly and irregularly, as if they, too, were waiting on the pleasure of the coming storm, are going to run no more, and the odds are heavily against today's train ever reaching its destination. It is true these trains have long ceased running as far as we are personally concerned, for the weariness of living forty-two hours during twenty-four dulls one's perception of everything excepting one's immediate surroundings. And even one's surroundings are somehow shrinking until they will soon be but the four walls of a courtyard. But about the trains— why are they stopping? Because the licking flames are approaching so near that they will soon overwhelm all who are concerned with the running of trains unless they disappear very nimbly.

One of the Chinese railway managers, an educated man in the Western sense who can quote Shakespeare, has been all over Legation Street yesterday and today, pointing out the hopelessness of the general position and almost openly urging the Legations to call on Europe to take steps. General Nieh, an intelligent general, with foreign-drilled troops, has indeed been fitfully ordered by Imperial Edict to "protect the railway," and to keep communication open, but this order has already come to nothing, and the position is worse than it was before. His troops, merely desirous of testing their brand-new Mausers, and as calmly cruel as only Easterns can be, did open a heavy fire a day or two ago on some Boxer marauders who had strayed into a station on the Tientsin-Peking line, and proposed to crucify the native stationmaster and beat all others, who were indirectly eating the foreign devils' rice by working on the railway, into lumps of jelly.

General Nieh's men let their rifles crash off, not because their sympathies were against the Boxers, but probably because every living man armed with a rifle loves to fire at another living man when he can do so without harm to himself. This is my brutal explanation. But in any case these soldiers have now been marched off in semi-disgrace to their camp at Lutai, a few miles to the north of Tientsin, and told never to do such rash and indiscreet things again. That means the end of any attempts to control. For the Boxer partisans in Peking allege that the soldiers actually hit and killed a good many men, which is quite without precedent, and is upsetting all plans. On such occasions it is always understood that you fire a little in the air, warwhoop a good deal, and then come back quietly to camp with captured flags and banners as undeniable evidences of your victory. This has been the old method of making domestic war in China—the only one.

But all this is many miles from the sacred capital. The cry is still that we of Peking are safe, and that even if this is to be a true rebellion we cannot be hurt. The cry, however, is not so lusty as it was even three or four days ago, and, indeed, has only become an official cry—that is, one you are permitted to contradict privately when you meet your dear colleagues in the street and wonder aloud what is really going to happen. In the despatches Peking is still quite safe, although unwholesome. Yet our own private political situations, of which we were so proud and talked so vauntingly, have all now disappeared, miserable things, and are quite lost and forgotten. No one cares to talk about them. People merely say that all business is temporarily suspended; that we must wait and merely mark time.

But we discovered something worth knowing at the last moment today which is, without any doubt, true. The Empress Dowager returned today from the Summer Palace, and is now actually in the Forbidden City. We are at a loss to know exactly as yet what this means, and whether it is an augury of good or of bad. The Winter Palace is so near us; it is just to the west of us. The fact that the redoubtable Tung Fu-hsiang rode behind his Imperial mistress with his banner-bearers flaunting their colours and his trumpets blaring as loudly as possible is, however, not very reassuring. It seemed like defiance and treachery.

But at first, in spite of the Empress's entry, there were not many rumours accompanying her; in the late afternoon they came so thick and fast that no one had time to write them down. But of rumours we have had more than our bellyful. Let me tell some of the facts.

First and foremost. The racecourse grand-stand where less than a month ago we were all watching the struggles for victory between our various short-legged ponies, has gone up in flames and puff—just like that—the social battle-ground is no more. The Boxers, for everybody who does anything nowadays is a Boxer, tried to grill our official caretakers on the red-hot bricks, but the neighbouring village came to the rescue and shouted the marauders out of the place. That is the nearest danger which has been heard of.

Immediately after this some Legation students, riding out on the sands under the Tartar Wall, were openly attacked by spear-armed men, and only escaped by galloping furiously and firing the revolvers which everyone now carries. Most important of all, however, to us is that aged Sir R—— H—— is hauling down his colours, and has been rapidly calling in all his scattered staff who live near the premises of the Tsung-li Yamen—China's Foreign Office. Here we are, the Legations of all Europe, with five hundred sailors and marines cleaning their rifles and marking out distances in the capital of a so-called friendly Power; with our *pro formâ* despatches still being despatched while our real messages are frightened; attempting to weather a storm which the Chinese Government is powerless to arrest. The very passers-by are becoming sheep-eyed and are looking at us askance.

Passers-by, did I say? But do not imagine from this that there are many of these, for the Chinese have been for days avoiding the Legation quarter as if it were plague-stricken, and sounds that were so roaring a few weeks ago are now daily becoming more and more scarce. A blight is settling on us, for we are accursed by the whole population of North China, and who knows what will be the fate of those seen lurking near the foreigner?

And now when we wander even in our own streets—that is, those abutting immediately on our compounds of the Legation area—a new nickname salutes our ears. No longer are we mere *yang kuei-tzu*, foreign devils; we have risen to the proud estate of *ta mao-tzu*, or long-haired ones of the first class. *Mao-tzu* is a term of some contemptuous strength, since *mao* is the hair of animals, and our barbarian heads are not even shaved. The *ta*—great or first class—is also significant, because behind our own detested class press two others deserving of almost equal contempt at the hands of all believers in divine Boxerism. These are *ehr-mao-tzu* and *san mao-tzu*, second and third class coarse-haired ones.

All good converts belong to the second class, and death awaits them, our servants say; while as to the third category, all having any sort of connection, direct or indirect with the foreigner and his works are lumped indiscriminately together in this one, and should be equally detested. The small talk of the tea-shops now even says that officials having a few sticks of European furniture in their houses are *san mao-tzu*. It is very significant, too, this open talk in the tea-shops, because in official Peking, the very centre of the enormous, loose-jointed Empire, political gossip is severely disliked and the four characters, "*mo t'an kuo shih*" (eschew political discussions), are skied in every public room. People in the old days of last month heeded this four-character warning, for a bambooing at the nearest police-station, *ting erh*, was always a possibility. Now everyone can do as he likes.

It is, therefore, becoming patent to the most blind that this is going to be something startling, something eclipsing any other anti-foreign movement ever heard of, because never before have the users of foreign imports and the mere friends of foreigners been labelled in a class just below that of the foreigners themselves. And then as it became dark today, a fresh wave of excitement broke over the city and produced almost a panic. The main body of Tung Fu-hsiang's savage Kansu braves—that is, his whole army—re-entered the capital and rapidly encamped on the open places in front of the Temples of Heaven and Agriculture in the outer ring of Peking. This settled it, I am glad to say. At last all the Legations shivered, and urgent telegrams were sent to the British admiral for reinforcements to be rushed up at all costs.

But too late—too late; the Manchu servants who have friends among the guards at the Palace gates have said this all the evening. For the Chinese Colossus, lumbering and lazy, sluggish and ill-equipped, has raised himself on his elbow, and with sheep-like and calculating eyes is looking down on us—a pigmy-like collection of foreigners and their guards—and soon will risk a kick—perhaps even will trample us quickly to pieces. How bitterly everyone is regretting our false confidence, and how our chiefs are being cursed!

7

The City of Peking and All Its Glories

11th June, 1900.

You do not know this Capital of Capitals, perhaps—that is, you do not know it as you should if the scenes which may presently move across the stage, now in shouting crowds of sword-armed men, now in pitiable incidents of small account, are to be properly understood, and their dramatic setting, stirring blood-thrilling, incongruous as they must be and can only be. I feel that something will come—I even know it. I have been talking vaguely about this and about that; have begun preparing colours, as it were, in the usual careless fashion without explanations or digressions—until you possibly wonder what it is all about. For you have not yet seen the barbaric frame which will hedge in the whole—the barbaric frame in all truth, since it is gradually closing in on us on every side until, like some medieval torture-room, we may have the very life crushed out of us by a cruel pressure. But enough of fine phrases; while there is time let me write something.

Peking is at least two thousand years old. Several hundred years before Christ, they say a Chinese kingdom made the present site the capital, and began building the outer walls; but the Chinese, the gentler Chinese who had all military spirit crushed out of them five thousand years before by having to tramp from Mesopotamia to where they now are in the eighteen provinces, these Chinese, I say, never had in Peking anything but a temporary trysting-place. For Peking stands for a sort of blatant barbarianism, mounted on sturdy ponies, pouring in from the far North; and the history of Peking can only be said to begin when Mongol-Tartars, who have always been freebooters and robbers, forced their way in and imposed their militarism on a nation of shopkeepers and collectors of taxes.

Even before the Christian era, the Chinese chronicles tell of the pressure of these fierce barbarians from the North being so much felt and their raids so constant, that Chi Huang-ti, the ruler of the powerful Chinese feudatory state which laid the foundations of the present Empire of China, began to build the Great Wall of China and to fortify old Peking as the only means of stopping these living waves. The Great Wall took ages to build, for the Northern barbarians always kept cunningly slipping round the uncompleted ends, and the Mings, the last purely Chinese sovereigns to reign in Peking, actually added three hundred miles to this colossal structure in the year 1547, or nearly two thousand years after the first bricks had been cemented. That shows you what people they were, and what the contest was.

For hundreds of years the war with the semi-nomadic hordes of the North continued. Sometimes isolated bands of Tartars broke through the Chinese defence and enslaved the people, but never for very long; instinctively by the use of every stratagem the cleverer Chinese compassed their destruction. While Attila and his Huns were ravaging Europe in the fifth century, other *Hwingnoo*, or Huns, veritable scourges of God, forced their way into China. In this fashion, while China itself was passing through a dozen different forms of government, and had a dozen capitals—sometimes owning allegiance to a single Emperor such as those of the T'ang dynasty who added Canton and the Cantonese to the Empire, sometimes split into petty kingdoms such as the "Ten States"—this curious frontier war continued and was handed down from father to son.

Chinese industrialism and socialism, content to accept whatever form of government Chinese strong men succeeded in imposing, instinctively kept up an iron resistance to these Northern invaders. Such was the fear inspired, that a proverb coined thousands of years ago is still current. "*Do not fear the cock from the South, but the wolf from the North,*" it says. Everybody is always quoting this saying. I have heard it twice today.

It was not until the tenth century that the Tartars finally broke through and established themselves definitively on Chinese soil. The Khitans, a Manchu-Tartar people, springing from Central Manchuria, then captured Peking and made it their capital. The Khitans were a cheerful people, with a peculiar sense of humour and a still greater conviction of the inferiority of women. To show their contempt for them, it is still recorded that they used to slit the back of their wives and drink their blood to give them strength. For two and a half centuries the Khitans, under the style of the Liao or Iron dynasty, maintained their position by the use of the sword, and then succumbing to the sapping influence of Chinese civilisation, they in turn were unable to resist a second Manchu-Mongol horde, the Kins. The Kins, under the style of the Silver dynasty, reigned in Northern China for a term of years, but there was nothing of a permanent character in their rule, since they were uncouth barbarians who soon drank themselves to death and destruction.

At the beginning of the thirteenth century Genghis Khan, the great Mongol, born in the bleak Hsing-an Mountains, gathered together all the restless bands of Mongolia, and sweeping down on Peking drove out the Kins and established the purely Mongol dynasty of the Yüan. Up till then Peking had consisted of what is today the Chinese city, or the older outer city. Kublai Khan, Genghis's grandson, fixed his residence definitively in Peking in 1264, and began building the *Ta-tu*, or Great Residence—the Tartar city of today. The Chinese city is oblong; the Tartar city is squat and square and overlaps and dominates the northern walls of the older city. Kublai Khan, by building the Tartar city on the northern edge of the Chinese city and fortifying it with immense strength, may be said to have fitted the spear-head on to the Chinese shaft, and to have given the key-note to the policy which exists to this day—the policy of the North of China dominating the South of China.

In time the Yüan dynasty of Mongols passed away—their strength sapped by confinement to walled cities because their power was only on the tented field. Ser Marco Polo, that audacious traveller, never tires of telling of the magnificence of the Mongol Khans and their resplendent courts. It requires no Marco Polo to assure us that the thirteenth century of the Far East was immeasurably in advance of the thirteenth century of Europe. The vast and magnificent works which remain to this day, weather-beaten though they be; the fierce reds, the wonderful greens, the boldness and size of everything, speak to us of an age which knew of mighty conquests of all Asia by invincible Mongol horsemen. . . .

The Mongols were succeeded by the Mings—a purely Chinese house; but the Mings, in some terror of the rough North, since for over four centuries Tartars or Manchu-Mongols had been the overlords of China, discreetly established their capital on the Yangtsze and called it Nanking, or the Southern capital. It was only the third Emperor of the Mings who dared to remove the court to Peking. His choice was ill made for his dynasty, since a century and a half had hardly passed before fresh hordes—the modern Manchus—began to gather strength in the mountains and valleys to the northeast of Moukden. Fighting stubbornly, Nurhachu, the founder of this new enterprise, steadily broke through Chinese resistance in the Liaotung, then a Chinese province colonised from Chihli, and slowly but surely reached out towards Peking, the goal which beckons to everyone.

The Great Wall, built eighteen hundred years before as a protection against other barbarians of the same stock, stopped Nurhachu a hundred times, and although he captured Moukden and made it a Manchu capital, he died worn out by half a century of warfare. His son, Tai Tsung, or Tien Tsung, nothing daunted, took up the struggle, and finding it impossible to break through the fortifications of the East, near Shan-hai-kwan, adopted Genghis Khan's route—the passes leading in from the great grassy plains of Mongolia many hundreds of miles to the West. Allying himself by marriage with Mongols, the Manchu monarch began a series of grand raids through their territory in the direction of Peking.

Once he actually reached Peking and sat down in front of its mighty walls to besiege it. But he found his strength unequal to the task, and once more was forced to retire. Then this second Manchu prince died, and was succeeded by a tiny grandson of five. The regent appointed by the Manchu nobles owed his final success to the fact that he was called in by the Chinese generals commanding the coveted Shan-hai-kwan gates to rescue Peking from the hands of Chinese insurgents, who had everywhere arisen; and in 1644, after seventy years of warfare, the Manchus seated themselves on the Dragon Throne, in defiance of the wishes of the people, but backed up by a vast concourse of Manchus and Mongols, and half the fierce blades of Eastern Asia.

The history of all these centuries of warfare is eloquently written on all the buildings, the fortifications, the monuments, the palaces and temples of Peking which surround us. Peking is the Delhi of China, and the grave of warlike barbarians. Four separate times have Tartars broken in and founded dynasties, and four separate times have Chinese culture and civilisation sapped rugged strength, and made the rulers the *de facto* servants of the ceremonious inhabitants. In the Tartar city there are Yellow Lama temples, with hundreds of bare-pated lama priests, the results of Buddhist Concordats guaranteeing

Thibetan semi-independence in return for a tacit acknowledgment of Chinese suzerainty.

Near the palace walls is a Mongolian Superintendency, where the Mongol hordes still grazing their herds and their flocks on the grassy plains of high Asia, as they have done for countless centuries, are divided up into Banners, or military divisions, showing the enormous strength in irregular cavalry they possessed two hundred and fifty years ago. Round the Forbidden City are the Six Boards and the Nine Ministries, the outward signs of those bonds of etiquette and procedure which bind the Manchu Throne to the eighteen provinces. The walls of the Tartar city heave up fifty feet in the air, and are forty feet thick. The circumference of the outer ring of fortifications is over twenty miles. Each gate is surmounted by a square three-storied tower or pagoda, vast and imposing.

Round the city and through the city run century-old canals and moats with water-gates shutting down with cruel iron prongs. In the Chinese city the two Temples of Heaven and Agriculture raise their altars to the skies, invoking the help of the deities for this decaying but proud Chinese Empire. Think of the millions of dead hands that fashioned such enormous strength and old-time magnificence! On the corner of the Tartar Wall is the old Jesuit Observatory with beautiful dragon-adorned instruments of bronze given by a Louis of France. There are temples with yellow-gowned or grey-gowned priests in their hundreds founded in the times of Kublai Khan. There are Mohammedan mosques, with Chinese *muezzins* in blue turbans on feast days; Manchu palaces with vermillion-red pillars and archways and green and gold ceilings.

There are unending lines of camels plodding slowly in from the Western deserts laden with all manner of merchandise; there are curious palanquins slung between two mules and escorted by sword-armed men that have journeyed all the way from Shansi and Kansu, which are a thousand miles away; a Mongol market with bare-pated and long-coated Mongols hawking venison and other products of their chase; comely Soochow harlots with reeking native scents rising from their hair; water-carriers and barbers from sturdy Shantung; cooks from epicurean Canton; bankers from Shansi—the whole Empire of China sending its best to its old-world barbaric capital, which has now no strength.

And right in the centre of it all is the Forbidden City, enclosing with its high pink walls the palaces which are full of warm-blooded

Manchu concubines, sleek eunuchs who speak in wheedling tones, and is always hot with intrigue. At the gates of the Palace lounge bow and jingal-armed Imperial guards. Inside is the Son of Heaven himself, the Emperor imprisoned in his own palace by the Empress Mother, who is as masterful as any man who ever lived . . .

I beg you, do you begin to see something of Peking and to understand the eleven miserable little Legations, each with its own particular ideas and intrigues, but crouching all together under the Tarter Wall and tremblingly awaiting with mock assurance the bursting of this storm? If you are so good as to see this you will realise the wonderful stage effects, the fierce Medievalism in senile decay, the superb distances, the red dust from the Gobi that has choked up all the drains and tarnished all the magnificence until it is no more magnificence at all—this dust which is such a herald of the coming storm—the new guns and pistols of Herr Krupp and the camels of the deserts and all the other things all mixed up together. . . .

Oh, I see that we are absurd and can only be made more ridiculous by coming events. Of course the Boxers coming in openly through the gates cannot be true, and yet—shades of Genghis Khan and all his Tartars, what is that? When I had got as far as this from all sides came a tremendous blaring of barbaric trumpets—those long brass trumpets that can make one's blood curdle horribly, a blaring which has now upset everything I was about to write and also my inkpot. I rushed out to inquire; it was only a portion of the Manchu Peking Field Force marching home, but the sounds have unsettled us all again, and in the tumult of one's emotions one does not know what to believe and what to fear. Everything seems a little impossible and absurd, especially what I am now writing from hour to hour.

8

Some Incidents and the One Man

12th June, 1900.

Even the British Legation—"the stoical, sceptical, ill-informed British Legation," as S—— of the American Legation calls it—is wringing its hands with annoyance, and were it Italian, and therefore dramatically articulate, its curses and *maladette* would ascend to the very heavens in a menacing cloud like our Peking dust. For on England we have all been waiting because of an ancient prestige; and England, everyone says, is mainly responsible for our present plight. Everybody is lowering at England and the British Legation along Legation Street, because S—— was not sent for two weeks ago, and the language of the minor missions, who could not possibly expect to receive protecting guards unless they swam all the way from Europe, is sulphurous. They ask with much reason why we do not lead events instead of being lead by them; why are we so foolish, so confident. What has happened to justify all this, you will ask? Well, permit me to speak.

The day before yesterday several Englishmen rode down to the Machiapu railway station, which is just outside the Chinese city, and is our Peking station, to welcome, as they thought, Admiral S—— and his reinforcements, so despairingly telegraphed for by the British Legation just fourteen days later than should have been done. Their passage to the station was unmarked by incidents, excepting that they noted with apprehension the thickly clustering tents of Kansu soldiery in the open spaces fronting the vast Temples of Heaven and Agriculture. Once the station was reached a weary wait began, with nothing to relieve the tedium, for the vast crowds which usually surround the "fire-cart stopping-place," to translate the vernacular, all had disappeared, and in place of the former noisiness there was nothing but silence.

At last, somewhat downcast, our Englishmen were forced to return without a word of news, passing into the Chinese city when it was almost dusk. Alas! the Kansu soldiery, after the manner of all Celestials, were taking the air in the twilight; and no sooner did they spy the hated foreigner than hoots and curses rose louder and louder. The horsemen quickened their pace, stones flew, and had it not been for the presence of mind of one man they would have been torn to pieces. They left the great main street of the outer city in a tremendous uproar and seemed glad to be back among friends.

Yesterday, the 11th, it seemed absolutely certain S—— would arrive, since he must have left Tientsin on the 10th, and it is only ninety miles by rail. The Legations wished to despatch a messenger, but the Kansu soldiery on those open spaces were not attractive, and nobody was very anxious to brave them. Who was to go? No sooner was it mentioned in the Japanese Legation than, of course, a Japanese was found ready to go; in fact, several Japanese almost came to blows on the subject. Sugiyama, the *chancelier*, somehow managed to prove that he had the best right, and go he did, but never to return.

It was dark before his carter turned up in Legation Street, covered with dust and bespattered with blood, while I happened to be there. It was an ugly story he unfolded, and it is hardly good to tell it. On the open spaces facing the supplicating altars of Heaven and Agriculture this little Japanese, Sugiyama, met his death in a horrid way. The Kansu soldiery were waiting for more cursed foreigners to appear, and this time they had their arms with them and were determined to have blood. So they killed the Japanese brutally while he shielded himself with his small hands. They hacked off all his limbs, barbarians that they are, decapitated him, then mutilated his body. It now lies half-buried where it was smitten down.

The carter who drove him was eloquent as only Orientals can be when tragedy flings their customary reserve aside: "May my tongue be torn out if I scatter falsehoods," he said again and again, using the customary phrase, as he showed how it all happened. And late into the night he was still reciting his story to fresh crowds of listeners, who gaped with terror and astonishment. Squatting in a great Peking courtyard on his hams and calling on the unseen powers to tear out his tongue if he lied, he was a figure of some moment, this Peking carter, for those that thought; for everybody realises that we are now caught and cannot be driven out....

This was the 11th. On the 12th, the day was still more startling, for somehow the shadow which has been lurking so near us seems to have been thrown more forward and become more intense. The hero of the affair is the one really brave man among our chiefs, of course—the Baron von K——, the *Kaiser's* Minister to the Court of Peking.

The baron is no stranger in Peking, although he has been here but a twelvemonth in his new capacity as Minister. Fifteen years ago his handsome face charmed more than one fair lady in the old pre-political situation days, when there was plenty of time for picnics and love-making. Then he was only an irresponsible *attaché*; now he is here as a very full-blooded plenipotentiary, with the burden of a special German political mission in China, bequeathed him by his pompous and mannerless predecessor, Baron von H——, to support. But a man is the present German Minister if there was ever one, and it was in the newly macadamised Legation Street that the incident I am about to relate occurred.

Walking out in the morning, the German Minister saw one of the ordinary hooded Peking carts trotting carelessly along, with the mule all ears, because the carter was urging him along with many digs near the tail. But it was not the cart, nor the carter, nor yet the mule, which attracted His Excellency's immediate attention, but the passenger seated on the customary place of the off-shaft. For a moment Baron von K—— could not believe his eyes. It was nothing less than a full-fledged Boxer with his hair tied up in red cloth, red ribbons round his wrists and ankles, and a flaming red girdle tightening his loose white tunic; and, to cap all, the man was audaciously and calmly sharpening a big carver knife on his boots!

It was sublime insolence, riding down Legation Street like this in the full glare of day, with a knife and regalia proclaiming the dawn of Boxerism in the Capital of Capitals, and withal, was a very ugly sign. What did K—— do—go home and invite someone to write a despatch for him to his government deprecating the growth of the Boxer movement, and the impossibility of carrying out conciliatory instructions, as some of his colleagues, including my own chief, would have done? Not a bit of it! He tilted full at the man with his walking stick, and before he could escape had beaten a regular roll of kettledrums on his hide. Then the Boxer, after a short struggle, abandoned his knife, and ran with some fleetness of foot into a neighbouring lane.

The gallant German Minister raised the hue and cry, and then discovered yet another Boxer inside the cart, whom he duly secured by falling on top of him; and this last one was handed over to his own Legation Guards. The fugitive was followed into Prince Su's grounds, which run right through the Legation area, and there cornered in a house. The mysterious Dr. M—— then suddenly appeared on the scenes and insisted upon searching the Manchu Prince's entire grounds and most private apartments. But time was wasted in *pourparlers,* and in spite of a minute inspection, which extended even to the concubine apartments, the Boxer vanished in some mysterious way like a breath, and is even now untraced. This shows us conclusively that there are accomplices right in our midst.

No sooner had this incident occurred and been bandied round with sundry exaggerations, than the life of the Legations and the nondescripts who have been coming in from the country became more abnormal than ever. For in spite of our extraordinary position, even up to today we were attempting to work—that is, writing three lines of a despatch, and then rushing madly out to hear the latest news. Now not so much as one word is written, and our eleven Legations are openly terribly perturbed in body and mind and conscious of their intense impotence, although we have all the so-called resources of diplomacy still at our command, and we are officially still on the friendliest terms with the Chinese Government.

This morning, the 12th, there was another commotion—this time in Customs Street, as it is called. Three more Boxers, armed with swords and followed by a crowd of loafers, fearful but curious, ran rapidly past the post-office, which faces the Customs Inspectorate, and got into a small temple a few hundred feet away, where they began their incantations. It was decided to attack them only with riding-whips, so as to avoid drawing first blood. But when a party of us arrived, we could not get into their retreat, as they had barricaded themselves in. So marines and sailors were requisitioned with axes; after a lot of exhausting work it was discovered that the birds had flown. This was another proof that there is treachery among friendly natives, for without help these Boxers could never have escaped.

And now imagine our excitement and general perturbation. Since the 8th or 9th, I really forget which date, we have been acting on a more or less preconcerted plan—that is, as far as our defences are concerned, as we have been quite cut off from the outer world. The commanders of the British, American, German, French, Italian, Russian, Austrian and Japanese detachments have met and conferred—each carefully instructed by his own minister just how far he is to acquiesce in his colleagues' proposals, which is, roughly speaking, not at all. We can have no effective council of war thus, because there is no commander-in-chief, and everybody is a claimant to the post.

There is first an Austrian captain of a man-of-war lying off the Taku bar, who was merely up in Peking on a pleasure trip when he was caught by the storm, but this has not hindered him taking over command of the Austrian sailors from the lieutenant who brought them up; and everybody knows that a captain in the navy ranks with a colonel in the army. There are no military men in Peking excepting three captains of British marines, one Japanese lieutenant-colonel and his *aide-de-camp*, and some unimportant military *attachés*, who are very junior.

So on paper the command should lie between two men—the Austrian naval captain and the Japanese lieutenant-colonel. But, then, the Japanese have instructions to follow the British lead, and the senior British marine captain has orders to follow, his own ideas, and his own ideas do not fancy the unattached Austrian captain of a man-of-war. So the concerted plan of defence has only been evolved very suddenly, a plan which has resolved itself naturally into each detachment-commander holding his own Legation as long as he could, and being vaguely linked to his neighbour by picquets of two or three men. But about this you will understand more later on.

The point I wish you now to realise is that the counsels of the allied countries of Europe in the persons of their Legation Guards' commanders are as effective as those of very juvenile kindergartens. Everybody is intensely jealous of everybody else and determined not to give way on the question of the supreme command. Of course, if the storm comes suddenly, without any warning, we are doomed, because you cannot hold an area a mile square with a lot of men who are fighting among themselves, and who have fallen too quickly into our miserably petty Peking scheme of things.

9

The Coming of the Boxers

14th June, 1900.

I had risen yesterday somewhat late in the day with the oddness and uncomfortableness—I do not mean discomfort—which comes from too much boots, too much disturbance of one's ordinary routine, too much listening to people airing their opinions and recounting rumours, and, last of all, very wearied by the uncustomary task of transporting a terrible battery of hand artillery (for we are at last all heavily armed); and consequent of these varied things, I, like everybody else, was a good deal out of temper and rather sick of it all. I began to ask myself this question: Were we really playing an immense comedy, or was there a great and terrible peril menacing us? I could never get beyond asking the question. I could not think sanely long enough for the answer.

The day passed slowly, and very late in the afternoon, when some of us had completed a tour of the Legations, and looked at their various picquets, I finished up at the Austrian Legation and the Customs Street. Men were everywhere sitting about, idly watching the dusty and deserted streets, half hoping that something was going to happen shortly, when suddenly there was a shout and a fierce running of feet. Something had happened.

We all jumped up as if we had been shot, for we had been sitting very democratically on the sidewalk, and round the corner, running with the speed of the scared, came a youthful English postal carrier. That was all at first.

But behind him were Chinese, and ponies and carts ridden or driven with recklessness that was amazing. The English youth had started gasping exclamations as he ran in, and tried to fetch his breath, when from the back of the Austrian Legation came a rapid roll of musketry.

Austrian marines, who were spread-eagled along the roofs of their Legation residences, and on the top of the high surrounding wall, had evidently caught sight of the edge of an advancing storm, and were firing fiercely. We seized our rifles—everybody has been armed *cap-à-pie* for days—and in a disorderly crowd we ran down to the end of the great wall surrounding the Austrian compounds to view the broad street which runs towards the city gates.

The firing ceased as suddenly as it had begun, and in its place arose a perfect storm of distant roaring and shouting. Soon we could see flames shooting up not more than half a mile from where we stood; but the intervening houses and trees, the din and the excitement, coupled with the stern order of an Austrian officer, shouted from the top of an outhouse, not to move as their machine-gun was coming into action over our heads, made it impossible for us to understand or move forward. What was it?

Presently somebody trotted up from behind us on a pony, and, waiting his opportunity, rode into the open, and with considerable skill seized a fleeing Chinaman by the neck. This prisoner was dragged in more dead than alive with fear, and he told us that all he knew was that as he had passed into the Tartar city through the Ha-ta Gate a quarter of an hour before, myriads of Boxers—those were his words—armed with swords and spears, and with their red sashes and insignia openly worn, had rushed into the Tartar city from the Chinese city, slashing and stabbing at everyone indiscriminately. The foreigners' guns had caught them, he said, and dusted them badly, and they were now running towards the north, setting fire to chapels and churches, and any evidences of the European they could find. He knew nothing more.

We let our prisoner go, and no sooner had he disappeared than fresh waves of fugitives appeared sobbing and weeping with excitement. The Boxers, deflected from the Legation quarter, were spreading rapidly down the Ha-ta Great Street which runs due north, and everybody was fleeing west past our quarter. Never have I seen such fast galloping and driving in the Peking streets; never would I have believed that small-footed women, of whom there are a goodly number even in the large-footed Manchu city, could get so nimbly over the ground. Everybody was panic-stricken and distraught, and we could do nothing but look on. They went on running, running, running. Then the waves of men, women and animals disappeared as suddenly as they had come, and the roads became once again silent and deserted. Far away the din of the Boxers could still be heard, and flames shooting up to the skies now marked their track; but of the dreaded men themselves we had not seen a single one.

We had now time to breathe, and to run round making inquiries. We found the Italian picquet at the Ha-ta end of Legation Street nearly mad with excitement; the men were crimson and shouting at one another. But there was nothing new to learn. Bands of Boxers had passed the Italian line only eighty or a hundred yards off, and a number of dark spots on the ground testified to some slaughter by small-bore Mausers. They had been given a taste of our guns, that was all; and, fearing the worst, every able-bodied man in the Legations fell in at the prearranged posts and waited for fresh developments.

At eight o'clock, while we were hurriedly eating some food, word was passed that fires to the north and east were recommencing with renewed vigour. The Boxers, having passed two miles of neutral territory, had reached the belt of abandoned foreign houses and grounds belonging to the foreign Customs, to missionaries, and to some other people. Pillaging and burning and unopposed, they were spreading everywhere. Flames were now leaping up from a dozen different quarters, ever higher and higher. The night was inky black, and these points of fire, gathering strength as their progress was unchecked, soon met and formed a vast line of flame half a mile long.

There is nothing which can make such a splendid but fearful spectacle as fire at night. The wind, which had been blowing gently from the north, veered to the east, as if the god's wished us to realise our plight; and on the breeze leading towards the Legations, some sound of the vast tumult and excitement was wafted to us. The whole city seemed now to be alive with hoarse noises, which spoke of the force of disorder unloosed. Orders for every man to stand by and for reinforcements to be massed near the Austrian quarter were issued, and impatient, yet impotent, we waited the upshot of it all. Chinese officialdom gave no sign; not a single word did or could the Chinese Government dare to send us. We were abandoned to our own resources, as was inevitable.

Suddenly a tremor passed over all who were watching the brilliant scene. The flames, which till then had been confined to a broad belt at least three thousand yards from our eastern picquets, began leaping up a mile nearer. The Boxers, having destroyed all the foreign houses in the Tsung-li Yamen quarter, were advancing up rapidly on the Tung T'ang—the Roman Catholic Eastern Cathedral, which was but fifteen minutes' walk from our lines. We knew that hundreds of native Christians lived around the cathedral, and that as soon as their lives were threatened they would at once seek refuge in their church, and we knew, also, what that would mean.

The roar increased in vigour, and then hundreds of torches, dancing like will-o'-the-wisps in front of our straining eyes, appeared far down the Wang-ta, or so-called Customs Street, which separates Sir R—— H——'s Inspectorate from the Austrian Legation. They were less than a thousand yards away. The Boxers, casting discretion to the winds, appeared to be once more advancing on the Legations. But then came a shout from the Austrian Legation, some hoarse cries in guttural German, and the big gates of the Legation were thrown open near us. The night was inky black, and you could see nothing. A confused banging of feet followed, then some more orders, and with a rattling of gun-wheels a machine-gun was run out and planted in the very centre of the street.

"At two thousand yards," sang out the naval lieutenant unexpectedly and jarringly as we stood watching, "slow fire."

I was surprised at such decision. *Tang, tang, tang, tang, tang,* spat the machine-gun in the black night, now rasping out bullets at the rate of three hundred a minute, as the gunner under the excitement of the hour and his surroundings forgot his instructions, now steadying to a slow second fire. This was something like a counter-excitement; we were beginning to speak at last. We were delighted. It was not so much the gun reports which thrilled us as the resonant echoes which, crackling like very dry fagots in a fierce fire as the bullets sped down the long, straight street, made us realise their destroying power. Have you ever heard a high-velocity machine-gun firing down deserted and gloomy thorough-fares? It crackles all over your body in electrical shocks as powerful as those of a galvanic battery; it stimulates the brain as nothing else can do; it is extraordinary.

The will-o'-the-wisp torches had stopped dancing forward now, but still they remained there, quite inexplicable in their fixity. We imagined that our five minutes' bombardment must have carried death and destruction to everyone and everything. And yet what did this mean? The flames, which had been licking round near the cathedral, suddenly burst up in a great pillar of fire. That was the answer; the cathedral was at last alight. At this we all gave a howl of rage, for we knew what that meant.

The picquets had been mysteriously reinforced by Frenchmen,

Englishmen, and men of half a dozen other nationalities, all chattering together in all the languages of Europe. "*Que faire, que faire,*" somebody kept bawling. "Get your damned gun out of the way," shouted other angry voices, "and let us charge the beggars." But Captain T——, the Austrian commander, was already conferring with a dear colleague whom he had discovered in the dark. Even in this storm of excitement the protocol could not be forgotten. Marines, sailors, and Legation juniors groaned; was this opportunity to be missed? At last they arranged it; it should be a charge of volunteers.

"Volunteers to the front," shouted somebody. Everybody sprang forward like one man. A French squad was already fixing bayonets noisily and excusing their rattle and cursing on account of the dark; the Austrians had deployed and were already advancing. *"Pas de charge,"* called a French middy. Somebody started tootling a bugle, and helter-skelter we were off down the street, with fixed bayonets and loaded magazines, a veritable massacre for ourselves in the dark. . . .

The charge blew itself out in less than four hundred yards, and we pulled up panting, swearing and laughing. Somebody had stuck someone else through the seat of the trousers, and the someone else was making a horrid noise about this trivial detail. Some rifles had also gone off by themselves, how, why and at whom no one would explain. A very fine night counter-attack we were, and the rear was the safest place. Yet that run did us good. It was like a good drink of strong wine.

But we had now reached the first torches and understood why they remained stationary. The Boxers, met by the Austrian machine-gun, had stuck them in long lines along the edge of the raised driving road, and had then sneaked back quietly in the dark. Every minute we expected to have our progress checked by the dead bodies of those we had slain, but not a corpse could you see. The Austrian commander was now once again holding a council of war, and this time he urged a prompt retreat. We had certainly lost touch with our own lines, and for all we knew we might suddenly be greeted with a volley from our own people coming out to reinforce us.

Our commanders wobbled this way and that for a few minutes, but then, goaded by the general desire, we pushed forward again, with a common movement, without orders this time. We moved more slowly, firing heavily at every shadow along the sides of the road. Here it seemed more black than ever, for the spluttering torches, which cast a dim light on the raised road itself, left the neighbouring houses in an impenetrable gloom. Whole battalions of Boxers could have lurked there unmarked by us; perhaps they were only waiting until they could safely cut us off. It was very uncanny.

In front of us the flames of the burning Roman Catholic Cathedral rose higher and higher, and the shouts and roars, becoming ever fiercer and fiercer, could be plainly heard. Just then a Frenchman stumbled with a muttered oath, and, bending down, jumped back with a cry of alarm. At his feet lay a native woman trussed tightly with ropes, with her body already half-charred and reeking with kerosene, but still alive and moaning faintly. The Boxers, inhuman brutes, had caught her, set fire to her, and then flung her on the road to light their way. She was the first victim of their rage we had as yet come across. That made us feel like savages. We were now not more than three hundred yards from the cathedral, and in the light of the flames, which were now burning more brightly than ever, we could see hundreds of figures dancing about busily.

We had just halted to prepare for a final charge when something moved in front of us. "Halt," we all cried, marking our different nationalities by our different intonations of the word. A sobbing Chinese voice called back to us: "*Wo pu shih; wo pu shih*," which merely means, "I am not," leaving us to infer that he was referring to the Boxers; and then without waiting for an answer the night wanderer, whoever he might be, scampered away hurriedly. The immediate result was that we opened a terrible fusillade in the direction he had fled, our men firing at least a hundred shots. Many mocking voices then called back to us from the shadows. There was laughter, too. It was obviously hopeless trying to do anything in this dark; so when a bugler trotted up from our lines with stern orders from the French commandant for his men to retire, we all stumbled back more than willingly We had gone out of our depth.

Meanwhile the flames spread farther and farther, until half the Tartar city seemed on fire. All Peking awoke, and from every part confused noises and a vast barking of dogs was borne down on us. What course should we take, if the attack was suddenly carried all round our area?

The French Minister was by this time officially informed that native Catholics were being butchered wholesale; that there were plenty of men who were willing to go and rescue them, but that no one seemed to have any orders, and that everyone was swearing at the general incompetence. Absolute confusion reigned within our lines;

the picquets broke away from their posts; the different nationalities fraternised under the excitement of the hour and lost themselves; and it would have been child's play to have rushed the whole Legation area. We felt that clearly enough.

It was not until well past midnight, and after several heated discussions, that a relief party was finally organised; but when they got to the cathedral there was hardly anything to see, for the butchery was nearly over and the ruin completed. Several hundred native Roman Catholics had disappeared, only a few Boxers were seen and shot and a few converts rescued.

How well I remember the scene when this second expedition returned, excited and garrulous as only Frenchmen can be. The French Minister led them in. He explained to us that the Boxers had already absolutely demolished everything—that it was no use risking one's self so far from one's own lines any more—that it was a terrible business, but *que faire*. . . . The French Minister did not hurry away, but stood there talking endlessly. It was at once dramatic and absurd. Sir R—— H——, in company with many others, stood listening, however, with an awestruck expression on his face. He carried a somewhat formidable armament—at least two large Colt revolvers strapped on to his thin body, and possibly a third stowed away in his hip pocket. From midnight to the small hours there was a constant stream of our most distinguished personages coming and looking down this street and wondering what would happen next. It was not a very valiant spectacle.

In this curious fashion the memorable night of the 12th passed away, with sometimes one picquet firing, sometimes another, and with everybody waiting wearily for the morning. We had almost lost interest by that time.

At half-past four the pink light began chasing away the gloom; the shadows lightened, and day at last broke. At six o'clock native refugees from the foreign houses that had been burned came slinking silently in with white faces and trembling hands, all quite broken down by terrible experiences. One gate-keeper, whose case was tragically unique, had lost everything and everybody belonging to him, and was weeping in a curious Chinese way, without tears and without much contortion of features, but persistently, without any break or intermission, in a somewhat terrifying fashion. His wife, six children, his father and mother, and a number of relations had all been burned alive—thirteen in all. They had been driven into the flames with spears.

Moaning like a sick dog, and making us all feel cowardly because we had not attempted a rescue, the man sought refuge in an outhouse. Sir R—— H—— was still standing at his post, looking terribly old and hardly less distressed than the wretched fugitives pouring in. His old offices and residences, where forty years before he had painfully begun a life-long work, were all stamped out of existence, and the iron had entered into his soul. A number of the officers commanding detachments, and people belonging to various Legations, attempted to glean details as to the strength of the Boxer detachments from these survivors, but nobody could give any information worth having. I noticed that no Ministers came; they were all in bed!

At eight o'clock, still afoot, we heard that there was a deuce of a row going on at the Ha-ta Gate, because it was still locked and the key was gone. It now transpired that a party of volunteers, led by the Swiss hotel-keeper of the place and his wife, had marched down to the gate after the Boxers had rushed in, had locked it, and taken the key home to bed, so that no one else could pay us their attentions from this quarter. This is the simplest and the most sensible thing which has been yet done, and it shows how we will have to take the law into our own hands if we are to survive.

In this fashion the Boxers were ushered in on us. Most of us kept awake until ten or eleven in the morning for fear that by sleeping we might miss some incidents. But even the Boxers had apparently become tired, for there was not a sign of a disturbance after midnight. In spite of the quiet, however, the streets remain absolutely deserted, and we have no means of knowing what is going to happen next.

10

Barricades and Reliefs

16th June, 1900.

We have entered quite naturally in these unnatural times on a new phase of existence. It is the time of barricades and punitive expeditions; of the Legations tardily bestirring themselves in their own defence, and realising that they must try and forget their private politics if they are even to live, not to say one day to resume their various rivalries and animosities. Imperceptibly we are being impelled to take action; we must do something.

We woke up late on the 14th to the fact that loopholed barricades had been everywhere begun on our streets, as effective bars to the inrush of savage torch-bearing desperadoes, each Legation doing its own work; and that the Chinese Government, with its likes and dislikes, would have to be seriously and cynically disregarded if we wished to preserve the breath of life. So barricades have been going up on all sides, excepting near the British Legation, where the same indifference and sloth, which have so greatly contributed to this *impasse*, still remain undisturbed.

Near the Austrian, French, American, Italian and Russian Legations barricade-builders are at work, capturing stray Peking carts, turning them over and filling them full of bricks. So quickly has the work been pushed on, that in some places there are already loopholed walls three feet thick stretching across our streets, and so cleverly constructed that carts can still pass in and out without great difficulty. We are still on speaking terms with the Chinese Government, but who knows what the morrow may bring?

But although you may have gathered some idea of the general aspect of Peking from what I have written, it is more than probable that you have no clear conception of the Legation quarter and what this barricading means. It seems certain that we will have to fight someone in time, so I will try and explain.

Legation Street, or the *Chiao Min hsiang*, to give it the native appellation, runs parallel to the Tartar Wall. Beginning at the west end of the street—that is, the end nearest the Imperial City and the great Ch'ien Men Gate—the Legations run as follows: Dutch, American, Russian, German, Spanish, Japanese, French, Italian. Of the eleven Legations, therefore, eight are in the one street, some on one side, some on the other; some adjoining one another, with their enormous compounds actually meeting, others standing more or less alone with nests of Chinese houses in between.

Apart from the eight Legations, there are a number of other buildings belonging to Europeans in this street, such as banks, the club, the hotel, and a few stores and nondescript houses. Taking the remaining three Legations, the Belgian is hopelessly far away beyond the Ha-ta Gate line; the Austrian is two hundred yards down a side street on which is also the Customs Inspectorate; and, finally, the British is at the back of the other Legations—that is, to the north of the south Tartar Wall. The extent of this Legation and its sheltered position make it a sort of natural sanctuary for all non-combatants, since it is masked on two sides by the other Legations, and is only really exposed on two sides, the north and the west. Already many missionaries and nondescripts have been coming in and claiming protection, and in the natural course of events it must become the central base of any defence. Everyone sees and acknowledges that.

At the two ends of Legation Street, the western Russo-American end and the eastern Italian end, heavy barricades have already gone up. The Dutch Legation, lying beyond the Russian and American Legations at this west end of the street, being without any guards and protectors, will, therefore, have to be abandoned immediately there is a rush from the Ch'ien Men Gate. The Belgian Legation is naturally untenable, and will also have to be sacrificed. The Austrian Legation is likewise a little too far away; but for the time being a triple line of barricades have gone up, having been constructed along the road between this Legation and the Customs inspectorate. Today, the 16th, carts are no more to be seen on these streets; foot traffic is likewise almost at an end. There is a tacit understanding that everybody must act on the defensive.

Also every Chinaman passing our barricades is forced to provide himself with a pass, which shows clearly his reason for wandering abroad in times like this. There has already been trouble on this score, for our system has had no proper trial. . . .

Since the 14th and that dreadful first Boxer night, we have begun to take affairs a good deal into our own hands, and have attempted to strike blows at this growing movement, which remains so unexplained, whenever an occasion warranted it—that is, those of us who have any spirit. Thus, on the afternoon of the 14th, Baron von K—— took a party of his marines on top of the Tartar Wall, pointed out to them a party of Boxer recruits openly drilling below on the sandy stretch, and gave orders to fire without a moment's hesitation. So the German rifles cracked off, and the sands were spotted with about twenty dead and dying. This action of the German Minister's at once created an immense controversy.

The timid ministers unhesitatingly condemned the action; all those who understand that you must prick an ulcer with a lancet instead of pegging at it with despatch-pens, as nearly all our chiefs have been doing, approved and began to follow the example set. This is the only way to act when the time for action comes in the East, and the net result is that we have been unendingly busy. There have been expeditions, raids, and native Christians pouring in and demanding sanctuary within our lines. One story is worth telling, as showing how we are being forced to act.

Word came to us suddenly that the Boxers had caught a lot of native Christians, and had taken them to a temple where they were engaged in torturing them with a refinement of cruelty. One of our leaders collected a few marines and some volunteers, marched out and surrounded the temple and captured everybody red-handed. The Boxers were given short shrift—those that had their insignia on; but in the sorting-out process it was impossible to tell everybody right at first sight. Christians and Boxers were all of them gory with the blood which had flown from the torturing and brutalities that had been going on; so the Christians were told to line up against the wall of the temple to facilitate the summary execution in progress.

Then a big fellow rushed out of a corner, yelling, "I have received the faith." Our leader looked at the man with a critical eye, and then said to him in his quietest tones, "Stand up against the wall." The Boxer stood up and a revolver belched the top of his head off. With that quickness of eye for which he is distinguished, our leader had seen a few red threads hanging below the fellow's tunic. The man, as he fell with a cry, disclosed his sash underneath. He was a Boxer chief.

At least thirty men were killed here.

But it was at the Western Roman Catholic Cathedral that the most exciting times up till now have been had, for there, as at the other cathedral, the Boxers have been at work. The first relief expedition went out during the night—that is, last night. Headed by someone from the French Legation, the expedition managed to bring in all the priests and nuns attached to the cathedral mission. Old Father d'A——, a charming Italian priest, was the most important man rescued. After having been forty years here, he surveys the present scenes of devastation and pillage with the remark, "*En Chine il n'y a ni Chrétiens ni civilisation. Ce ne sont là que des phrases.*" That is what he said.

This morning a second relief corps, containing the most miscellaneous elements, tramped away stolidly in the direction of the still smoking cathedral ruins in the hopes of saving some more unfortunates, and our expectations were soon realised. After a walk of a mile and a half, we rounded a corner with the sound of much wailing on all sides, and ran suddenly full tilt into at least two or three dozen Boxers, who have been allowed to do exactly as they like for days. There was a fierce scuffle, for we were down on them in a wild rush before they could get away, and they showed some fight. I marked down one man and drove an old sword at his chest.

The fellow howled frightfully, and just as I was going to despatch him, a French sailor saved me the trouble by stretching him out with a resounding thump on the head from his Lebel rifle. The Boxer curled over like a sick worm and expired. There was not much time, however, to take stock of such minor incidents as the slaying of individual men, even when one was the principal actor, for everywhere men were running frantically in and out of houses, shouting and screaming, and the confusion was such that no one knew what to do. The Boxers had been calmly butchering all people who seemed to them to be Christians—had been engaged in this work for many hours—and all were now mixed up in such a confused crowd that it was impossible to distinguish friends and foes.

As they caught sight of us, many of the marauders tore off their red sashes and fell howling to the ground, in the hope that they would be passed by. Dozens of narrow lanes round the ruined cathedral, which was still smoking, were full of Christian families hiding in the most impossible places, and everywhere Boxers and *banditti*, sometimes in groups, sometimes singly, still chased them and cut them down. Numbers had already been massacred, and several lanes looked like veritable shambles. The stench of human blood in the hot June air was almost intolerable, and the sights more than we could bear. Men, women and children lay indiscriminately heaped together, some hacked to pieces, others with their throats cut from ear to ear, some still moving, others quite motionless.

Gradually we collected an ever-growing mob of terror stricken people who had escaped this massacre. Some of the girls seemed quite paralysed with fear; others were apparently temporarily bereft and kept on shrieking with a persistency that was maddening. A young French sailor who did not look more than seventeen, and was splashed all over with blood from having fallen in one of the worst places, kept striking them two and three at a time, and cursing them in fluent Breton, in the hope of bringing them to reason. "*Eh bien, mes belles! Vous ne finissez pas,*" he ended despairingly, and rushed off again to see whether he could find any more.

The blood was rising to our men's heads badly by now, and I saw several who could stand it no longer stabbing at the few dead Boxers we had secured. We had none of us imagined we were coming to such scenes as these; for nobody would have believed that such brutal things were possible. When we judged we had finished rescuing every one alive, a man in the most pitiable condition ran out from behind the smouldering cathedral carrying a newly severed human head in either hand. He seemed but little abashed when he saw us, but came forward rapidly enough towards us, glancing the while over his shoulder.

Several sailors were rushing at him with their bayonets, ready to spit him, when he fell on his knees, and, tearing open his tunic, disclosed to our astonished eyes a bronze crucifix with a silver Christ hung on it. "*Je suis catholique,*" he cried to us repeatedly and rapidly in fair French, and the sailors stayed their cold steel until we had extracted an explication.

Then it transpired that he had used this horrible device to escape the notice of some Boxers who were still at work in a street on the other side of the cathedral. We ran round promptly on hearing this, and caught sight of a few fellows stripped to the waist, and gory with blood as I have never seen men before. Instead of fleeing, they met our charge with resolution, and one tall fellow put me in considerable danger of my life with a long spear, finally escaping before we could shoot him down.

On this side the ruins of the cathedral were covered with corpses burned black from the heat of the flames and exposure to the sun.

One woman, by some freak of nature, had her arms poised above her head as she sat dead, shrivelled almost beyond human recognition. It was probable that the Boxers had pitched many of their victims alive into the flames and driven them back with their swords and spears whenever they attempted to escape. . . .

At last we got away with everybody who was still alive, as far as we could judge. Tramping back slowly and painfully, the rescued looked the most pitiable concourse I have ever seen. Somehow it was exactly like that eloquent picture in *Michael Serogoff*, showing the crowds of Siberian prisoners being driven away by Feofar Khan's Tartars after the capture of Omsk. Among our people there were the same old granddames, wrinkled and white haired, supporting themselves with crooked sticks and hobbling painfully on their mutilated feet; the same mothers with their children sucking their breasts; the same little boys and little girls laden with a few miserable rags; the same able-bodied men carrying the food they had saved. The older people gazed straight in front of them with the stolid despair of the fatalist East, and did not utter a word. A woman who had given birth to a child the very night before was being carried on a single plank slung on ropes, with a green-white pallor of death on her features. I have never taken part in such a remarkable procession as this.

Thus bloodstained and very weary we finally reached our Legation quarter, and once again the energy and resolution of Dr. M——— expressed themselves. The grounds of the Su wang-fu, belonging to the Manchu prince Su, where the first Boxer we had openly seen had sought refuge a few days previously, were commandeered by him, and by evening nearly a thousand Catholic refugees were crowded into its precincts. All day people were labouring to bring in rice and food for their people, and camp-fires were soon built at which they could cook their meals.

Several of the *chefs de mission* were again much alarmed at this action of ours in openly rescuing Chinese simply because they were doubtful co-religionists. They say that this action will make us pay dearly with our own lives; that the Legations will be attacked; that we cannot possibly defend ourselves against the numbers which will be brought to bear against us; that we are fools. Perhaps we are, but still there is some comfort in discovering that this nest of diplomacy still contains a few men.

Meanwhile there is not a word of news from S———, and there are indications that our despatches to the Chinese Government, which are being sent from every Legation more and more urgently, are hardly read. The situation is becoming more and more impossible, and our servants say it is useless bringing in any news, as there is such confusion in the palace that nobody knows anything reliable.

11

Some Men and Things

16th June, 1900.

No developments have taken place during the past few hours. So far very few men have been conspicuous; and as it is these few who have brought about the only developments, and outlined our position, and that they are today all terribly tired, we have absolute monotony. I have not heard what the German Minister has been doing, but it is rumoured that he is engaged in trying to re-establish communication with Tientsin and the sea by bribing the Tsung-li Yamen smaller officials to take down packets of his despatches by pony-express. It seems doubtful whether this will succeed. For all communication has absolutely ceased now, and the Customs postal carriers say that it is impossible to get through by any stratagem, as all the roads are swarming with Boxers and *banditti*. The Chinese Government, in its few despatches to some of the Legations, is clearly temporising and trying to save itself.

There is no means of knowing what is going on inside the Palace, or of understanding what the Empress Dowager has decided. Everybody says it is all topsy-turvydom now in the capital, and that the most extraordinary reports are coming in from the provinces. Our Chinese despatch writers, our Manchu servants, and the few natives who come through our barricaded streets, all say the same thing—that it is too soon to speak, but that the dangers are enormous. Meanwhile the more timid of these people attached to the Legation area are sending word that they are sick and cannot come any more. It is a polite way of saying that they are afraid. I do not blame them, since anything now is possible. You cannot surely ask men to sacrifice themselves when they are only bound to you by the hire system. Such is the external and general situation.

Within our own quarter things are much the same, developing naturally along the line of least resistance.

Now that Prince Su's palace grounds have been openly converted into a Roman Catholic sanctuary, hundreds of converts are pouring in on us from everywhere, laden with their pots and pans, their beds, and their bundles of rice; indeed, carrying every imaginable thing. The great Northern Cathedral and Monseigneur F—— are in no danger, for the time being at least, since the cathedral and its extensive grounds are surrounded by powerful walls and the bishop has now got his fifty guards and possibly a couple of thousand young native Catholics, who can probably be armed and fight. So although it seems as if the whole Roman Catholic population of Peking is pouring in on us, we are in reality only getting a few hundred miserables who had no time to fly to their chief priest when the storm caught them; we have to prepare for the worst, as everything is developing very slowly.

Even in this matter of Chinese refugees the attitude of our foolish Legations is rather inexplicable. Actually up to within a few days ago some of the Ministers were still resolutely refusing to entertain the idea that native Christians—men who have been estranged from their own countrymen and marked as pariahs because they have listened to the white man's gospel—could be brought within the Legation area. In consequence of this hardly any Chinese Protestants have as yet come in.

Of course circumstance, the force of example, and a timidity in the face of the growing irritation, have at length broken down this weak-kneed attitude, but people have not yet finished discussing it. For instance, there is a remarkable story about the well-known S——, who wrote that celebrated book, *Chinese Characteristics*. He turned up at the British Legation late one evening, long before the Boxers entered the Tartar city, and brought positive proof that unless S—— was hurried in we would all be murdered by a conspiracy headed by the most powerful men. S—— was kept waiting for an hour, and then told that no time could be spared to see him as everybody was busy writing despatches!

This is indeed our whole situation expressed in a trivial incident; all the plenipotentiaries are trying to save their positions and their careers by violent despatch-writing at the eleventh hour. They know perfectly well that it is they alone who are responsible for the present *impasse*, and that even if they come out alive they are all hopelessly compromised. Young O—— told me that in their Legation they were actually antedating their despatches so as to be on the safe side! This shows how absolutely inexcusable has been the whole policy for three entire weeks.

We do not know what is going on around us; we do not know of what the Peking Court is thinking; we do not know by whom S—— has been stopped. We know nothing now excepting that we are gradually but surely getting so dirty that our tempers cannot but be vile. One never realises how great a part soap and water play in one's scheme of things until times like these. With upturned Peking carts blocking the ingresses to our quarter; with everything disgruntled and out of order; with native Christians crowding in on us, sensible heathen servants bolting as hard as they can, ice running short, we, the eleven Legations of Peking, await with some fear and trepidation and an ever-increasing discomfort our various fates under the shadow of the gloomy Tartar Wall. What is to be the next thing? I could possibly imagine and write something about this were I not so tired.

12
Hell Hounds

Night, 17th June 1900.

It is past twelve o'clock at night, but in spite of the late hour and my fatigue—I have been dead tired for a week now—I am writing this with the greatest ease, my pen gliding, as it were, over a surface of ice-like slippiness, although my fingers are all blistered from manual work. Why, you will ask? Well, simply because my imagination is afire, and taking complete control of such minor things as the nerves and muscles of my right arm, my eyes and my general person, it speeds me along with astonishing celerity. Let your imagination be aflame and you can do anything. . . .

It began last night. No sooner had the gates which pierce the Tartar Wall been closed by the Imperial guards, who still remain openly faithful to their duties, than there arose such a shouting and roaring as I have never heard before and never thought possible. It was the Boxers. The first time the Boxers had rushed in on us, it was through the Ha-ta Gate to the east of the Legations. Last night, after having for three days toured the Tartar city pillaging, looting, burning and slaying, with their progress quite unchecked except for those few hundred rifle shots of our own, the major part of the Boxer fraternity, to whom had joined themselves all the many rapscallions of Peking, found themselves in the Chinese or outer city after dark, and consequently debarred from coming near their legitimate prey. (The gates are still always closed as before.)

Somebody must have told them that they could do as they liked with Christians and Europeans; for, mad with rage, they began shouting and roaring in chorus two single words, "*Sha-shao,*" kill and burn, in an ever-increasing crescendo. I have heard a very big mass of Russian soldiery give a roar of welcome to the Czar some years ago, a roar which rose in a very extraordinary manner to the empyrean; but never have I heard such a blood-curdling volume of sound, such a vast bellowing as began then and there, and went on persistently, hour after hour, without ever a break, in a maddening sort of way which filled one with evil thoughts. Sometimes for a few moments the sound sank imperceptibly lower and lower and seemed making ready to stop.

Then reinforced by fresh thousands of throats, doubtless wetted by copious drafts of *samshu*, it grew again suddenly, rising stronger and stronger, hoarser and hoarser, more insane and more possessed, until the tympanums of our ears were so tortured that they seemed fit to burst. Could walls and gates have fallen by mere will and throat power, ours of Peking would have clattered down Jericho-like. Our women-folk were frozen with horror—the very sailors and marines muttered that this was not to be war, but an Inferno of Dante with fresh horrors. You could feel instinctively that if these men got in they would tear us from the scabbards of our limbs. It was pitch dark, too, and in the gloom the towers and battlements of the Tartar Wall loomed up so menacingly that they, too, seemed ready to fall in and crush us.

For possibly three or four hours this insane demonstration proceeded apace. The Manchu guards listened gloomily and curiously from the inside of the gates, but made no attempt to open them, but they equally refused sullenly to parley with a strong body of sailors and volunteers we sent with instructions to shoot anyone attempting to unlock the barriers. Yet it was evident that the guards had received special instructions, and that the gates would not be handed over to the mob.

A few minutes before midnight the sounds became more sullen, and beneath the general uproar another note, one of those in distress, began, as it were, like an undercurrent to this pandemonium. The cause we had not long to seek, for presently flames began to shoot up, a sight we were by now well accustomed to, though not in this purely trading quarter of the city. The fire, started with savage disregard in the very centre of the most densely populated street of the Chinese city, spread with terrible rapidity. Soon both sides of Ch'ien Men great street, just on the other side of the Tartar Wall, were enveloped in raging flames, and a lurid light, growing ever brighter and brighter, turned the dark night into an unnatural day.

Between the incendiaries and ourselves the great Tartar Wall stood firm, but though this ancient defence against other barbarians was an effective protection for us, it could not long remain immune itself. The *lou*, or square *pagoda*-like tower facing the Chinese city side, caught some of the thousands and tens of thousands of sparks flying skywards, and it was not long before the vast pile was burning as fiercely as the rest.

The great rafters of Burmese teak, brought by Mongol Khans six centuries before to Peking, were as dry as tinder with the dryness of ages; and thus almost before we had noted that the bottom of the tower was well alight the flames were shooting through the roof and out through the hundreds of little square windows which in olden days were lined by archers. Higher and higher the flames leaped, until the top of the longest tongues of fire, pouring out through a funnel of brick, was hundreds of feet above the ground level. Only Vereschagin could have done justice to this holocaust; I have never seen anything so barbarically splendid.

Meanwhile below this in the Chinese city all had become quiet, except for the increasing and growing roar of the all-devouring flames. The Boxers, as if appalled by their own handiwork and the mournful sight of the capital in flames, had retreated into their haunts and had left the unfortunate townfolk to battle with this disaster as they could. From the top of the wall, which I hastily climbed as soon as I obtained permission to leave my post, thousands and tens of thousands of figures could be seen moving hurriedly about laden with merchandise, which they were attempting to save. Busy as ants, these wonderful Chinese traders were rescuing as much of their invested capital from the very embrace of the flames as they could at a moment when the Boxer patriots, menacing and killing them with sword and spears as *san mao-tzu*, or third-class barbarians who sold the cursed foreigners' stuffs and products, had hardly disappeared.

Yet it seemed vain, indeed, to talk of salvage with half the city in flames, for other fires now began mysteriously in other places, which "lighted" the horizon. "*Tout Pékin brûlé*," muttered a French sailor to me as I passed back to my post, and his careless remark made me think that this was the Commune and Sansculottism intermixed—the ends of two centuries tumbled together—because we foreigners had upset the equilibrium of the Far East with our importunities and our covetousness of the Yellow Man's possessions. . . .

And what of S——, what of the Peking Government—what is everybody in the outside world doing—the distant world of which we have so suddenly lost all trace, while we are passing through such times? We do not know; we have no idea; we have almost forgotten to think about it. S—— was heard of twice some days ago from Langfang, a station only forty miles from Peking, but why he does not advance, why there is this intolerable delay, we do not know.

The Peking Government is still decreeing and counter-decreeing night and day according to the Government *Gazettes*. The ministers of our eleven Legations are meeting one another almost hourly, and are eternally discussing, but are doing nothing else. We have blocked our roads with barricades and provided our servants and dependents with passes written in English, French, German, Italian, Russian and Chinese—so that everyone can understand. We are now sick of such a multitude of languages and wish all the world spoken Volapük.

Thus with our rescued native Christians, our few butchered Boxers, our score and more of fires lighting the whole of the horizon, here in the middle of the night of the 16th of June we are no further forward in our political situation than we were two and a half weeks ago, when our Legation Guards arrived, and we esteemed ourselves so secure. Two and a half weeks ago! It seems at least two and a half months; but that is merely the direct fault of having to live nearly twice the proper number of hours in twenty-four.

13

A Few Crumbs

18th June, 1900.

It has just transpired that Hsü Tung, an infamous Manchu high official, who has been the Emperor's tutor, and whose house is actually on Legation Street some fifty yards inside the lines of the Italian Legation, has been allowed to pass out of our barricaded quarter, going quite openly in his blue and red official chair. This is a terrible mistake which we may pay for dearly.

Hsü Tung is a scoundrel who is at least thorough in his convictions as far as we are concerned. It is he who has long been boasting—and all Peking has been repeating his boast—that in the near future he is going to line his sedan chair with the hides of foreign devils and fill his harem with their women; and it is he, above all other men, who should have been seized by us, held as hostage, and shot out of hand the very moment the Chinese Government gives its open official sanction to this insane Boxer policy. Had we acted in this way and taken charge of a number of other high officials who live just around us, we might have shown the trembling government that a day of retribution is certain to come.

And yet listen what happened. Either on the 15th or 16th Hsü Tung sent the *major-domo* of his household cringing to the French Legation for a *passepartout*. He had already tried once to escape by way of the Italian barricades, but had been sternly ordered back, and his house placed under watch. Somehow, through the foolishness of an interpreter of the French Legation, he got his safe-conduct pass, and started out bold as brass in the morning, seated in his official chair and accompanied by his official outriders. He passed a first French barricade and reached an outer second barrier manned by volunteers, who challenged him roughly and then refused to let him pass.

The outriders then tried to ride our men down, and it needed a rifle-shot to bring them to their senses. Fortunately nobody was hurt, and presently the youthful volunteers had Hsü Tung himself out of the chair, and kept him seated on the ground while they debated whether they should respect the French pass or strap the great man up and send him to their own quarters as a prisoner of war.

In the end, however, one of the secretaries came up and inquired what it all meant, and then, of course, weak counsels prevailed, and Hsü Tung was allowed to sneak off unmolested down a side lane.

This incident is typical as showing the stamp of men who have commanding voices in our beleaguered quarter.

God help us if any considerable force is sent against us, for we can never help ourselves. Every proper-minded young man is a natural soldier methinks, even in *Anno Domini* 1900, but every elderly person in the same year of grace is quite valueless—that is what we have already discovered.

And yet even today all the senior people in our Legation area—those who are our guides and mentors—though they be secretly much alarmed, are comforting themselves with a great deal of garrulous talk because a letter has arrived from Tientsin—in fact, several letters have arrived. This is the first reliable news we have had for many days, and everybody seems now to imagine that we are safe. The chief item in these fateful missives seems to be that the Roman Catholic Cathedral at Tientsin has also been burned; that this was accompanied by massacres of native converts; and that the riverine port is swarming with Boxers.

And there is no news of S——, no news of anything good. What has become of him we cannot imagine. Yet Ministers, secretaries, and elderly nondescripts are somewhat relieved, and go about nervously smiling in a very ridiculous way. No one can quite make out why they are relieved, excepting perhaps, that they are delighted to find that the visible world still exists elsewhere, and goes on revolving on its own axis in spite of our dilemma. Why should the obvious be so often discovered?

Our poor Legation Guards and their commanding officers, with whom we were so pleased a fortnight ago, are quite as crushed as everyone else now—perhaps even more. You see the rank and file are merely a crowd of uneducated sailors, who have not yet made head or tail of what all this Peking *bouleversement* means. They were suddenly entrained and rushed up to Peking many days ago; they arrived in the dark; they were crammed into their respective Legations as quickly as possible; they have done a little patrol and picquet work on the streets, and have stood expectantly behind barricades which they were told to erect; but otherwise they are as completely at sea again as if they were back to their ships.... In all the clouds of dust and smoke around them, how can they understand?

It is true I have rather a grudge against some persons of the Legation defenders as yet unknown, and think of them perhaps a little angrily, for, like all soldiery, they loot. They have already taken my field-glasses, an excellent revolver, and several other things during the confusion of the nights. Of course this is the fortune of war, as all old campaigners will tell you, but a more decent interval should have been allowed to elapse before beginning the inevitable stripping process...

As for the detachment officers, some of them are very good fellows and some of them are not; but already they have each of them instinctively adopted the old attitude of the Legations towards one another. They are mutually suspicious. The detachment officers are also considerably tired and in very bad tempers, for the night has been turned into day with a regularity which cannot leave anybody very happy. Then dirt is accumulating, too, sad truth; and in the East you cannot feel dirty in the summer and be happy. That is quite impossible....

Thus we are all in a very grunting frame of mind. The British Legation appears to be at length hopelessly crowded with perspiring missionaries of all denominations and creeds, who have suddenly come in from beyond the barricades. Life must be quite impossible there. The novelty of this experience has been worn off, and I for one would welcome any change, either for better or worse. So long as it is only a change....

14

The Ultimatum

19th June, 1900.

How foolish we can be! Only last night I was bewailing the dullness and the dirt of it all, and the general absurdity and discomfort, and now without one qualm I confess I would willingly exchange yesterday's uncertainty for today's certainty—that we are all going to be made into mincemeat. But I do not even feel serious or desperate now; it has got beyond that.

I do not know at what hour the ultimatum came today; it may have been eleven in the morning or one in the afternoon; but one thing I do know is, that here, at four in the afternoon, the great majority of one thousand Europeans are shaking, absolutely distraught. It is evident therefrom that there is something impressive and demoralising to most people in the idea of finality, and that on the threshold of the twentieth century, courage, since it is seldom dealt in, is hardly a great living force. It makes one realise, too, that with all their faults, the aristocrats of France, who, a hundred years ago, were condemned to the shameful death of the guillotine and went in their tumbrils through streets filled with cursing crowds of *sans-culottes*, with scorn and contempt written on their features, were rather exceptional people. Things have changed since then, and the so-called Americanisation of the world has not conduced to gallantry.

Fortunate are we that there is no white man's audience to watch us impassively, and to witness the effects of this bombshell of an ultimatum which has come today. There is nothing so humiliating as abject fear. Curiously enough, the women bear it much better than the elder men, who are openly distraught; and when I say women, I mean all the women, both those belonging to the Legations and the dozens of missionary women who have crowded in. Nearly everyone of them is better than the elderly men; at least, they try and say nothing so as not to add to the terrible confusion....

But the ultimatum—what is it, and against whom is it so summarily directed? Briefly the ultimatum is a neat-looking document written on striped Chinese despatch-paper, and comes from the Tsung-li Yamen, or office charged with the overseeing of "the outside nations' affairs"—which are the affairs of Europe. After very briefly referring to a demand made by the allied admirals for a surrender of the Taku forts off the muddy bar of the Tientsin River—about which we know nothing—it goes on to say that as China can no longer protect the Legations, the Legations will have to protect themselves by leaving Peking within twenty-four hours, dating from today at four o'clock. That is all. Not another word.

Yet in other words this document means this: that the demand of the admirals must have been refused; that they would not have made it unless something disastrous had happened to S—— and to Tientsin; that acts of war have already been committed, and that it will be no longer a Boxer affair, but a government affair. This makes our position desperate enough in all truth. There is to be war.... The ultimatum was conveyed to the eleven Legations and the Inspectorate-General of Foreign Customs in twelve neat red envelopes by trembling *t'ing ch'ai* of the Chinese Government, and in spite of some attempt at first to hide its contents was soon known by everyone.

The twelve copies, indeed, were exactly alike, twelve bombshells, which, bursting in twelve different parts of our barricaded quarter, finally united their fumes until we were all fairly suffocated. For we have either got to flee now or be butchered. Mechanically all eyes were turned at once to the chiefs of the eleven missions to China, who have brought things to such a pass, and everybody demanded frantically that something should be done. People lost control themselves and behaved insanely. It was not long before the whole diplomatic body met—in a terrible gloom—at the Legation of the Spanish Minister, who is the *doyen* of the Corps, and soon a tremendous discussion was raging.

There were mutual recriminations, and proposal after proposal was taken up and rejected as being too dangerous. Nobody had for a moment dreamed that such a menace would come so swiftly. Expectant crowds soon gathered round the gates of the Spanish Legation, and attempted to find out what was being decided, but the only thing I could learn was that brave Von K—— proposed at once that the ministers should go in a body to the Yamen and force the Chinese Government to agree to an armistice.

This was vetoed by all, of course, and one gentleman openly wept at the idea. In the end, at seven o'clock, when it was nearly dark, a joint Note was prepared, saying that the ministers could only accept the demand made on them and prepare to leave Peking at once, but that twenty-four hours was too short a notice in which to pack their trunks, and that, besides, they must have some guarantees as to the ninety miles road to Tientsin, which were so swarming with bandits that communication had been completely interrupted. That is to say, the Ministers were prepared to accept. . . .

No sooner had this weak reply been despatched than a fresh wave of consternation passed over the whole Legation quarter, for we now number nearly a thousand white people in all, and we could never march that distance to Tientsin unbroken. But beneath that wave of consternation a fiercer note steadily rose—the note of revolt against the decrees of eleven men. I cannot describe to you what an intensity of passion was suddenly revealed. Muttering first, this revolt became quite open and almost unanimous.

All of us would have a fair fight behind barricades and entrenchments, but no massacre of a long, unending convoy. For picture to yourself what this convoy would be crawling out of giant Peking in carts, on ponies and afoot, if it were forced to go; we would be a thousand white people with a vast trail of native Christians following us, and calling on us not to abandon them and their children. Do you think we could run ahead, while a cowardly massacre by Boxers and savage soldiery was hourly thinning out the stragglers and defenceless people in the rear? Never!

Hardly anybody thought of eating all that long evening. Most of us were trying to find out whether some sensible understanding could not be arrived at; whether we could not prepare before it was too late. But it was quite in vain to plan anything or attempt to think of anything. Everything was so topsy-turvy, everybody so panic-stricken.

But as the night grew later and later, some people began busying themselves packing boxes, still deluding themselves that they were going to leave comfortably on the morrow as if nothing had happened. Yet the world is really upside down as far as we are concerned, and it is quite absolutely impossible that the situation should end so normally as to find us quietly retreating down the Tientsin road.

Others kept sending out servants to discover at what price carts would undertake to drive the whole way down to the sea, or at least to Tientsin. Forty, fifty, and even one hundred *taels* were demanded for three days' work; and then, although the carters said they would come if the government sends proper escorts of soldiers as has been promised, Heaven only knows if they will ever dare to move near our stricken quarter. Still in some Legations they ordered fifty carts at any price, with the most lavish promises of reward for those that could manage to secure them.

All the official servants soon came back trembling, saying that they had found a few carts, but that it was *pu yi t'ing*—not at all sure whether the carters would dare to move when daylight came. For the whole city is already in a fresh uproar; people are flying in every direction in the night. Stories come in of officials who have been pulled out of their chairs and forced to *K'et'ou* to Boxers to show their respect to the new power. Prince Tuan has been appointed President of the Tsung-li Yamen, high Manchus have been placed in charge of the Boxer commands, and rice is being issued to them from the Imperial granaries.

There is no end to the tales that now come in, since everybody has understood that there is no need for concealment and that there is going to be some sort of war. At two o'clock I even began to get news of what the Empress Dowager had been doing, and how the Boxer partisans had become so strong that it was absolutely impossible to hope for anything but the worst.

Once when I got some details which I thought of importance, I tried to find my chief in order to communicate it to him. But he was lost in the middle of the night, conferring unofficially with some of his colleagues; and I could but feel immensely amused when in his office I saw that he had been scribbling some frenzied notes on the back of a completed despatch, dealing with one of those petty little affairs which were so important only the other day.

Ah, where are the dear little political situations of only a few weeks ago; those safe little political situations which redounded so much to the credit of those that made them and did not contain any of the dread elements of our present very real and terrible one! Like soldiers who have degenerated from the chasing of mere vagabonds of mediocre importance, so have our Peking Ministers Plenipotentiary and Envoys Extraordinary fallen from their proud estate to mere diplomatic make-beliefs full of wind—wind-blown from much tilting at windmills, with their Governments rescuing them Sancho Panza-like at the eleventh hour....

But though for us there is still some hope, there is very little for the wretched native Christians quartered in the palace grounds of Prince Su, whom we have saved from the Boxers.

They soon heard the news, too, that the foreigner who has once saved them is going—going away because he has been ordered to. All night long there was an awful panic among these people which made one's heart sick, for they understood better than us how quickly they would be massacred once they left our care.

I shall never forget the night of the 19th of June, 1900, with all its tragedy and tragi-comedy, though I live to be a hundred. It allowed me to see something of real human nature in momentary flashes; of how mean and full of fear we really are, how small and how easily impressed. A hundred times I longed to have the time and the power to set down exactly so that everyone might understand the incidents and the sudden impulses which took place—all prompted by that master of human beings—FEAR. That is why we worship heroes, or we pretend we worship them, because it is the *culte*. For a moment these people who have been set on pedestals were not afraid. Is it only the power not to be afraid which makes one a hero?

15

The Debacle Begins

20th June, 1900.

It is notorious that in moments of tension, when the mind has been stimulated to too great an activity by unhealthy excitement, you think of the most curiously assorted things—in fact, of absurd things which are quite out of place. I have been thinking the whole time of something very stupid which is only fiction: That a Zulu, named Umslopagas, rode and ran one hundred miles in a single night and then refreshed himself sufficiently by a couple of hours' sleep to deliver battle with such vigour at the head of a marble staircase, that he saved the haggard hero. That is what I have been thinking of....

We of Peking are, unfortunately, not of the mettle of Zulus, and as far as I am personally concerned, three hours' sleep is but the appetite-giver for five hours more. And so on this fateful 20th June, with the time limit of our ultimatum expiring at four o'clock, I got up in no sort of valorous spirit, and with the feeling that tragedies outside the theatre—at least those that spin themselves out for an indefinite number of days—are quite impossible for us Moderns. But, then, probably everybody has always thought the same thing—even those who lived before the Renaissance.

At eight o'clock everyone was once more afoot, although most have hardly had a wink of sleep. All over our Legation quarter, dusty and dirty men, unwashed and unbathed, now squatted along the edge of the streets, hanging their weary heads against their rifles, with their faces very white from too much sentry-go and too little sleep. There is little distinction between sailors and Legation people, for we are all in the same dilemma. On this eventful 20th of June, instead of being resolute and alert, everybody is merely tired and weakened by a couple of weeks' watchfulness against Boxers during an unofficial semi-siege, a state of affairs which has quite unfitted us for fresh strains. Yet beyond our barricades of upturned carts and stolen building-bricks all was quiet and peaceful, and hardly a thing moves.

It seemed as if we had been only dreaming.... Wandering down beyond the eastern end of Legation Street, which gives you the most view of the mysterious world around the great Ha-ta Street, which the Boxers have conquered, indeed you find everything practically deserted, the people having learned that it is best to stay indoors until this crisis is solved in some manner. Occasionally a rag-picker, or some humble person so little separated from the life hereafter that to push a trifle closer does not spell much peril, can be seen hooking up rags and whatnots from the piles of Peking offal. If you speak to him he gives an unintelligent *pu chih tao*— "I do not know"—and moves boorishly on. As my old Chinese writer said a week ago, Peking has never been in such a state of topsy-turvydom since the robber who unseated the Ming dynasty rushed in two and a half centuries ago....

Going on top of the great Tartar Wall and gazing down on the scene of devastation and ruin beyond the Ch'ien Men Gate, one can hardly believe one's eyes, for where there was once a mighty bustle one now sees thousands of houses with nothing but their walls standing and charred timbers strewing the grounds. The great burned tower which blazed so wondrously a few nights ago is still half standing, its mighty brickwork too powerful and too proud to succumb totally to the flames' destroying energy. Gaunt and hollow-eyed, the old Tartar tower surveys the scene somewhat contemptuously, as if saying that the pigmy men of today are far removed from the paladins of old and their works....

Quiet and perfectly silent it all looks—but below the tower, and, indeed, on all sides as far as the eyes can see, some search shows little ants of men are at work in the ruins—not moving much, but bobbing up and down with unending energy and regularity. They are the beggars of Peking in their hundreds and thousands salving what they can from all this immense destruction by poking deep holes into the ruins and pulling out all manner of things from under the mass of bricks and rubbish. In the conserving hands of the Chinaman nothing is ever irremediably destroyed....

Looking far to the east, even the Ha-ta Gate, where no harm has been done, does not show much movement. The carts passing in and out are very few and far between, and the dust which in ordinary times floats above the din and roar of the gates in heavy clouds is today seemingly absent. Even our Peking dust is awed by the approaching storm and nestles close to Mother Earth, so that it may come to no harm.

The more I looked the more observant I became. The sun lolling up in a red ball, the birds, twittering and flying about while the heat of the day is not severe, showed themselves in a new light; and thus the 20th June is ushered in so complaisantly, when all the world of men appear merely tired and watchful, that the contrast makes one wonder, and at nine o'clock once more our Ministers Plenipotentiary and our *Chargés d'Affaires* gather their eleven estimable persons together at the Legation of the *doyen*. For yesterday's Ministerial reply agreeing to the Manchu order to vacate the capital, if certain conditions were fulfilled, had begged for an urgent answer by nine o'clock regarding the little counter-demands for a time-extension, and a definite arrangement concerning the Chinese troops who are to be the safe conduct along the Tientsin road.

Nine o'clock has come, but alas! with it there is no neat Chinese despatch on striped paper which would so relieve our ministerial feelings. The Chinese Government remains grimly silent, for the Chinese Government has spoken plainly once, and never within the memory of man has it done so on two consecutive occasions. So the eleven Ministers meet once more in anything but a happy frame of mind—eleven sorely tried and wholly fearful persons, except for two or three who vainly try to instil some courage into the others. All idea of completing the packing commenced last night has vanished; even that would demand action and resolution.

A proposal to visit the Tsung-li Yamen in a body is set aside with nervous protestations once more. The meeting thereupon became very stormy, and the French Minister was kind enough to report afterwards that the British Minister became thereafter very red—*il est devenu soudainement très rouge*, for what reason is unknown. S——, who did the minutes afterwards, said that the French Minister volunteered to go with the others if they would proceed in a body, and became very pale at the idea, that he confessed himself. Here we have, then, a red Minister and a white Minister, and if we add those who were most certainly blue and green, the national flags of the entire assembly could be fitly made up.

The French Minister, although simply a *citoyen* sent by the Republic to intrigue in times of peace, and aid his Russian colleague to the best of his ability, is a man withal, although quite unfitted *de carrière* for wars and sieges. In the French Legation he has been receiving such tearful instructions from his wife during the past three weeks that it is a wonder he has any backbone at all....

The meeting became stormier and stormier as it went on, S—— says, until old C—— argued that the only way to decide was to put everything to the vote. Every vote put was promptly lost, and after an hour's haggling they had got no farther than at the beginning!

The dramatic moment came when Baron Von K—— got up and stated shortly that as he had a previous appointment with the Tsung-li Yamen at eleven o'clock, in spite of the ultimatum and a possible state of war—in fact, in spite of everything—it was his intention to keep his appointment, cost what it might. The others urged him not to go, for they must have been feeling rather ashamed of themselves and their overvalued lives. But K—— insisted he would go; he had said so once, and did not intend to allow the Chinese Government to say he broke an appointment through fear.

S——, who told me the whole story a few hours afterwards, said that he added that as soon as his own personal business was finished, he would attend to the general question of the Legations' departure from Peking, if the diplomatic corps would give him authority. As time was pressing they gave it to him promptly enough. I remember everything that happened afterwards with a very extraordinary accuracy of detail, because I had just walked past the Spanish Legation when the Ministerial meeting broke up, and I had determined to follow any move in person so as to know what our fate was to be.

The German Minister turned into his Legation, and after a time he reappeared in his green and red official chair, with C——, the dragon-man, in a similar conveyance. There were only two Chinese outriders with them, as Von K—— had refused to take any of his guards. I remember Von K—— was smoking and leaning his arms on the front bar of his sedan, for all the world as if he were going on a picnic. The little *cortège* soon turned a corner and was swallowed up. I walked out some distance beyond our barricades with Baron R——, of the Russian Legation, and we wondered how long he would take to come back. We soon knew! How terrible that was! For not more than fifteen minutes passed before, crashing their Manchu riding-sticks terror-stricken on to their ponies' hides, the two outriders appeared alone in a mad gallop and nearly rode us down. Through the barricades they passed, yelling desperately. It was impossible to understand what they were saying, but disaster was written in the air.

At this we started running after these two men, but when we reached the corner of the French Legation the people there had already understood, and said the German Minister had been shot down and was stone-dead. Everybody was paralysed.

Meanwhile the outriders had reached the German Legation and had flung themselves, disordered, from their sweating ponies. The men of the Legation Guard were swarming round them and questioning them roughly when I came up, but there was nothing further to be learned about Von K——. A shot had passed through his chair and he had never moved again, while other shots struck all round. C——, the dragonman, dripping with blood, had run round a corner closely pursued by Chinese riflemen. What happened to him they cannot say, for they, too, would have been shot had they not fled. The tragedy was so simple, but so crushing, that we all stood dazed. Our one man of character and decision was dead—lost beyond recall!

A quarter of an hour after this half the German detachment was marching rapidly down Customs Street, with fixed bayonets and an air of desperation on their harsh Teutonic faces. They were determined to try and at least save the body. I thought of going with them, too, but a moment's thought told me there were other things which were now more pressing. I went and gave some attention to the contents of despatch-boxes which no one else had a right to see....

The detachment reached the scene of the murder led by a trembling outrider. Drops of blood were found on the ground; the Peking dust was scraped this way and that, as if it had only been made an accomplice unwillingly and with a violent struggle too; but the sedan-chairs, the bearers, the murderous soldiers, and every other trace had vanished completely. To question people was impossible, since everyone was keeping closely indoors and barred entrances everywhere met the eye. The Peking streets have become so lonely and deserted that not even a dog allows himself to be entrapped in the open. Later I heard that C—— had escaped, although terribly wounded.

The detachment tramped back stolidly, and would not answer a word when spoken to, for German despair is very gloomy. The remaining Plenipotentiaries at last understood the nature of the game that was being played, and realised that we were down to the naked and crude facts of life and death. Their confounded vacillation has alone brought us to this pass. They do realise it now, and they are made to realise it more and more by the savage looks everyone has been giving them ....

The departure for Tientsin half-acquiesced in but fifteen short hours ago is no longer thought of, for what the Ministers propose to do now interests no one. After impotently attempting to deal with questions for which they were in no wise fitted they have resigned themselves to the inevitable, and have become mere pawns like the rest of us. Fortunately the men who are men begin to work with frenzied energy, rushing about collecting food and materials. S——, the first Secretary of the American Legation, began it, and soon stood out with some insistence. He guesses with no one contradicting him that rice is useful, that flour is still more useful, and that every pound we can find in the native shops should be taken.

The obvious is often somewhat obscure in times like these, and the men who act are very laudable. There is no denying it that on this 20th the Americans showed more energy than anybody else, and pushed everybody to sending out their carts and bringing in tons upon tons of food. Every shop containing grain was raided, payment being made in some cases and in others postponed to a more propitious moment. The American missionaries concentrated in a fortified missionary compound a couple of miles from us, and the last people to remain outside were hastily sent for, given twenty minutes in which to pack their things, and marched in as quickly as possible by a guard of American marines.

There were seventy white men, women and children, and countless herds of native schoolgirls and converts. Their reports were the last we got. Vast crowds of silent people had watched them pass through the eastern Tartar city to our Legation lines without comment or without hostility. Gloomily the Peking crowd must have watched this strange convoy curling its way to a safer place, the missionaries armed in a droll fashion with Remingtons and revolvers, and some of the converts carrying pikes and carving-knives in their hands, for the Peking crowd and Peking itself has been, and is being, terrorised by the Boxers and the Manchu extremists, and is not really allied to them—of that we all are now convinced. But C——, who was so nearly massacred, came in too with the American missionaries. He managed somehow, after he was shot in a deadly place, to half-run and half-crawl until he was picked up and carried into the American missionary compound. From what I heard, he knows nothing more about the death of the German Minister. It was only a few hours ago, and yet it already seems days!

All the non-combatants were now rushed into the British Legation, and to the women and children join themselves dozens of men, whose place should be in the fighting-line, but who have no idea of being there. Lines of carts conveying stores, clothing, trunks and miscellaneous belongings were soon pouring towards the British Legation, and long before nightfall the spacious compounds were so crowded with impedimenta and masses of human beings that one could hardly move there. It was a memorable and an extraordinary sight.

The few Chinese shops that had been until now carrying on business in our Legation quarter in spite of the semi-siege and the barricades in a furtive way, were soon quietly putting up their shutters—not entirely, but what they call three-quarters shut after the custom on their New Year holidays, when they are not supposed to trade, but do trade all the same. The shop-boys, slipping their arms into their long coats and dusting off their trousers and shoes after the Peking manner with their long sleeves, made one feel in a rather laughable sort of way that finality had been reached! They had that curious half-laugh on their faces which signifies an intense nervousness being politely concealed.

Up to three o'clock these complaisant shopmen were still selling things at a purely nominal price, which was not entered in the books, but quietly pocketed by them for their own benefit. Having completed my own arrangements, I began idly watching their actions, they were so curious. At three o'clock sharp the last shutters went up, the last shopman pasted a diamond-shaped Fu, or Happiness, of red paper over the wooden bars, and vanished silently and mysteriously. It was for all the world once again exactly like the telegraph-operator in *Michael Strogoff*, when the Tartars smash in the front doors of his office and seize the person of the hero, while the clerk coolly takes up his hat and disappears through a back door. These Chinese had done business in the very same way, until the very last moment—the very last.

And not only are the few shopmen slipping away, but also numbers of others within our lines who had been half-imprisoned during the past week by our barricades and incessant patrolling. Men, women, and children, each with a single blue-cloth bundle tied across their backs containing a few belongings, slip away; gliding, as it were, rapidly across the open spaces where a shot could reach them, and scuttling down mysterious back alleys and holes in the walls, the existence of which has been unknown to most of us. This time the rats are leaving the sinking ship quietly and silently, for a quiet word passed round had informed everyone of what is coming, and no one wishes to be caught. This is the sort of silent play I love to watch.

Just before this, however, down beyond the Austrian Legation came a flourish of hoarse-throated trumpets—those wonderful Chinese trumpets. Blare, blare, in a half-chorus they first hang on a high note; then suddenly tumbling an octave, they roar a bassoon-like challenge in unison like a lot of enraged bulls. Nearer and nearer, as if challenging us with these hoarse sounds, came a large body of soldiery; we could distinctly see the bright cluster of banners round the squadron commander. Pushing through the clouds of dust which floated high above them, the horses and their riders appeared and skirted the edge of our square. We noted the colour of their tunics and the blackness of the turbans. Two horsemen who dismounted for some reason, swung themselves rapidly into their saddles, carbine in hand, and galloped madly to rejoin their comrades in a very significant way.

For a moment they half turned and waved their Mannlichers at us, showing their breast-circle of characters. They were the soldiers of savage Tung Fu-hsiang, and were going west—that is, into the Imperial city. The manner in which they so coolly rode past fifty yards away must have frightened someone, for when I passed here an hour later the Austrian Legation and its street defences had been suddenly abandoned by our men. We had surrendered, without striking a blow, a quarter of our ground! I remember that I was only mildly interested at this; everything was so *bouleversé* and curious that a little more could not matter. It was like in a dream. Tramping back, the Austrian sailors crowded into the French Legation and all round their lines and threw themselves down. One man was so drunk from lack of sleep that he tumbled on the ground and could not be made to move again. Everybody kicked him, but he was dead-finished and could be counted out. This was beginning our warfare cheerfully.

On top of the Austrians a lot of volunteers came in at a double, very angry, and cursing the Austrians for a retreat which was only discovered by them by chance. Like so many units in war-time, these volunteers had been forgotten along a line of positions which could have been held for days. Nobody could give any explanation excepting that Captain T——, the Austrian commander, said that he was not going to sacrifice his men and risk being cut off, when there was nobody in command over the whole area. T—— was very excited, and did not seem to realise one thing of immense importance—that half our north-eastern defences have been surrendered without a shot being fired.

At the big French barricades facing north an angry altercation soon began between the French and Austrian commanders. The French line of barricades was but the third line of defence here, and only the streets had been fortified, not the houses; but by the Austrian retreat it had become the first, and the worn-out French sailors would have hastily to do more weary fatigue-work carting more materials to strengthen this contact point. I remember I began to get interested in the discussion, when I found that there was an unfortified alley leading right into the rear of this. It would be easy at night-time to rush the whole line.

Meanwhile nobody knew what was going to happen. All the Ministers, their wives and belongings, and the secretaries and nondescripts had disappeared into the British Legation, and the sailors and the volunteers became more and more bitter with rage. A number of young Englishmen belonging to the Customs volunteers began telling the French and Austrian sailors that we had been *trahis*, in order to make them swear louder. I know that it was becoming funny, because it was so absurd when . . . *bang-ping, bang-ping*, came three or four scattered shots from far down the street beyond the Austrian Legation. It was just where Tung Fu-hsiang's men had passed. That stopped us talking, and as I took a wad of waste out of the end of my rifle I looked at my watch—3.49 exactly, or eleven minutes too soon. I ran forward, pushing home the top cartridge on my clip, but I was too late. "*A quatre-cents mètres*," L——, the French commander, called, and then a volley was loosed off down that long dusty street—our first volley of the siege.

Our barricades were full of men here, and it was no use trying to push in. I postponed my own shooting, for after a brisk fusillade here, urgent summons came from other quarters, and I had to rush away. . . . The siege had begun in earnest. I record these things just as they seemed to happen. We are so tired, my account cannot seem very sensible. Yet it is the truth.

PART 2—THE SIEGE

1

Chaos

21st June, 1900.

I passed the night in half a dozen different places, assimilating all there was to assimilate; gazing and noting the thousand things there were to be seen and heard, and sleeping exactly three hours. Few people would believe the extraordinary condition to which twelve hours of chaos can reduce a large number of civilised people who have been forced into an unnatural life. It is indeed extraordinary. Half the Legations are abandoned, excepting for a few sailors; others are being evacuated, and most people have even none of the necessities of life with them. For instance, at eight o'clock I discovered that I had had no breakfast, and on finding that it would be impossible for me to get any for some hours, I forthwith became so ravenously hungry that I determined I would steal some if necessary. What a position for a budding diplomatist!

Fortunately I thought of the Hôtel de Pékin before I had done anything startling, and soon C——, the genial and energetic Swiss, who is the master of this wonderful hostelry, had given me coffee. He told me then to go into his private rooms, ransack the place and take what I liked. I found I was not alone in his private apartments. Baron R——, the Russian commandant, had just come in before me, and had fallen asleep from sheer fatigue as he was in the act of eating something. He looked so ridiculous lying in a chair with his mouth wide open and his sword and revolver mixed up with the things he had been eating, that I began laughing loudly, and, aroused by this sound, two more men appeared suddenly—Marquis P——, the cousin of the Italian *chargé*, and K——, the Dutch Minister.

What they were doing there I did not inquire. The Dutch Minister was in a frightful rage at everything and everybody, and began talking so loudly that R—— woke up, and commenced eating again in the most natural way in the world, without saying a single word. As soon as he had finished he went to sleep again. He was plainly a man of some character; the whole position was so ridiculous and yet he paid no attention.

I soon got tired of this, as plenty of other people now came in, all calling for food, and I was really so weary from lack of sleep and proper rest that I could not remember what they were talking about two seconds after they had finished speaking. Most of the men were angry at the "muddle," as they called it, and said it was hopeless going on this way. One of the Austrian midshipmen told me that there had been altogether very little firing, and not more than a few dozen Chinese skirmishers engaged, but that the whole northern and eastern fronts of our square were so imperfectly garrisoned that they could be rushed in a few minutes. Everybody agreed with him, but nobody appeared to know who was in supreme command, or who was responsible for a distribution of our defending forces, which would total at least six hundred or seven hundred men if every able-bodied man was forced into the fighting-line. Fortunately the Chinese Government appears to be hesitating again; we have been all driven into our square and can be safely left there for the time being—that seems to be the point of view.

I now became anxious about a trunk containing a few valuables, which I had sent into the British Legation, and I determined to go in person and see how things were looking there. What confusion! I soon learned that it had been very gay at the British Legation during the night. At four o'clock of the previous afternoon, when the first shots had already been dropping in at the northern and eastern defences, not a thing had been done in the way of barricading and sandbagging—that everybody admitted. The flood of people coming in from the other Legations, almost weeping and wailing, had driven them half insane. At the Main Gate, a majestic structure of stone and brick, a few sandbags had actually been got together, as if suggesting that later on something might be done.

But for the time being this Legation, where all the women and children have rushed for safety, is quite defenceless. Yet it has long been an understood thing that it was to become the general base. It was not surprising, then, that at six in the evening yesterday a tragedy had occurred within eyesight of everybody at the Main Gate. A

European, who afterwards turned out to be Professor J——, of the Imperial University, an eccentric of pronounced type, had attempted to cross the north bridge, which connects the extreme north of Prince Su's palace walls with a road passing just one hundred yards from the British Legation northern wall, and perhaps three hundred yards from the Main Gate itself.

It was seen that the European was running, onlookers told me, and that after him came a Chinese brave in full war-paint, with his rifle at the trail. Instead of charging his men down the street to save this wretched man, the British officer, Captain W——, ordered the Main Gate to be closed, and everybody to go inside except himself and his file of marines. He then commanded volley-firing, apparently at the pink walls of the Imperial city, which form a background to the bridge, although he might as well have ordered musical drill.

Meanwhile the unfortunate J—— was caught half way across the stone bridge by some other Chinese snipers, who had been lying concealed there all the time behind some piles of stones. He was hit several times, though not killed, as several people swear they saw him crawling down into the canal bed on his hands and knees. Volley-firing continued at the Main Gate, and the aforesaid British officer cursed himself into a fever of rage over his men. Even when J—— had finally disappeared, no steps were taken to see what had become of him; he was calmly reported lost. This was the opening of the ball at the British Legation.

No sooner was it dark than M——, the chief, appeared on the scenes, smoking a cigarette reminiscent of his Egyptian campaign, and clad in orthodox evening dress. This completed everyone's anger, but the end was not yet. At ten in the evening a scare developed among the women, and it was decided to begin fortifying some of the more exposed points. Everybody who could be found was turned on to this work, but in the dark little progress could be made excepting in removing all possibility of any one going to sleep.

But the sublimely ridiculous was reached in an out-of-the-way building facing the canal, an incident displaying even more than anything else the attitude of some of the *personnel* of our missions to China. Sleeping peacefully in his nice pyjamas under a mosquito net was found a sleek official of the London Board of Works, who wanted to know what was meant by waking him up in the middle of the night. Investigations elsewhere found other members of this Legation asleep in their beds; everybody said the young men were all right, but those above a certain age...!

The night thus spent itself very uneasily. They were only learning what should have been known days before.

When day broke in the British Legation things had seemed more impossible than ever. Orders and counter-orders came from every side; the place was choked with women, missionaries, puling children, and whole hosts of lamb-faced converts, whose presence in such close proximity was intolerable. Heaven only knew how the matter would end. The night before people had been only too glad to rush frantically to a place of safety; with daylight they remembered that they were terribly uncomfortable—that this might have to go on for days or for weeks. It is very hard to die uncomfortably. I thought then that things would never be shaken into proper shape.

In this wise has our siege commenced; with all the men angry and discontented; with no responsible head; with the one man among those high-placed dead; with hundreds of converts crowding us at every turn—in a word, with everything just the natural outcome of the vacillation and ignorance displayed during the past weeks by those who should have been the leaders. Fortunately, as I have already said, so far there has been no fighting or no firing worth speaking of. Only along the French and Italian barricades, facing east and north, a dropping fire has continued since yesterday, and one Frenchman has been shot through the head and one Austrian wounded.

It is worth while noting, now that I think of it, that the French, the Italians, the Germans, and, of course, the Austrians, have accepted Captain T——, the cruiser captain, as their commander-in-chief, and that the Japanese have signified their willingness to do so, too, as soon as the British and Americans do likewise. Thus already there are signs that a pretty storm is brewing over this question of a responsible commander; and, of course, so long as things remain as they are at present, there can be no question of an adequate defence. Each detachment is acting independently and swearing at all the others, excepting the French and Austrians, for the good reason that as the Austrians have taken refuge in the French lines they must remain polite. Half the officers are also at loggerheads; volunteers have been roaming about at will and sniping at anything they have happened to see moving in the distance; ammunition is being wasted; there are great gaps in our defences, which any resolute foe could rush in five minutes were they so inclined; there is not a single accurate map of the area we have to defend!

All this I discovered in the course of the morning, and by afternoon I had nothing better to do than go over to the great Su wang-fu, or Prince Su's palace grounds, now filled with Chinese refugees, both Catholic and Protestant, and there watch the Japanese at work. The Japanese Legation is squashed in between Prince Su's palace grounds and buildings and the French Legation lines, and, consequently, to be on the outer rim of our defences the little Japanese have been shifted north and now hold the northeast side of our quadrilateral. Prince Su, together with his various wives and concubines and their eunuchs, has days ago fled inside the Imperial city, abandoning this palace with its valuables to the tender mercies of the first comers; and thus the Japanese sailor detachment, reinforced by a couple of dozen Japanese and other volunteers, has made itself free with everything, and is holding an immense line of high walls, requiring at least five hundred men to be made tolerably safe.

But they have an extraordinary little fellow in command, Colonel S——, the military *attaché*. He is awkward and stiff-legged, as are most Japanese, but he is very much in earnest, and already understands exactly what he can do and what he cannot. After a search of many hours, I found here the first evidences of system. This little man, working quietly, is reducing things to order, and in the few hours which have gone by since the dreadful occurrences of yesterday he has succeeded in attending to the thousand small details which demanded his attention. He is organising his dependents into a little self-contained camp; he is making the hordes of converts come to his aid and strengthen his lines; in fact, he is doing everything that he should do. Already I honour this little man; soon I feel I shall be his slave.

But not only is there order within these Japanese lines; attempts are being made to find out what is going on beyond—that is, to discover what is being done in this deserted corner of the city, which is abandoned to the European. Although all is quiet without, it is not possible that everyone has fled, because some rifle-firing is going on... When I arrived the Japanese had already discovered that a Chinese camp had been quietly established less than a quarter of a mile away. Half an hour afterwards a breathless Japanese sailor brought in a report that snipers had been seen stealthily approaching. I was just in the nick of time, as Colonel S—— immediately decided on a reconnaissance in force; anyone who liked could go. Would I go?

We slipped out under command of the colonel himself and worked through tortuous lanes down towards the abandoned Customs Inspectorate and the Austrian Legation. We reached the rear of the Customs compounds without a sound being heard or a living thing seen. All along hundreds of yards of twisting alleyways the native houses stood empty and silent, abandoned by their owners just as they are. Even the Peking dog, a cur of great ferocity, who in peaceful times abounds everywhere and is the terror of our riding-parties, had fled, as if driven away by the fear of the coming storm. In the distance, as we stealthily moved, we could hear an occasional rattle of musketry, probably directed against the French Legation and the Italian barricade, where it has been going on for twenty-four hours; but so isolated is one street in Peking from the rest by the high walls of the numberless compounds and the thick trees which intercept all sounds that we could be certain of nothing. Perhaps the firing was not even the enemy at work, whoever he may be; it might be our men. . . .

But directly in front of us all was still, and just as we thought of stealing on, a Japanese whispered "Hush," and pointed a warning finger. We flattened ourselves against houses and scurried into open doors. Suddenly it was getting exciting. Down another lane then came a noisy sound of feet, incautiously pattering on the hard ground to the accompaniment of some raucous talk. It is the very devil in this network of lanes and blind alleys which twist round the Legations, and no force could properly patrol them. . . .

Without any warning two men came round the corner, peering everywhere with sharp eyes and bobbing up and down. Simultaneously with the sob of surprise they gave our rifles crashed off. And this time, owing to the short range and the Japanese warning, we got them fair and square, and both of them rolled over. But no, one fellow jumped to his feet again, and before we could stop him was down another lane like a flash of lighting. We promptly gave chase, yelling blue murder in an incautious manner, which might have brought hundreds of the enemy on our heels. But we did not care.

Round a corner, as we followed the man up, a high wall rose sheer, but nothing daunted, the fellow took a tremendous leap, and by the aid of the lattice-work on a window, climbed to a roof. Then *bang, bang, bang,* seven shots went at him rapidly, one after another. In spite of the volley the man still crawled upwards, but as he reached the top of the low house and passed his legs over he gave a feeble moan and then. . . . *flopper-ti flop, flopper-ti flop,* he crashed down the other side and ended with a dull thud on the ground. On the other side there he was dead as a door-nail and all covered with blood.

It was our first proper work. But he was not a soldier, he was a Boxer; and in place of the former incomplete attire of red sashes and strings, this true patriot wore a long red tunic edged with blue, and had his head tied up in the regulation *bonnet rouge* of the French Revolution. Round his waist he had also girded on a blue cartridge-belt of cloth, with great thick Martini bullets jammed into the thumb holes. This we thought very curious at the time, as the Boxers were supposed to laugh at firearms. Elated by this little affair, we pushed on, and came upon other men working round our lines in small bands, and exchanged shots with them. All were Boxers in this new uniform; but although we tried to entice them on and corner them in houses, they were too cunning for us, and broke back each time. In the end we had so stirred up this hornet's nest that the scattered firing became more and more persistent, and stern orders came for us to fall back.

We came in feeling elated, but Colonel S—— was looking serious, for he had discovered that the extent of Prince Su's outer walls, which have to be held in their entirety, is so much greater than was expected, and every part can be so easily attacked from the outside, that the task is desperate. There are less than fifty men in all for these long Japanese lines, and if we take more from elsewhere it will be merely creating fresh gaps.... Decidedly it is not enticing. The whole line from the north right round to the south, where the Japanese, French, Austrians, Italians and Germans are distributed, ending on the Tartar Wall itself, is terribly weak. And as I began to understand this, an hour after this afternoon adventure I became quite gloomy at the outlook.

Everything, indeed, was upside down. Matters in the British Legation were not improving, and the fighting air which exists elsewhere is not to be found here. Men, women and children; ponies, mules and packing-cases; sandbags and Ministers Plenipotentiary—are still all engaged in attempting to sort themselves out and keep distinct from one another. Already the British Legation has surrendered itself, not to the enemy, but to committees. There are general committees, food committees, fortifications committees, and what other committees I do not know, except that American missionaries, who appear at least to have more energy than anyone else, are practically ruling them.

This is all very well in its way, but it is curious to see that dozens of able bodied men, armed with rifles, are hiding away in corners so that they shall not be drafted away to the outer defences. Everywhere a contemptible spirit is being displayed, because a feeling prevails that there are no responsible chiefs in whom absolute trust can be placed.

A pleasant mess in all truth. It is now everyone for himself and nobody looking after the others....

Some of the people, however, have begun dividing themselves up, and now are billeted, nationality by nationality, in separate quarters. But many persons seem lost and distraught. H——, the great director of Chinese affairs, was sitting on an old mattress looking quite paralysed; P——, his counterpart in the Russian bank, was striding about excitedly and muttering to himself. The Belgian Legation has disappeared entirely; whether they have run away or been lost in the confusion I could not for the life of me tell. What a position, what a condition!

Already it is a great feat to be on speaking terms with a dozen people, and if we could only instil some of the savageness we all feel towards one another into our defence, it would become so vigorous and unconquerable that not all the legions of the Boxer Empire, massed in serried ranks, could break in on us. But this very defence, which should be so determined, is the most half-hearted thing imaginable. It has no real leader, and merely resolves itself into the old policy of each Legation holding its own in an irregular half-circle round the British Legation, which itself is a mass of disorder. I feel certain that if we have a night attack at once the Chinese will break in with the greatest ease, and then.... *Tant pis!*

The last thing I saw in the British Legation was M——, the great correspondent, sitting on a great stack of his books, looking wearily around him. His former energy and resolution have all departed, sapped by the spectacle of extraordinary incompetence around him. Of what good has all that rescuing of native Christians been—all that energy in dragging them more dead than alive into our lines in the face of Ministerial opposition, when we cannot even protect ourselves? But just when I began this moralising, the hundred and fifty mules and ponies that have been collected together all broke loose, frightened by some stray shots, and went careering madly around us. It was pitch dark and most gloomy before they had been all tied up again, and although firing became heavier and heavier as Chinese snipers found they could approach our outer lines in safety, I finally sought out a spot for myself and fell asleep with my rifle on my chest—cursing everybody. It is a sign of the times—my nerves are becoming Ministerial!

2

The Retreat and the Return

23rd June, 1900.

Yesterday the inevitable happened, and only Heaven and the foolishness of the attacking forces, who are only playing with us, and do not seem to have settled down to their work, saved us from complete annihilation. Without a word of explanation, Captain T——, the Austrian commander, suddenly ordered all the French, Italians and Austrians to fall back on the British Legation, sending word meanwhile to the Japanese and the Germans to follow his example. This meant that the whole vast semicircle to the northeast and the southeast was being thrown up. The result was that for ten minutes armed men of all nationalities poured into the British Legation, until every rifle-bearing effective was standing there, all jabbering in a mass, and not knowing what it was all about.

The Americans, who had established themselves on the Tartar Wall as the main point in the western defence, guessed they were not going to be left there cut off from salvation by a failure to remember their existence; and presently they, too, ran in, openly swearing at their officers. These American marines have never quite liked this idea of being planted on the Tartar Wall; for with that smartness for which their race is distinguished, they see it is quite on the cards that they are forgotten up there if a rush occurs while the others are sitting safe in the main base. And the Americans are not going to be forgotten—we soon found that out. They are the people of the future.

Depict to yourself, if you can, the blind fear of all the Plenipotentiaries, of all the missionaries and their lamb-faced converts, on seeing the gallant defenders of the outer lines rushing in on them at a fast trot, and then falling into line and standing very much at ease awaiting the next move. I may be brutal, but I relished that scene a little;

it was a lesson that was sadly needed. It was the British Minister who remained the most calm; perhaps he immediately understood that the game was now in his hands. But the other ministers, I wish you could have but seen them! They crowded round his British Excellency in an adoring and trembling ring, and without subterfuge offered him the supreme command; that was exactly what we had been expecting.

Underneath their manner you could easily see they meant to say that they knew it was the British Legation in which they had taken refuge; that they had had enough of all these alarums and excursions; and that so long as they were left in peace they did not care about the rest. What mean little people we are in this world! The French, the Russian, the Italian and the Japanese Ministers were the first to act thus, and as they represented a majority of the detachments, the others who had Legation Guards had pretty well to follow suit, whether they liked it or not, and some did not like it, as I shall show hereafter. M—— had been hinting very plainly that he had been in a kilted regiment, and that the British Legation was the hub of the defence—the asylum for all; and so with a satisfied smile, he was pleased to accept the proffered appointment.

Yet it was one only in name. For just as he was writing out his first *ordre du jour* the various Plenipotentiaries showed their appreciation of the office they had conferred on him by ordering, each one of them separately, their respective detachments to return to their respective Legations so hurriedly abandoned. So the sailors and the marines, and the fighting volunteers who bear them company, bundled back to the outer lines and barricades again, finding all just as it had been before, except that the Italian Legation was in flames and the Italian barricades therefore useless. The snipers had found that they could suddenly work in peace, and had thrown blazing torches. Four Legations are now destroyed and abandoned, for the Belgian, the Austrian and the Dutch have all gone up in flames at different times during the last days. Seven Legations remain and ten ministers.

The defence is thus getting into reasonable limits and so long as our attacks are confined to what they have been up till now, we may really pull through. Incendiary fires round the outer lines, lighted by means of torches stuck on long poles, a heavy rifle-fire poured into the most exposed barricades by an unseen enemy, and very occasionally a faint-hearted rush forward, which a fusillade on our part turns into a rout—these have so far been the dangers with which we have had to contend. But the very worst feature of the defence is that no one trusts the neighbouring detachment sufficiently to believe that it will stand firm under all circumstances and not abandon its ground; consequently this fear that a sudden breakdown along some barricades will allow of an inrush of Chinese troops and Boxers makes men fight all the time with their eyes over their shoulders, which is the very worst way of fighting I can possibly imagine.

And another hardly less important point is that the burden is not evenly apportioned, and that the men know it. For instance, the British Legation, which is as yet not in the slightest exposed, is full of able-bodied men doing nothing—whereas on the outer lines of the other Legations many men are so dead with sleep that they can hardly sit awake two hours. It can easily be seen from the rude sketches I have made and re-made, what I mean. I have been over every inch on my own legs; there can be no mistake.

From the main sketch you will see that the holding of the Tartar Wall, together with the American and Russian Legations, protects the British Legation effectively from the south and partially, from the west; that the Franco-German-Austrian lines, and the Su wang-fu, with the Japanese, mask the east; and that of the other two sides on which the British Legation walls and outbuildings really constitute the actual defence line directly in touch with the enemy, the Imperial Carriage Park, a vast grass-grown area with but half a dozen yellow-roofed buildings in it, makes the western approaches very difficult to attack, since they are easily swept by our rifle-fire; and that the northern side is so filled with buildings belonging to the Chinese Government (which it now seems cannot be destroyed), that I do not apprehend attacks here. The only real dangers to the British Legation in any case are these two corners to the north and the southwest. . . .

Passing over to the Su wang-fu, you realise the extraordinary difference between the danger points along the British Legation northern and western barricades, and little Colonel S——'s command. Here you are in direct touch with the enemy, for the snipers of forty-eight hours ago have been strongly reinforced, doubtless attracted by the possibility of loot.

Soldiers and all sorts of *banditti* must have joined hands with the Boxers, for it is clear that every hour is mysteriously adding more and more men round our lines. You can hear the men talking, and you can see bricks moving but fifty or sixty yards from where you are squinting through a loophole as fresh barricades, that are gradually surrounding us in a vise which may yet crush us to death, are

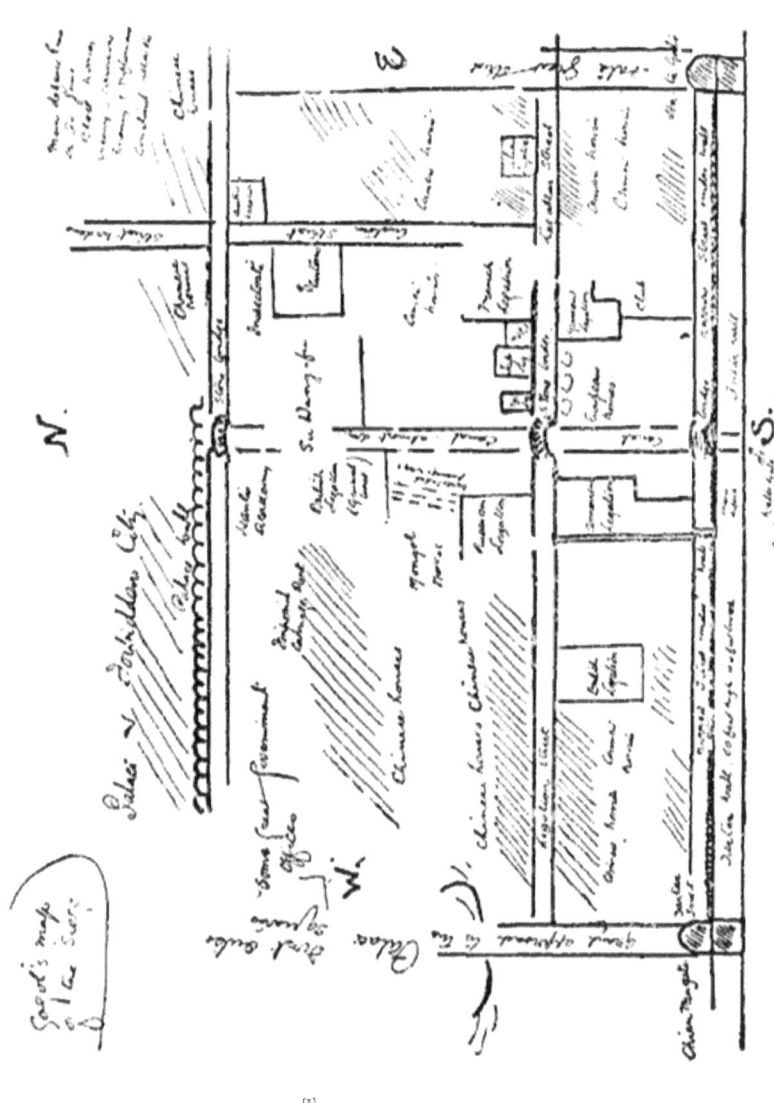

MAP OF THE SIEGE

silently built. The forty or fifty Japanese, and the few volunteers who are with them, have now been reinforced by all the Italians, who have been given a big strip of outer wall and a fortified hillock in Prince Su's ornamental garden—a hillock which commands a great stretch of territory, as territory goes in our wall split area. For here in the Su wang-fu the number of walls and buildings is terrible, and Heaven only knows how seventy or eighty men can even make a pretence of holding such positions. First there is the great outer wall eighteen feet high and three feet thick.

Then from this outer wall, other thick walls run inwards at right angles, splitting up the place into little squares, in which as likely as not there will be a group of houses with great dragon-adorned roofs. Further towards the centre of the Fu is Prince Su's own palace and his retainers' quarters; to the south of this is an ornamental garden full of trees, a vast and mournful enclosure, standing in which the crack of outpost rifles can only be distantly heard. Moving across to the southern side—that is, the side near the French Legation and the protected Legation Street—the Christian refugees are found gathered here in huge droves. In one building there are alone four hundred native schoolgirls, rows upon rows of them that never seem to come to an end, sitting on the ground in their sober blue coats and trousers, peacefully combing each other's hair, or working on sandbags with the imperturbability of the Easterner who is placid under death. Farther on, again, you come on families, sometimes three generations huddling together on a six-foot straw mat.

A mother trying to feed a child from her half-dry breasts tells you quietly that it is no use, since the meagre fare she is already getting does not make sustenance enough for her, let alone her child. Yet everything possible is being done to feed them. All the able-bodied converts have long ago been drafted off for barricade-building and loophole-making in the endless walls, and here the curious Japanese passion for order and detail is shown on the coats of the older men. The boss-shifts, each responsible for so many men who have to accomplish a given amount of work in a specified time, have big white labels with characters written squarely across them, telling everyone clearly what they are.

At a little table nearby writers, who have been carefully sorted out from this incongruous gathering, are provided with brush and ink, and have been set to work making up reports and lists of all the people. These are handed to a Japanese Secretary of Legation, who has been evolved into an engineer-in-chief and overseer of native labour, and thus at every hour of the day the distribution of the barricaders is known. Amid these crowds of native refugees, who number at least a couple of thousand people, two or three Japanese occasionally wander to see that all's well, and give the babies little things they have looted from Prince Su's palace to play with. Content to be where they are and assured that the European will not abandon them, these natives exhibit in a strange manner that inexplicable thing—Faith. Poor people—they little know! Is it always thus with faith?

So the Su wang-fu, which is but the north-western part of our lines, is now a city in itself, inhabited by the most unlikely people in the world. Three days have sufficed to give it an entity of its own. The nature of the defence and the fighting value of the Japanese as compared to the Italians, are fitly illustrated by the distribution of forces which little Colonel S—— has already made. The Italians hold perhaps a hundred feet of the outer wall and one hillock of some importance.

The Japanese have at least a thousand feet of loopholed and un-loop-holed wall, and are quite ready to take another thousand if someone would be kind enough to give it to them. In posts of three and four men, distant sometimes hundreds of feet apart, the little Japanese takes his two hours on and his four hours off night and day without a murmur or without ever a break. Only at one place are there more than three or four little men together. At the eastern end of the Fu there is a big post grouped round the fortified Main Gate, where there are actually eight or nine men under the command of a Japanese naval lieutenant.

But the genius who has organised all this system, the little Japanese colonel, does not waste time walking around. He is at work at an eternal map decorated with green, blue and red spots, which show the distribution of his forces and their respective strength and fighting value. Somehow I could not tear myself away from this quarter. It was so orderly. . . .

Behind the commanding hillock in the Italian centre I found Lieutenant P——, the Italian naval officer, dining off bread and Bologna sausage, which he was stripping after the Italian fashion, inelegantly using his knife both to punctuate his sentences and to assist the passage of his food. "Look out," he cried, as soon as I had appeared, "it is very warm here; the bullets are flying low." The leaves of the trees under which he was sitting were indeed falling thickly, cut down by snipers' fire. But still I wish he would walk down to a Japanese post not more than five hundred feet away and watch a little Jap and a half dozen Chinese snipers at work against each other. That is where I had just been—convoying some supplies.

The little Japanese had ostentatiously placed his sailor cap just in front of an empty loophole twenty feet from where he actually squatted, and where he had probably been a few seconds before I had arrived. The snipers saw this and promptly fired, *bang, bang, bang,* a long line of shots following one after the other in quick succession. Hum! they must be reloading now, said the little Jap plainly by the expression on his face; and jumping straight on top of the wall in front of him he hastily snapped at one of his enemies. Then down he came again, but hardly quick enough, for bricks were dislodged all around him, and once he received one on the head. The little man rubbed his cranium ruefully, shook himself like a dog to get rid of the sting, and then with a little more caution began his strange performance again.

This is what is going on all round the Japanese posts—men bobbing up and firing rapidly, in some cases only fifty feet away from one another. The Italians are lying comfortably on their stomachs completely out of sight, and wildly volleying far too often. Already their ammunition is running low, although there is hardly any need really to reply at all to our enemies. They have crept closer, it is true, and without surprising any one, or even causing notice, their numbers of riflemen have grown from hour to hour. Now I come to think of it, there must be many hundreds of men lying all round us and firing just as they please. But they are hidden behind walls and ruined houses; they belong to our curious state; they are the essential things after all. How foolish one becomes!

Threading your way due south you come suddenly on a French picquet, four Frenchmen and two Austrians behind a heavy barricade. This precious Su wang-fu is merely linked to the French Legation by a system of such posts audaciously feeble when you consider the duty they have to undertake—to keep up a connection hundreds of yards long which any moment may be broken in a dozen places by a determined rush of the enemy. This first French post is the extreme left of the French defence, and it is only after some long alleyways that you come on the centre itself. Here on roofs, squatting behind loopholes, and even on tree-tops, though these are very dangerous, French and Austrian sailors exchange shots with the enemy.

Half a dozen men have been already hit here, but in spite of the strictest orders men are fearlessly exposing themselves and reaping the inevitable result. It is only at the beginning that one is so unwise. One giant Austrian had spread himself across the top of a roof near which I passed, with two sandbags to protect his head, and looked in his blue-black sailors clothes like an enormous fly squashed flat up there by the anger of the gods. Now leaning this way, now that, he flashed off a Mannlicher there towards the Italian Legation, where only one hundred hours ago no one ever dreamed that Chinese desperadoes would have made our normal life such a distant memory.

As I came up the French commander allowed the remark to drop that the position did not please him—*ça ne me dit rien* is the exact expression he used—and that his defence was too thin to be capable of resisting a single determined rush. The abandoned Italian barricade, with the Italian Legation still smouldering behind it, is indeed now filling up with more and more Chinese sharpshooters, who continually pour in a hot fire only fifty feet from the French lines. Occasionally a reckless Chinese brave dashes across from the hiding-place he has selected to cover his advance into the nest of Chinese houses which are only separated by a twenty-foot lane from the French Legation wall, and coolly applies the torch. Then *puff*; first there is a small cloud of smoke, then a volley of crackling wood, and finally flames leaping skyward. You can see this here at all hours. Aided by fire and rifle-shots the Chinese are pushing nearer and nearer the French. It is clear that they will have a worse time than the Japanese if the situation develops as quietly but as rapidly as it has been doing. . . .

Across Legation Street connection with the Germans is now had by means of more loopholed barricades; for the Germans link hands with the French and Austrians, just as they on their part link up with the little colonel of the Su wang-fu. But the Germans are not in force at their own Legation; they are merely using it as their base, for it is only by means of the Peking Club, whose grounds run sheer back, that they touch the priceless Tartar Wall. Spread-eagled along a very indifferently barricaded line, the marines of the German Sea Battalion now lie in an angry frame of mind dangerous for everyone. They have felt hurt ever since the loss of their Minister, and the men are recklessly desperate. On the Tartar Wall itself they are exposed to a dusting fire from the great Ha-ta Towers that loom up half a mile from them, and men are already falling.

A three-inch gun commenced firing in the morning—nobody but the Wall posts noticed it at first—and now overhead *whiz* with that odd shaking of the air so hard to explain these light but dangerous projectiles. Happily it is rather a modern gun, and the Chinese, unaccustomed to the flat trajectory, are firing far too high. I noticed as I crept along that the shells fell screaming into the Imperial city a mile or two away. If they only get the range!

Far along the Tartar Wall, towards the Ch'ien Men Gate, yellow dots could be indistinctly seen. These were the Americans, in their slouch hats and khaki suits, lying on the ground and facing the enemy's fire in the other direction. Held in check by the Germans and Americans in two feeble posts of a few men each, the Chinese commanders cannot get their men along the Tartar Wall, and command the Legations that crouch below. Perhaps that is why playing is only going on and no assaults. Now sobbing, now gurgling, the bullets pass thickly enough overhead here, sometimes in dense flights like angry wild-fowl, sometimes speeding in quick succession after one another as if they were all late and were frantically endeavouring to make up for lost time.... I am certain now that this fusillade is increasing from hour to hour—almost from minute to minute. I do not think playing will soon be the right expression....

To get to the Russo-American side of the defence, there is no help for it, you have to make a long voyage; to climb down off the Wall, pass through the German Legation, cross Legation Street into the French lines, and work your way slowly through acres of compounds and deserted houses. Yesterday I would have made a dash, but after watching the four hundred yards of wall between the German and American posts, you are easily convinced that even to sneak along, hugging the protecting parapet, would be an undertaking of utter foolishness. For as I stood looking, the rank undergrowth, which Chinese sloth has allowed in past years to grow up along the top of the Tartar Wall, was apparently alive, now swinging this way, now swaying that, and sometimes even jumping into the air in pieces as if galvanised into madness by the rush of bullets. The number of riflemen is growing fast.

So passing into the French Legation, great holes let you into the next compound, which happens to be that of my friend C——, the Peking hotel-keeper. Here there is a new sight; everybody is at work quite peacefully, milling wheat, washing rice, slaughtering animals, barricading windows—doing everything, in fact at once. This fellow C—— is an original, who knows how to make his Chinese slave with the greatest industry and sets them an admirable example himself. A rather desperate lot are these servants, although most of them are professed Roman Catholics, and can gabble French learned years ago at Monseigneur F———'s. And that reminds me: no one has thought of the gallant bishop during the past few days. That shows how indifferent the abnormal makes one; the French Legation has attempted once to get into communication with the distant cathedral and failed. Since then nobody I have seen has even mentioned the great Catholic mission.

These lonely and deserted compounds, merely connected with our bases and the outlying works by great holes rudely picked through their massive walls, are curiously mournful and passing strange. The houses are absolutely empty and silent; everything has been left exactly as it stood, when the occupants rushed off feverishly to the British Legation, where they now sit in idleness relying for protection on the thin outer lines I have described. In these abandoned Legations and residences you can scarcely hear more than a distant rattle of musketry, and when you think how great the distances are it is very easy to understand why the panic occurred yesterday morning among the men on the outer lines, at which those smugly safe in the British Legation were so indignant.

Occupying widely separated positions, imperfectly linked together, and with no responsible commander to watch them with a keen and discerning eye, the defenders of the eastern, southern and western lines could well suppose that the incompetence of the Ministers and the disorders which have reigned during the past few weeks would culminate in their being abandoned without a word of warning being sent them. It is so silly to say that because men are soldiers and sailors they must be prepared to do their duty everywhere. There must have been times when even the Roman soldier at Pompeii felt like revolting.

Pushing on, I crossed the southern bridge of stone, in order to reach the Russo-American lines and the rear of the British Legation, and marvelled more and more at our good luck. As yet nothing has been done to protect this very exposed connecting link; and so bending low you have once more to sneak rapidly along, using the stone parapet as a traverse to save you from the enfilading fire, which is coming from heavens know where. The bullets were singing in all manner of tones here as I ran, the iron ones of old-fashioned make muttering a deep bass; the nickel-headed modern devils spitting the thinnest kind of treble as they hastened along. It was almost amusing to gauge their speed. Some had already travelled so far that with a flop which raises a little cloud of dust they dropped exhausted at your feet.

The ricochets are in the majority, for with the vast number of intervening walls and trees and the sloping Chinese roofs which pen us in on all sides, the nickel, iron and lead of Mannlicher and Mauser rifles and Tower muskets are soon converted into mere discordant humming-birds, whose greatest inconvenience is their sound. Never have I heard such a humming as these spent ricochets make.

Fifty feet past this southern stone bridge you meet the first Russian barricade, with half a dozen tired Russian sailors sleeping on the ground and a sleepy-eyed lookout man leaning on his rifle. This barricade faces in both directions in the shape of a V, and under its protection this part of Legation Street is supposed to be safe from a rush, if the men stand firm. In the Russian and American Legations it is everywhere the same story—barricades and loopholed houses and outworks, now mostly crowned with sandbags, succeed one another with a regularity which becomes monotonous. But on this western side the bullets are few and far between as yet, and sometimes for a few seconds a curious quiet reigns, only broken by the distant and muffled hum of sound and crackling towards the east.

Decidedly up to date it is the Japanese and the French and their companions who have all the honours in the matter of cannonading and fusillading, and the Germans are soon going to be not far behind them. Right up on the Tartar Wall I found the American marines once again lying mutinously silent. They, too, do not like it, frankly and unreservedly; and as I lay up there and told them what I had seen elsewhere, an old fellow with a beard said it was S——, the first secretary, who had insisted on their stopping, and had almost had a fight with everyone about it.

The old marine told me that the other men would be damned—he used the word in a wistful sort of way which had nothing profane about it—if they stopped much longer. They wanted other people to share the honours; they did not see why every man should not have a turn at the same duty. . . . I was glad these Americans were making this fuss, for everything is just as unbalanced as it was at the beginning, and there is no sort of confidence anywhere. After three days of siege the only clear thing I can see is that there are a lot of bad tempers, and that the few good men are saving the situation by acting independently to the best of their ability and are not trying to understand anything else.

Much depressed, I at last slipped down through the back of the

Russian Legation into the British Legation. Yes! the others are right, for on reaching the English grounds you feel unconsciously that you have passed from the fighting line to the hospital and commissariat base. Here, mixed impartially with the women, crowds of vigorous men, belonging to the junior ranks of the Legations' staffs and to numbers of other institutions, are skulking, or getting themselves placed on committees so as to escape duty.

I suppose you could beat up a hundred, or even a hundred and fifty, rifle-bearing effectives in an hour. Many of the younger men were furious, and said they were quite willing to do anything, but that everybody should be turned out. . . . . In the afternoon some of them fell in with my idea—volunteering under independent command on the outer lines—and now the Japanese, the French and the Germans have got more men. But what I wish to show you in this rambling account is the unbalanced condition. Except in two or three places we can be rushed in ten minutes.

3

Fires and Food

24th June, 1900.
I am convinced that not only does everything come to him who knows how to wait, but that sooner or later everybody meets with their deserts.

The British Legation, allowed to sink into a somewhat somnolent condition owing to its immunity from direct attack, has been now rudely awakened. Fires commencing in earnest yesterday, after a few half-hearted attempts made previously, have been raging in half a dozen different places in this huge compound; and one incendiary, creeping in with the stealthiness of a cat, threw his torches so skilfully that for at least an hour the fate of the Ministerial residences hung in the balance, and Ministerial fears assumed alarming proportions. Again I was satisfied; everybody should sooner or later meet with their deserts.

I have already said how the British Legation is situated. Protected on the east and south entirely by the other Legations and linked defences, it can run no risk from these quarters until the defenders of these lines are beaten back by superior weight of numbers. Partially protected on the west, owing to the fact that an immense grass-grown park renders approach from this quarter without carefully entrenching and barricading simple suicide, there remain but two points of meagre dimensions at which the Chinese attack can be successfully developed without much preliminary preparation; the narrow northern end and a south-western point formed by a regular rabbit-warren of Chinese houses that push right up to the Legation walls. It is precisely at these two points that the Chinese, with their peculiar methods of attack, directed their best efforts.

Beginning in earnest at the northern end, after some inconsiderable efforts on the south-western corner, they set fire to the *sacrosanct* Hanlin Yuan, which is at once the Oxford and Cambridge, the Heidelberg and the Sorbonne of the eighteen provinces of China rolled into one, and is revered above all other earthly things by the Chinese scholar. In the spacious halls of the Hanlin Academy, which back against the flanking wall of the British Legation, are gathered in mighty piles the literature and labours of the premier scholars of the Celestial Empire.

Here complete editions of Gargantuan compass; vast cyclopædia copied by hand and running into thousands of volumes; essays dating from the time of dynasties now almost forgotten; woodblocks black with age crowded the endless unvarnished shelves. In an empire where scholarship has attained an untrammelled pedantry never dreamed of in the remote West, in a country where a perfect knowledge of the classics is respected by beggar and prince to such an extent that to attempt to convey an idea would cause laughter in Europe, all of us thought—even the pessimists—that it could never happen that this holy of holies would be desecrated by fire. Listen to what happened.

To the sound of a heavy rifle-fire, designed to frustrate all efforts at extinguishing the dread fire-demon, the flaming torch was applied by Chinese soldiery to half a dozen different places, and almost before anybody knew it, the holy of holies was lustily ablaze. As the flames shot skywards, advertising the danger to the most purblind, everybody at last became energetic and sank their feuds. British marines and volunteers were formed up and independent commands rushed over from the other lines; a hole was smashed through a wall, and the mixed force poured raggedly into the enclosures beyond. They had to clamber over obstacles, through tightly jammed doors, under falling beams, occasionally halting to volley heavily until they had cleared all the ground around the Hanlin, and found perhaps half a ton of empty brass cartridge cases left by the enemy, who had discreetly flown. From a safe distance snipers, hidden from view an untraceable, kept on firing steadily; but they were careful not to advance.

Meanwhile the flames were spreading rapidly, the century-old beams and rafters crackling with a most alarming fierceness which threatened to engulf the adjacent buildings of the Legation. What huge flames they were! The priceless literature was also catching fire, so the dragon-adorned pools and wells in the peaceful Hanlin courtyards were soon choked with the tens of thousands of books that were heaved in by many willing hands. At all costs this fire must be checked. Dozens of men from the British Legation, hastily whipped into action by sharp words, were now pushed into the burning Hanlin College, abandoning their tranquil occupation of committee meetings and commissariat work, which had been engaging their attention since the first shots had been fired on the 20th, and thus reinforced the marines and the volunteers soon made short work of twenty centuries of literature.

Beautiful silk-covered volumes, illumined by hand and written by masters of the Chinese brush, were pitched unceremoniously here and there by the thousand with utter disregard. Sometimes a Sinologue, of whom there are plenty in the Legations, unable to restrain himself at the sight of these literary riches which in any other times would be utterly beyond his reach, would select an armful of volumes and attempt to fight his way back through the flames to where he might deposit his burden in safety; but soon the way was barred by marines with stern orders to stop such literary looting. Some of these books were worth their weight in gold. A few managed to get through with their spoils, and it is possible that missing copies of China's literature may be some day resurrected in strange lands.

With such curious scenes proceeding these fires were checked in one direction only to break out in another. For later on, sneaking in under the cover of trees and the many massive buildings which pushed up so close, Chinese marauders finding that they could escape, threw torch after torch soaked in petroleum on the neighbouring roofs and rafters. In some cases they forced our posts to seek cover by firing on them very heavily, and then with a sudden dash they could accomplish their deadly work at ease. At one time, thanks to this policy, the outbuildings of the British Legation actually caught fire, and the flames, urged on by a sharp north wind, lolled out their tongues longingly towards the main buildings.

Lines of men, women, and children were hastily formed to our wells and hundreds of utensils of the most incongruous character were brought into play. I came back to find ladies of the Legations handing even *pots de chambre* full of water to the next person in the long chain which had been formed; and among all these people who were at length willing to work because of the imminent danger of their being smoked out, I found long-lost faces, including that of my own chief. Where they had all sprung from I could not make out. But to see Madame So-and-so, a Ministerial wife, handing these delectable utensils, and forced to labour hard, was worth a good many privations.

There are so many elements of the tragic-absurd now to be seen.

That work on the British Legation lines confined me for some time to this area, and determined to profit by it, I sought out Viscount T——, who loves delicacies, and offered to exchange champagne for a few tins of preserves. We have mules, we have ponies, and we have even donkeys, it is true, and a great mass of grain and rice which will last for weeks. But it is dry and sorrowful food, and I long for a few delicacies. Today my midday *tiffin* consisted of a rude curry made of pony meat; and in the evening, because I was busy and had no time to search out other things, I ate once again of pony—this time cold! I will frankly confess that I was not enchanted, and had it not been for the Monopole, of which there are great stores in the hotel and the club—thousand cases in all, I believe—I should have collapsed.

For as Monsieur la Fontaine has informed us, even the most willing of stomachs has certain rights, and there are times when a good deal of zeal is necessary. It is true we have now a narcotic to feed on which supports us at all times almost without the aid of anything else—the never-ending roll of rifle-fire now blazing forth with grim violence and sending a storm of bullets overhead, now muttering slowly and cautiously with merely a falling leaf or a snipped branch to show that it is directed at our devoted heads. You can live on that for many hours, but it is a bad thing to feed on, of course, for it must leave after-effects more hard to overcome than those of opium. Little d'A——, of the French Legation, swears he never feels hungry at all so long as the firing continues....

To perform this work of feeding so many mouths, there are committees—committees far too big, since everyone is anxious to join their safe ranks—committees which, although they number men of all nationalities, are simply standing examples, I opine, of the organising capacity of the Yankee and his masterfulness over other people. For it is the Yankee missionary who has invaded and taken charge of the British Legation; it is the Yankee missionary who is doing all the work there and getting all the credit. Beginning with the fortifications committee, there is an extraordinary man named G——, who is doing everything—absolutely everything. I believe there are actually other members of this committee—at least, there are some people who assist—but G—— is the man of the hour, and will brook no interference.

Already the British Legation, which at the commencement of the siege was utterly undefended by any entrenchments or sandbags, is rapidly being hustled into order by the masterful hand of this missionary. Coolies are evolved from the converts of all classes, who, although they protest that they are unaccustomed to manual work, are merely given shovels and picks, sandbags and bricks, and resolutely told to commence and learn. Already the discontented in the outer lines are sending for him and asking him to do this and that, and the hard-worked man always finds time for everything. It is a wonder.

And behind this one man fortifications committee there are many other committees now. There is a general committee which no one has yet fathomed; a fuel committee; a sanitary committee; nothing but committees, all noisily talking and quite safe in the British Legation. Out of the noise and chatter the American missionary emerges, sometimes odorous and unpleasant to look upon, but whose excuse for not shouldering a rifle and volunteering for the front is written on his tired face. It is the selfsame Yankee missionary who is grinding the wheat and seeing that it is not stolen; it is the American missionary who is surveying the butcher at work and seeing that not even the hoofs are wasted. And I am sad to confess that it is he who is feeding those thousands of Roman Catholics in the Su wang-fu, while the French and Italian priests and fathers, divorced from the dull routine of their ordinary life, sit helplessly with their hands folded, willingly abandoning their charges to these more energetic Anglo-Saxons.

This Protestantism is not my religion, but for masculine energy there is none other like it. I would not have you think by this and my constant irritation that there are no Englishmen doing well; it is merely that the ponderous atmosphere of the British Legation is such that very few men who live habitually there can shake themselves free from it even in such times as these. I know that half of them are much upset at the *rôle* they are being forced to play, but who can help them?

We are progressing more quietly now that the big fires are out; but still there is scant reason for any congratulations. S——, for instance, is quite forgotten, I assure you, for I mentioned his name to P——, the French Minister, only an hour ago, and the only reply he made was to spread out his hands in front of him and give vent to an immense sigh. Then he muttered as he went away, "*Il a disparu complètement—entièrement; c'est la fin*"....

All relief is now felt to be out of the question. Men are also beginning to fall with regularity, and are carried in bloodstained, as evidence that this is really a serious business. The British Chancery is now the hospital; despatch tables have been washed and covered with surgical cloth; cases are dropping in (seventeen up to date, I hear), and doctors are busy. Already in the night smothered cries burst from the walls of these torture-rooms, and make one conscious that it may be one's turn next. I have always felt that it is all right up in the firing line, but it is that dreadful afterwards on the operating-table. . . . But nurses and doctors are doing valiantly. There is a German army doctor who knows his business very well, they say; and his reputation has already spread so far among the men of our all-nation sailors and marines that they all ask for him. I have heard that request in four languages already.

To me it seems that by incontestable laws each actor is taking his proper place, and that each nationality is pushing out its best to the proper perspective. Ah! a siege is evidently the testing-room of the gods. If we could only in ordinary life apply the great siege test, what mistakes would be avoided, what reputations would be saved from being shattered! Because no weak man would ever be given advancement.

4

The Bonds Tighten

25th June, 1900.

On all sides our position has become less secure, less enviable, and the enemy more menacing, more daring and more intent in breaking in on us. The few dropping shots which opened the ball on the 20th have now duly blossomed into a rich harvest of bullets that sometimes continues for hours without intermission or break. The Japanese, unable to hold their huge line, consisting of Prince Su's outer wall, have already been forced to give way at several points, but in doing so they have each time managed to bite hard at the enemy's attacking head. The day before yesterday the little Japanese colonel decided he would have to give up a block of courts on the northeast—some of those courts I have already described, which, hemmed in by walls almost as high as the outer monster, itself eighteen or twenty feet high and three feet thick, form veritable death-traps if you can entice any one inside and hammer them to pieces by loophole fire. This is precisely the policy adopted by Colonel S——.

The battalion of the Peking Field Force which faces the northern front had been industriously pushing forward massive barricades until they almost touched Prince Su's outer wall. Secure behind these sharpshooter fortifications a distressing fire was concentrated on the half a dozen fortified Japanese posts that lined the outer wall. Here on high stagings, crudely made of timber and bamboo poles and protected by thick wedges of sandbags, Japanese sailors and some miscellaneous volunteers, grouped in posts of four and five men, lay hour after hour unable to show a finger or move a hand. Hundreds of Chinese rifles at the closest possible range poured in a never-ending fire on these facile targets, and the sandbagged positions, literally eaten away by old-fashioned iron bullets in company with the most modern nickel-headed variety, crumbled down to practically nothing.

Lying on your back at these advanced posts and looking at the sloping roofs of Prince Su's ornamental pavilions a few hundred feet within our lines was a droll sight. The Chinese riflemen, being on a slightly lower level and forced to fire upwards at the Japanese positions, caused many of their bullets to skim the sandbagged crest and strike the line of roofs behind. Many, I say; I should have said thousands and tens of thousands, for the roofs seemed alive and palpitating with strange feelings; and extraordinary as it may sound, big holes were soon eaten into the heavily tiled roofs by this simple rifle fusillade. It seemed as if the Chinese hoped to destroy us and our defences by this novel method. But there was a more ominous sign than this.

A Japanese sailor perched high up aloft on a roof five hundred feet inside these advance positions and armed with a telescope, had seen two guns being dragged forward. In a few hours at the most, even allowing for Chinese sloth and indifference as to time, the guns would be in position, and then the outer wall would be demolished, and possibly a disordered retirement would be the result. So the little Japanese colonel took the bull by the horns. Setting all the coolies he could muster from among the converts, he quickly formed a second line of defence by loopholing and sandbagging all the chess-board squares that flank the northern wall.

When night came the advanced positions were quietly abandoned, and as soon as the Chinese scouts, who always creep forward at daybreak, discovered that our men had flown, their leaders ordered a charge. A confused mass rushed forward, penetrated one of the courtyards, and finding it apparently deserted, incautiously pushed into the next square. Before they could fly, a murderous fire caught them on three sides and wiped out several dozens of them, the rifles and ammunition being taken by our men and the corpses thrown outside. This has apparently had a chilling effect on the policy of open charges in this quarter, and now the Chinese commanders are advancing their lines by means of ingenious parallels and zigzag barricades, which will take some time to construct.

Meanwhile, the Japanese main-gate fort, at the extreme Japanese east, with its outlying barricades, is being slowly reached for by the same means. Two or three times the French, who make connection with the Japanese lines a hundred feet to the south, have had to send as many men as they could spare to hold back a sudden rush. Each time the threatened Chinese charge has not come off, and the incipient attack has fizzled out to the accompaniment of a diminishing fusillade.

The commanding Italian knoll on the northwest corner of the Su wang-fu remains firm, but somehow no one has very much confidence in the Italians, and secondary lines are being formed behind them, towards which the Italians look with longing eyes. And yet next to the British Legation posts the Italians are having the easiest time of all. Lieutenant P——, their commander, is a brave fellow; but he is brave because he is educated. The uneducated Italian, unlike the uneducated Frenchman, has little stomach for fighting, and it is easy to understand in the light of our present experiences why the Austrians so long dominated Northern Italy, and why unlucky Baratieri and his men were seized with panic and overwhelmed at Adowa.

Opposite the French and German Legations, Chinese activity is not so intense as it has been heretofore. Everything in this quarter for thousands of yards is practically flat with the ground, for incendiaries have destroyed hundreds and hundreds of houses, and the Chinese commanders are favouring low-lying barricades, which are hard to pick out from the enormous mass of partially burned ruins which encumber the ground. Just as in South Africa we were reading only the other day, before this plight overtook us, that the hardest thing to see is a live Boer on the battlefield, so here it is the merest chance to make out the soldiery that is attacking us.

Sometimes dozens of men scuttle across from position to position, and for a moment a vision of dark, sunburned faces and brightly coloured uniforms waves in front of us; but in the main, so well has the enemy learned the art of taking cover, and of utilising every fold in the ground, that many, have not even seen a Boxer or a soldier or know what they look like, although their fire has been so assiduously pelting us. But some sharp-eyed men of the Legations have learned two things—that the Manchu Banners and Tung Fu-hsiang's Kansu soldiery now divide the honour of the attack. Tung Fu-hsiang fortunately has mostly cavalry, and a strong force of his dismounted men armed with Mannlicher carbines are on the northeast of the Japanese position, for two have been shot and dragged into our lines. These cavalrymen are not much to be feared.

Farther to the south the German position has become exceedingly curious. While from the American marines on the Tartar Wall round in a vast sweep on to the French Legation, each hour sees more defences go up, the Germans have to content themselves with what practically amounts to fighting in the open. There has been no time to give them enough coolies, and so they have only lookout men, with the main body entrenched in the centre of their position. But yesterday they surprised some Boxers, who had daringly pushed their way into a Chinese house a few yards from one outwork, and who were about to set fire to it, preparatory to calling forward their regular troops. The Germans charged with a tremendous rush, killed everyone of the marauders, and flung the dead bodies far out so that the enemy might see the reward for daring. Being certain that the Chinese commanders would attempt to revenge this blow, what driblets of men could be spared have been lent to make the German chain more continuous.

It is almost impossible now to follow the ebb and flow of reinforcements from one point to another; but it may be roughly said that the south-eastern, eastern, northern and north-western part of our square—that is, the Germans, French, Austrians, Japanese and Italians—feed one another with men whenever the rifle fire in any given direction along their lines and the flitting movements of the enemy make post commanders suppose a mass attack is coming; and that the British Legation and the western Russo-American front, together with the American posts on the Tartar Wall, work together.

It is, of course, self-evident from what I have written that the first, or Continental and Japanese lines, are having by far the worst time. For, apart from the American posts on the Tartar Wall, no outposts in the second section are as yet in direct touch with the enemy. The strain on those who are within a few yards of Chinese commands is at times terrible. At night many men can only be held in place by a system of patrols designed to give them confidence....

I have just said that no part of the second half of our irregular system was in direct touch with the enemy, but this, although true enough today, was not so yesterday. The Chinese pushed up a gun somewhere near the dangerous south-western corner of the British Legation, and the fire became so annoying that it was decided to make a sortie and effect a capture if possible. Captain H——, the second captain of the British detachment, was selected to command the sortie, and with a small force of British marines who have been pining at their enforced inaction and dull sentry-go, and are jealous of the greater glory the others have already earned by their successful butchery of the enemy, a wall was breached and our men rushed out.

Being off duty, I witnessed most of the affair. Of course, the sortie ended in failure, as every such movement is foredoomed to, when the nature of the ground which surrounds us is considered. There are nothing but small Chinese houses and walls on every side, making it impossible to move beyond our lines without demolishing and breaking through heavy brickwork. The marines went forward as gallantly as they could, and surprised some of the nests of sharpshooters protecting the gun; but the Chinese, as they retreated, set fire to the houses on all sides, and in the thick flames and smoke it was impossible to move save back by the way they had come. Under cover of the smoke the Chinese soldiery opened a tremendous fire on the sortie party, who were picking up some of the rifles and swords with which the ground was strewn, and seeing that our men could not possibly advance, the enemy pushed forward boldly, rapidly firing more and more energetically.

The British captain received a terrible wound, but refused to retire; a marine was shot through the groin and died in a few minutes; bullets cut the men's tunics to pieces; and in a hailstorm of fire, poured on them a few yards away, they retreated. H—— covered the retreat all the way, wounded as he was, and shot three men with his revolver, who were heading a last desperate rush at his men as they made for the hole in the wall. Dripping with blood, this brave man staggered all the way to the hospital alone, refusing all support, and gripping his smoking revolver to the last. His battered appearance so frightened all the miserables who swarm in the British Legation that everyone was very gloomy until the next meal had been eaten, and they had restored themselves by garrulous talk. The German doctor says that H—— will probably die.

Meanwhile the Americans on the Wall are behaving more erratically than ever. They have retired and reoccupied their position three or four times since the siege began, and the men are now more than mutinous. Yesterday they came down twice—no one could quite make out why—and after a lapse of an hour or two in each case, they returned. Matters reached a crisis this morning, and a council of war was called by the British Minister, composed of all the officers commanding detachments. The meeting took place under the American barricade on the Tartar Wall itself, apparently to give confidence to the men and to make them ashamed of themselves. But the most curious part of it all was that our commander-in-chief excused himself on the diplomatic ground that he was sick, and amid the smiles of all, Captain T——, the Austrian, presided and laid down the law.

This clearly shows how absurd is our whole system. Everyone says the Americans were quite ashamed of themselves when the meeting was over, for the general vote of all the detachment officers was that the position was well fortified, easy to retain, and absolutely essential to hold. They say the whole reason is that there is internal trouble in the American contingent, and that one of the officers is hated. Whether this is really so or not, I do not know; we never know anything certain now. But although the American has but little discipline, as a sharpshooter on the defensive he is quite unrivalled by reason of his superior intelligence and the interest he takes in devoting himself to the matter in hand.

You only have to see these mutinous marines at work for five minutes as snipers to be convinced of that. I saw a case in point only a few hours ago. Men were wanted to drive back, or at least intimidate, a whole nest of Chinese riflemen, who had cautiously established themselves in a big block of Chinese houses across the dry canal, which separates the British Legation from the Su wang-fu. This block of houses is so placed that an enfilading fire can reach a number of points which are hidden from the Japanese lines; and this enfilading fire was badly needed, as the Chinese riflemen were becoming more and more daring, and had already made several hits. Half a dozen of the best American shots were requisitioned.

The six men who came over went deliberately to work in a very characteristic way. They split into pairs, and each pair got, by some means binoculars. After a quarter of an hour they settled down to work, lying on their stomachs. First they stripped off their slouch hats and hung them up elsewhere, but instead of putting them a few feet to the right or left as everybody else, with a vague idea of Red Indian warfare, within our lines had been doing, they placed them in such a way as to attract the enemy's fire and make the enemy disclose himself, which is quite a different matter. This they did by adding their coats and decorating adjacent trees with them so far away from where they lay that there could be no chance of the enemy's bad shooting hitting them by mistake—as had been the case elsewhere where this device had been tried.

All this by-play took some time, but at last they were ready—one man armed with a pair of binoculars and the other with the American naval rifle—the Lee straight-pull, which fires the thinnest pin of a cartridge I have seen and has but a two-pound trigger pull. Even then nothing was done for perhaps another ten minutes, and in some cases for half an hour; it varied according to individual requirements. Then when the quarry was located by the man with the binoculars, and the man with the rifle had finished asking a lot of playful questions so as to gain time, the first shots were fired. The marines armed with binoculars were not unduly elated by any one shot, but merely reported progress in a characteristic American fashion—that is, by a system of chaffing. This provided tonic, and presently the bullets crept in so close to the marks that all chaff was forgotten.

Sometimes it took an hour, or even two, to bring down a single man; but no matter how long the time necessary might be, the Americans stayed patiently with their man until the sniper's life's blood was drilled out of him by these thin pencils of Lee straight-pull bullets. Once, and once only, did excitement overtake a linked pair I was watching. They had already knocked over two of the enemy aloft in trees, and were attacking a third, who only showed his head occasionally above a roof-line when he fired, and who bobbed up and down with lightning speed. The sole thing to do under the circumstances was to calculate when the head would reappear.

So the man with the binoculars calculated aloud for the benefit of the man with the rifle, and soon, in safety below the wall-line, a curious group had collected to see the end. But it was a hard shot and a disappointing one, since it was essential not to scare the quarry thoroughly by smashing the roof-line instead of the head. So the bullets flew high, and although the sharpshooter was comforted by the remarks of the other man, no progress was made. Then suddenly the rifleman fired, on an inspiration, he said afterwards, and lo! and behold, the head and shoulders of a Chinese brave rose clear in the air and then tumbled backwards. "Killed, by G——; killed, by G——!" swore the man with the binoculars irreverently; and well content with their morning's work, the two climbed down and went away.

You will realise from all these things that everything is still very erratic, and that the men remain badly distributed. Nor is this all. The general command over the whole of the Legation area is now plainly modelled on the Chinese plan—that is, the officer commanding does not interfere with the others, excepting when he can do so with impunity to himself. As I have shown, orders which are distasteful are simply ignored. There is a spirit of rebellion which can only spring from one cause. People who have read a lot say that every siege in history has been like this—with everything incomplete and in disorder. If this is so, I wonder how history has been made! Certainly in this age there is very little of real valour and bravery. Perhaps there has been a little in the past, and it is only the glozing-over of time which makes it seem otherwise.

5

The Mysterious Board of Truce

25th June, 1900 (night-time).
It is always true that the unexpected affords relief when least awaited. In our case it has been amply proved.

The sun, which had been shining fiercely all day long until we felt fairly baked and very disconsolate, was heaving down slowly towards the west, flooding the pink walls of the Imperial city with a golden light and sinking the black outline of the sombre Tartar Wall that towers so high above us, when all round our battered lines the dropping rifle-fire drooped more and more until single shots alone punctuated the silence. Our outposts, grouping together, leaned on their rifles and gave vent to sighs of relief. Perhaps something had at last really happened, for though five days only have passed since the beginning of the real siege, they seemed to everyone more like five weeks, or even five months, so clearly do startling events separate one by huge gaps from the dull routine of every-day life.

All of us listened attentively, and presently on all sides the fierce music of the long Chinese trumpets blared out uproariously—blare, blare, sobbing on a high note tremulously, and then, *boom, boom,* suddenly dropping to a thrilling *basso profondissimo.* Even the children know that sound now. Louder and louder the trumpet-calls rang out to one another in answering voice, imperatively calling off the attacking forces. Impelled to retire by this constant clamour, all the Chinese soldiery must have retreated, except a few straggling snipers, who remained for a few minutes longer, dully and methodically loosing off their rifles at our barricades.

Ten or fifteen minutes passed, and then, as if the growing solitude were oppressing them, these last snipers desisted, and, coolly rising and disclosing their brightly coloured tunics and sombre turbans, they sauntered off in full view. I saw half a dozen go off in this way. Clearly something remarkable was happening and our astonishment deepened.

Presently the word ran round our half-mile of barricades that a board, with big Chinese characters written across it, had been placed by a Chinese soldier bearing the conventional white flag of truce on the parapet of the north bridge, where J——, the first man killed, had fallen, and that the curious board was exciting everyone's astonishment. Getting leave to absent myself, I ran into the British Legation, and from a scaffolding not a hundred yards from the bridge I saw the mysterious placard with my own eyes. Already binoculars and telescopes had been busily adjusted, and all the Sinologues mustered in the British Legation had roughly written copies of the message in their hands and were disputing as to the exact meaning. It was only then that I realised what a strange medley of nationalities had been collected together in this siege. Frenchmen, Russians, Germans, Japanese, English, Americans, and many others were all arguing together, until finally H——, the great administrator, was called upon to decide. The legend ran:

> In accordance with the Imperial commands to protect the Ministers, firing will cease immediately and a despatch will be delivered at the Imperial canal-bridge.

A vast commotion was created, as you may judge, when this news circulated among the refugee ministers and all the heterogeneous crowd who have been behaving so strangely since the serious business began. Not one of us had relished the idea of being massacred after the manner of the Indian Mutiny, but there are different ways of behaving under such perils; some of those we had witnessed would not bear relating.

In a very short time, indeed, a suitable reply had been written briefly in Chinese on another board, but the finding of a messenger was more difficult. We must send a proper man. A Chinaman was at length discovered, who, after having been invested with the customary official hat and the long official coat, was persuaded to advance towards the bridge bearing our message and piteously waving a white flag to show that he likewise was a harbinger of peace. The man progressed but slowly towards the Imperial bridge, and twice he gave unmistakable signs of wishing to bolt; but urged on by cries and a frantic waving, he at last reached the parapet on which leaned our enemy's placard.

Then depositing our own reply, his courage left him completely, and he incontinently bolted for our lines as hard as he could run, casting his dignity to the winds. In his haste he had set his board all askew, and the enemy could not possibly have understood it. But no arguments could induce our messenger to return. He swore, indeed, that he had just escaped in time, as the enemy's rifles were all pointed towards him from a number of positions just beneath the Imperial city wall, which we could not see from our lines. So nothing more was done by our headquarters, and an hour passed away with all the world waiting, but with no Imperial despatch brought to us.

The sun was now down only six inches above the pink walls—in another hour it would be dark and our position would be exactly the same as before. On all sides our fighting line had clambered over their barricades and were examining the enemy's silent ones with curiosity. Beyond the fortified Hanlin courtyards, to the north of the British Legation courtyards, which had been occupied and heavily sandbagged after the big fires there, so as to keep the enemy at a safe distance—the mass of ruins were indeed as silent and as deserted as a graveyard. Cautiously escalading walls and pushing down narrow alleyways, some of us advanced several hundred yards to see what was happening beyond; and presently, standing on the top of an unbroken wall line, there were the palace gates and the mysterious pink walls almost within a stone's throw of us.

The sun had moved still farther west, and its slanting rays now struck the Imperial city, under whose orders we had been so lustily bombarded, with a wonderful light. Just outside the palace gates were crowds of Manchu and Chinese soldiery—infantry, cavalry, and gunners grouped all together in one vast mass of colour. Never in my life have I seen such a wonderful panorama—such a brilliant blaze in such rude and barbaric surroundings. There were jackets and tunics of every colour; trouserings of blood red embroidered with black dragons; great two-handed swords in some hands; men armed with bows and arrows mixing with Tung Fu-hsian's Kansu horsemen, who had the most modern carbines slung across their backs.

There were blue banners, yellow banners embroidered with black, white and red flags, both triangular and square, all presented in a jumble to our wondering eyes. The Kansu soldiery of Tung Fu-hsiang's command were easy to pick out from among the milder looking Peking Banner troops. Tanned almost to a colour of chocolate by years of campaigning in the sun, of sturdy and muscular physique, these men who desired to be our butchers showed by their aspect what little pity we should meet with if they were allowed to break in on us. Men from all the Peking Banners seemed to be there with their plain and bordered jackets showing their divisions; but of Boxers there was not a sign. Where had the famed Boxers vanished to?

Thus we stood for some time, the enemy gazing as eagerly at us as we at them. Strict orders must have come from the palace, for not a hostile sign was made. It was almost worth five days of siege just to see that unique sight, which took one back to times when savage hordes were overrunning the world. Peking is still so barbaric!

We sent back word that it might be possible to parley with the enemy, and to learn, perhaps, the reason for this sudden truce; and soon several members of the so-called general committee, whose organisation and duties I confess I do not clearly understand, came out from our lines and stood waving their handkerchiefs. But it was some time before the gaudy-coated enemy would pay any attention to these advances, and finally one of our committeemen, to show that he was a man of peace and really wished to speak with them, went slowly forward with his hands held high above his head.

Then a thin, sallow Chinese, throwing a sword to the ground, advanced from the Palace walls, and finally these two were standing thirty or forty yards apart and within hail of one another. Then a parley began which led to nothing, but gave us some news. The board ordering firing to cease had been carried out under instructions from Jung Lu—Jung Lu being the *generalissimo* of the Peking field forces. A despatch would certainly follow, because even now a Palace meeting was being held. The Empress Dowager, the man continued, was much distressed, and had given orders to stop the fighting; the Boxers were fools. . . .

Then the soldier waved a farewell, and retreated cautiously, picking his way back through the ruins and masses of *débris*. Several times he stopped and raised the head of some dead man that lay there, victim to our rifles, and peered at the face to see whether it was recognisable. In five days we have accounted for very many killed and wounded, and numbers still lie in the exposed positions where they fell.

The disappearing figure of that man was the end to the last clue we came across regarding the meaning of this sudden quiet. The shadows gradually lengthened and night suddenly fell, and around us were nothing but these strangely silent ruins. There was barricade for barricade, loophole for loophole, and sandbag for sandbag. What has been levelled to the ground by fire has been heaped up once more so that the ruins themselves may bring more ruin!

But although we exhausted ourselves with questions, and many of us hoped against hope, the hours sped slowly by and no message came. The palace, enclosed in its pink walls, had slunk to sleep, or forgotten us—or, perhaps, had even found that there could be no truce. Then midnight came, and as we were preparing, half incredulously, to go to sleep, we truly knew. *Crack, crack,* went the first shots from some distant barricade, and bang went an answering rifle on our side. Awakened by these echoes, the firing grew naturally and mechanically to the storm of sound we have become so accustomed to, and the short truce was forgotten. It is no use; we must go through to the end. . . . .

6

Shells and Sorties

3rd July, 1900.

For a week I have written nothing, absolutely nothing, and have not even taken a note, nor cared what happened to me or to anybody else. How could I when I have been so crushed by unending sentry-go, by such an unending roar of rifles and crash of shells, that I merely mechanically wake at the appointed hour, mechanically perform my duty and as mechanically fall asleep again. My *ego* has been crushed out of me, and I have become, doubtless, quite rightly so, an insignificant atom in a curious thing called a siege. No mortal under such circumstances, no matter how faithful to an appointed task, can put pencil to paper, and attempt to sketch the confusion and smoke around him. You may try, perhaps, as I have tried, and then, suddenly, before you can realise it, you fall half asleep and pencil and paper are thrice damned.

For we have been worked so hard, those of us who do not care and are young, and the enemy is pushing in so close and so persistently, that we have not much farther to run if the signs that I see about me go for anything. Artillery, to the number of some eight or ten pieces, is now grinding our barricades to pieces and making our outworks more and more untenable. Rifle bullets float overhead in such swarms that by a comparison of notes I now estimate that there must be from five to six thousand infantry and dismounted cavalry ranged against us. Mines are being already run under so many parts of our advanced lines, and their dangers are so near that on the outworks we fall asleep ready to be blown up....

.....Nor are the dangers merely prospective. They are actual and grimly disgusting. During the past week the casualty list has gone on rapidly increasing, and today our total is close on one hundred killed and wounded in less than two weeks' intermittent fighting out of a force of four hundred and fifty rifles. The shells occasionally fly low and take you on the head; the bullets flick through loopholes or as often take you in the back from some enfilading barricades, and thus through two agencies you can be hastened towards the Unknown.

As far as I am personally concerned, it is largely a matter of food whether this affects one acutely or not. If you have a full stomach you do not mind so much, and even shrug your shoulders should the man next to you be hit; but at four or five in the morning, when everything is pale and damp, and you are stomach-sick, it is nerve-shaking to see a man brutally struck and gasping under the blow. I have seen this happen three times; once it was truly horrible, for I was so splashed with blood....

It is also largely a matter of days. On some days, you think, in a curious sort of a way, that your turn has come, and that it will be all over in a few minutes. You try to convince yourself by silent arguing that such thoughts are the merest foolishness, that you are at heart a real coward; but in spite of every device the feeling remains, and in place of your former unconcern a nervousness takes possession of you. This nervousness is not exactly the nervousness of yourself, for your outer self surveys your inner depths with some contempt, but the slight fear remains. You do not know what it is—it is inexplicable. Yet it is there.

Yesterday I had the experience in full force, just as a line of us in extended order were galloping up to a threatened position. My boots untied and twice nearly tripped me. I had to stop, perhaps two seconds, perhaps five, dropping on my knee with my head low beside it. For some reason I did not finish tying the laces. I sprang up, threw my right leg forward preparatory to doubling, and then *ping*—I was spinning on the ground, laughing at my own clumsiness in falling down.

Then I glanced to see why my right knee-cap stung me so much. I stopped laughing. A bullet had split across the skin—*raflé*, the French call it—and a shred of my trousers, mixed with some shreds of skin, was hanging down covered with blood. Half a second before my head had been exactly where my knee was, and had I not moved, spurred by some curious intuition, I would have been dead on the ground. Perhaps one's inner consciousness knows more than one thinks....

But such personal experiences are trivial compared with what is going on around us generally. I should not speak of them. For if the Chinese commands are closing in on us on every side, our fighting line is biting back as savagely as it can, and is giving them better than they give us when we get to grips. But in spite of this our position is less enviable than ever, and it requires no genius to see that if the Chinese commanders persist in their present policy the Legations must fall unless relief comes in another two weeks.

Look at the Su wang-fu and the plucky little Japanese colonel! You will, perhaps, remember that I said that the great flanking wall of the Su wang-fu was far too big a task for the Japanese command, and that sooner or later they would have to give way. It has been proved days ago that what I said was correct, for slowly but surely the fire of two Chinese guns has demolished successively the outer wall, the enclosed courtyards behind it, and then a line of houses linked together by field-works hastily constructed from the rubble lying around. It was my duty to be one of a post six men hastily sent here and entrenched on the fringe of our defence in one of these Chinese houses. It was a curious experience. It lasted for hours.

Inside the partly demolished wall of one house we were forced to squat on a staging, peeping at the enemy, who was not more than twenty yards off, lying *perdu* just behind a confused mass of low-lying barricades. These riflemen, flung far forward of the main Chinese positions in this quarter, lay very silent, hardly moving hour after hour. A couple of hundred yards or so behind them, the main body of the enemy, secure behind massive earthen and brick works, poured in an unending fire on our devoted heads with a vigour which never seemed to flag. Our loopholes, which we had carefully blocked up with loose bricks so that the merest cracks remained, spat dust at us as the enemy's bullets persistently pecked at the outside, but could gain no entrance. Sometimes a single missile would slue its way in through everything and end with a sob against the inside wall.

Once one came crash through and struck the Japanese who was next to me full in the face. It knocked out two teeth, cut his mouth and his cheek so that they bled red blood hour after hour, making him hideous to look on; but the Japanese, calmly untying the clout which encased his head, bound it instead across the wound, merely cursing the enemy and not stirring an inch. The rest of us had not time to note much even of that which was taking place right alongside of us; for we had orders to be ready at any moment for a forward rush. If it had come we should have been caught in a trap and lost. That I knew and understood.

We had stood this storm for a couple of hours, and were beginning to revenge ourselves on the advanced line of skirmishers by winging them whenever an incautious movement disclosed an arm or a leg, although we had the strictest orders not to fire except to check a rush, when a new danger presented itself, and was added to our already uncomfortable position. An antiquated gun that had been sending screeching shells over our heads, had evidently been given orders to drive us from where we lay, for the shells which had been flying high moved lower and lower, and buzzed more and more fiercely, until at last one struck the roof. The aim, however, was still too high, for the *débris* of tiles, timber and mortar clattered down the other side of the house and did us no harm.

It may have been five or ten minutes when a tremendous blow shook our staging, and a vast shower of falling tiles and bricks drowned all other sound. A shell, aimed well and low, had taken the roof full and fair, and brought a big piece in on top of us. For some time we could see nothing, nor realise the extent of the damage done, for clouds of choking dust filled our improvised fort, and made us oblivious to everything except a supreme desire for fresh air. Pushing our loopholes open, regardless of the enemy's fire, we gasped for breath; never have I been so choked and so distressed, and presently, the air clearing a little, a huge rent in the roof was disclosed.

On the ground behind lay piles upon piles of rubbish and broken tiles, and perilously near our heads a huge rafter sagged downwards, half split in two. We were debating how long we could stand under such circumstances, when a second shock shook the building, and once more we were deluged with dust and dirt. This time the hanging rafter was dislodged and fell sullenly with a heavy crash to the ground; and now, in addition to the gap in the roof, a long rent appeared in the rear wall. Our top line of loopholes was obviously, worse than useless, and as it seemed more than likely that with the accurate range they had got the Chinese gunners would soon be pitching their shells right into our faces, we decided to climb down off the staging and man a lower line of loopholes pierced two feet above the ground line.

Here we could see very little in front on account of the ruins. We were not a minute too soon, for the very next missile struck our front wall fairly and squarely, and showered bricks and ragged bits of segment on to the platform above us. Luckily the planks and timber with which this edifice was stoutly constructed saved our heads, and the loosened bricks, piling up on the improvised flooring above us, made our position below even more secure. Seizing the breathing time the clumsy reloading of the gun attacking us gave, we pulled spare rafters and bricks around us in the shape of a blockhouse, and thus apparently buried in the ruins of the house, we were soon in reality quite comfortably and securely ensconced.

Slowly and methodically the artillerymen demolished the upper part of our fort, and brought tons and tons of bricks and slates rattling about our ears; but with the exception of many bruises impartially distributed among all of us, no one was further hurt. After two hours' bombardment and throwing forty or fifty shells right on top of us, the enemy apparently tired of the amusement, and we, on our part, seeing no good in remaining where we were, sallied out of the side of the building and suddenly faced the skirmishers, who were still lying on the sunburned bricks.

The Chinese soldiery, alarmed at this sudden appearance when they must have thought us dead, took precipitously to flight, and in their haste to escape so exposed themselves that we had no difficulty in rolling over a couple. As soon as they had retreated we reoccupied a little position slightly in advance of the house, and lay there contentedly munching biscuit and having a pull at the water bottles. It is extraordinary how callous you become.

It was not until four or five o'clock in the afternoon that we were relieved, and then in a fashion that highly flattered our vanity. The little Japanese colonel appeared in person with a small force of riflemen and some stretcher bearers, and he fell back in astonishment when he saw our occupation. We had pushed forward a lookout a few yards in advance, and the rest of us were playing noughts and crosses on some broken tiles. In front of us the barricades were silent, and the Japanese sailor so curiously wounded in the earlier part of the day was fiercely wrangling with an English volunteer, who had taught him the game and had just insulted him by saying he was cheating. The colonel declared he had thought us all dead, but that although he had sent twice to find out how we were faring, the tremendous storm of shells and bullets raging round our entire lines had made it impossible to reinforce us.

The French, he said, had been so heavily beaten that he had had to prepare for a general retreat into the British Legation; the Germans had been swept off the Tartar Wall; the Americans had been shaken and almost driven back; and had not the Chinese themselves tired of the game, another hour would have seen a general retreat sounded. We were much commended for not having fallen back, but we pointed out that it had been really nothing, since we had only had one man slightly wounded. Still, it was an experience hard to beat to be left in a house practically levelled to the ground by shell-fire, and as I got eighteen hours off duty granted me, during which time I slept solidly without waking once, the whole affair remains most firmly impressed on the tablets of my memory. It is only when you have been through it that you understand what you can endure.

All this was some days ago, and was really nothing to what we had the day before yesterday, which happened to be the 1st of July.

The Chinese artillery practice, although poor, the guns and shells being hopelessly ancient, had become so annoying and so distressing that it was determined to adopt a policy of reprisals, taking the form of sorties, and by bayonetting the gunners and damaging the guns if we could not drag them off, to induce the enemy to make his offensive less galling. The ball was opened by an attack which was miserably conducted on the selfsame gun that had so harshly treated that little post I have described a few days before.

On the 1st of the month, Lieutenant P——, the commander of the Italian hillock, laid a plan of sortie before headquarters to which consent was given. Supported by British marines and volunteers, the Italians were to make a sortie in force from their position and seize the gun. The Japanese were to co-operate from their barricades and trenches by opening a heavy fire, and moving slowly forward in extended order as soon as the Italian charge had commenced. All the morning the Italians were noisily preparing, and as soon as their attack was delivered, it justified all we had already thought about them. They issued from their lines with a wild rush, but no sooner did the Chinese fire strike them than they broke and fled, losing several killed and wounded, and fighting like madmen to escape through a passageway which led back. P—— was very severely wounded in the arm, and had to give up his command, and the bodies of the Italians killed were never recovered.

A section of the British Legation students, who had gone forward with the Italians, had a man badly wounded, and the sight of this young fellow staggering back with his clothes literally dripping with blood gave the British Legation inmates a start it took some time to recover from. Later, it turned out that P——'s sortie plan was based on a faulty map; that the whole command found itself being fired on from a dozen quarters before fifty yards had been covered; and that there were nothing but impossible walls and barricades. But still this does not excuse the fact that while the Italians were behaving like madmen the young students stood stock-still and awaited orders to retire. In truth, we are being educated by events.

The loss of the Italian commander has made the Italian posts more useless than ever. These men are now nervous, and have hardly a round of ammunition left, although they were given some of the captured Chinese Mausers and a fresh stock of cartridges three days ago. Every shadow is fired at by them at night, and the vague uneasiness which overcomes everyone when dozens of the enemy are moving in the inky black only a few feet off seems more than they can stand.

Meanwhile the French Legation, thanks to this gunfire, is now but a ruined mass of buildings, a portion of which has fallen into Chinese hands. Alarmed at the progress which has been made everywhere, M——, the British Minister, who is still the nominal commander-in-chief, has for days been pestering the French commandant to send him men to reinforce other points.

The same stubborn answer has been sent back, that not a sailor can be spared, and that none will be sent. This curious contest between the commander of the French lines and the British Minister has ended in a species of deadlock, which bodes ill for us all. The Frenchman believes that the remains of the French lines form a vital part in the defence; the British Minister, invested with military rank by his colleagues, instead of examining the entire area of the defence carefully with his own eyes and seeing exactly whether this is so or not, never ventures beyond the limits of the British Legation. At least, no one has ever seen him. Even the so-called chief of the staff, who is the commander of the British marines, does not regularly visit the French lines. Practically, it may be said that while there is death and murder outside there is only armed neutrality within. It is an extraordinary position.

In spite of the way they have been treated up to the 1st Of July, the French and Austrians still sullenly cling to the ruins of the French barricades. But on the 1st the Chinese, elated at their success in capturing the eastern half of the French Legation, pushed their barricades nearer and nearer, and only one hundred yards behind their advanced lines they brought two guns into action, firing segment and shrapnel alternately. Under this devastating bombardment, almost *à bout portant*, as the French say, the last line of French trenches and their main-gate blockhouse became untenable. Pieces of shell tore through everything; men were wounded more and more quickly, and in the most sheltered part a French volunteer, Wagner, had his entire face blown off him, dying a horrible death.

The French commander, disheartened by the treatment he had received from the commander-in-chief, and convinced that all his men would be blown to pieces if they remained where they were, ordered his bugler to sound the retire. The clarion's notes rose shrilly above this storm of fire, and dragging their dead with them, the Franco-American survivors retreated into the fortified line behind them—the Peking hotel. Here they manned the windows and barricades of the intrepid Swiss' hostelry, which had already been heavily damaged by the Chinese guns.

A determination was arrived at not to be driven out of this hotel until the last man had been killed; it was necessary at all costs to prevent the enemy from breaking in so far. More volunteers were brought to reinforce this line, and the sinking spirits of the French were restored; for within half an hour of their retreat the bugler had sounded the advance again, and with a rush the abandoned positions were reoccupied and the Chinese driven back. Then the guns stopped their cannonade, and a breathing space was given which was sufficient to repair some of the damage done.

While these stirring events had been following each other in quick succession down on level ground, the grim Tartar Wall has been at once our salvation and destroyer of men. The Germans have been having a terrible time, and although they have borne themselves with soldiery composure, they have been at last driven clean down with heart-breaking losses. The guns, which the Chinese had been firing from the great Ha-ta Gate half a mile off, were advanced during the night of the 30th June to within a hundred yards of the imperfect German defences, and on the 1st of July four marines were killed and six wounded out of a post of fifteen men with nerve-shaking rapidity.

The Chinese soldiers, then swarming forward under the Tartar Wall itself, threatened the little blockhouse at the base, which kept up connection with the Club and the German Legation line of barricades, and soon there was no help for it, the eastern Tartar Wall posts had to be abandoned. With the German retirement the Americans abandoned their positions facing west and rushed down to safety below. It cannot be said that the Americans are afraid; they have merely realised from the beginning what a few of us have understood. The motley crowd gathered in the British Legation, as well as our commander-in-chief, were much stirred by the American retirement, for they already saw themselves directly bombarded from the menacing height of the city walls—a prospect which can enchant no one, as the confusion already reigning would have been worse confounded had all the elderly persons been given a taste of what the outworks are experiencing.

So a council of war was hastily convened very much after the style of the Boer commandoes, with everybody talking at once, and it was at once decided that the blessed Tartar Wall must be at once reoccupied at any cost. A mixed force, under the command of the American captain, stormed back again, and with a rush found themselves back in their old quarters with everything intact. The representation of the American marines had at last made themselves felt, for British marines took the places of half the Americans, who were given duty elsewhere. We thought that that had solved the question.

But this was on the 1st of the month. Today, the 3rd of the month, the position became once more untenable, for the Chinese now being able to attack the Wall defences from both sides, were pushing their barricades rapidly closer and closer until only a few feet separated them from their prey. So more men were called for, and this morning, after a short harangue, a storming-party, numbering sixty bayonets and composed of British, Americans and Russians, dashed over into the Chinese lines killing thirty of the enemy and driving the rest back in great confusion. It was a brilliant little affair and well conducted, but unfortunately Captain M———, who commanded, was wounded in the foot, and the Americans have no officer now fit to lead them.

It is a curious fact worth recording that owing to wounds and staff work, neither the British nor Americans have any good officers left. It is only many days of this close-quarter fighting that shows you that without good officers no men care for moving out of shelter. Unless there are men who will sacrifice themselves, the ordinary rank and file feel under no obligation to do anything more arduous than to lie comfortably firing at the enemy. You can have no idea how hard it is to get men to make sorties; on the slightest provocation, once they have left their own barricades, they rush back to safety....

Fortunately with all these events, we have been given something else to think about, and it is a thing of this sort which re-establishes confidence more than any warlike deeds. I mention it because it is the simple truth. It is also a pretty commentary on *la bête humaine*.

You remember the V-shaped barricade garrisoned by Russian sailors, I spoke about a few days ago? Well, if you do not happen to remember, I merely need say again, that it is a barricade facing both ways on Legation Street, which now in the fullness of time has blossomed into a whole network of barricades which protect our inner lines and the British Legation base from any rush of the enemy which might succeed momentarily in getting past our outworks. The Russian sailors who furnish these posts have been having a very easy time with nothing to do but to eat and to sleep, and to mount guard, turn and turn about. Of course, this comparative idleness in all the storm and stress around us gave them time to look around and to loot the vacant houses near them.

Not content with this, some of them discovered that a large number of buxom Chinese schoolgirls from the American missions were lodged but a stone's throw from their barricades. The missionaries, fearing that some scandal might occur, had placed some elderly native Christians in charge of the schoolgirls, with the strictest orders to prevent anyone from entering their retreat. This was effective for some time. One dark night, however, when the usual fusillade along the outer lines began, the sailors made tremendous preparations for an attack which they said was bound to reach them. At eleven o'clock they developed the threatened attack by emptying a warning rifle or two in the air. Then warming to their work, and with their dramatic Slav imaginations charmed with the *mise en scène*, they emptied all their rifles into the air.

Then they started firing volley after volley that crashed horribly in the narrow lanes, retreating the while into the forbidden area. Fiercely fighting their imaginary foe they fell back slowly; and as soon as the elderly native converts had sufficiently realised the perils to which they were exposed, these cowardly males fled hurriedly through the passageways which have been cut into the British Legation. The sailors then placed their rifles against a wall and disappeared. Unfortunately for them a strong guard sent to investigate this unexpected firing almost immediately appeared, and presently the sailors were rescued, some with much scratched faces. The girls, catlike, had known how to protect themselves!

The next day there was a terrible scene, which everybody soon heard about. Baron von R——, the Russian commander, on being acquainted with the facts of the affair, swore that his honour and the honour of Russia demanded that the culprits be shot. I shall never forget that absurd scene when R——, who speaks the vilest English, demanded with terrible gestures that the ring-leaders be identified by the victims. It was pointed out to him that the affair had occurred when all was dark—that the whole post was implicated—that it was impossible to name any one man.

Then R—— swore he would shoot the whole lot of them as a lesson; he would not tolerate such things. But the very next day, when a notice was posted on the bell-tower of the British Legation forbidding everyone under severe penalties to approach this delectable building, R—— had his *révanche à la Russe*, as he called it. Taking off his cap, and assuming a very polite air of doubt and perplexity, he inquired of the lady missionary committee which over-sees the welfare of these girls, "*Pardon, mesdames,*" he said purposely in French, "*cette affiche est-ce seulement pour les civiles ou aussi pour les militaires!*"

7

The Hospital and the Graveyard

5th July, 1900.

It depends very much on moments as to whether one has time to laugh or to cry. The last time I wrote, we were nearly all laughing—when we had the time; today most of us are doing the reverse. Be one ever so hardened, it is impossible to go to the humble hospital and the little graveyard of our battered lines without tender feelings welling up, and perhaps even a silent tear dropping. We have all been to either one or the other place today; our losses are mounting up. In the hospital alone there are now fifty sorely wounded and tortured men, groaning and moving this way and that. The bullet and shell wounds have so far been distinguished for their deadliness, probably because of the close ranges at which we are fighting.

It is a strange assembly, in all truth, to be mustered within the precincts of a diplomatic Chancery, wherein were prepared only a few short weeks ago dry-as-dust documents, which so hastened the storm by not promptly arresting it. For the Chancery of the British Legation is now the hospital, and on despatch tables, lately littered with diplomatic documents, operations are now almost hourly performed and muttered groans wrung from maimed men. It is a curious thought this—to think that the vengeance of foolish despatches overtakes innocent men and lays them groaning and bleeding on the very spot where the ink which framed them flowed. It does not often happen that cause and effect meet like this.

It is a wretched hospital, too, even though it is the best which can be made. Every window has to be bricked in partially; every entrance where bullets might flick in must be closed; and in the heat and dust of a Peking summer the stench is terrible. Worse still are the flies, which, attracted by the newly spilt blood of strong men, swarm so thickly that another torture is added. Half the nationalities of Europe lie groaning together, each calling in his native tongue for water, or for help to loosen a bandage which in the shimmering heat has become unbearable. And as the rifle cracking rises to the storm it always does every few hours, more men will be brought in and laid on that gruesome operating table. The very passageways have been already invaded by men lying on long chairs, because there are no more beds. Even they are happy; they have crept to a place where they can gasp in quiet; that is all they ask for.

In a hideous little room at the back the dead are prepared for their last resting place—prepared in a manner which is shocking, but is the best that can be done. I cannot describe it. In the cool of the evening, when perhaps the enemy's fire has slackened a little, and the bullets only sob very faintly overhead, and the shells have ceased their brutal attentions, stretcher parties come quietly and carry out the corpses. That is the worst sight of all.

There are no coffins, and the dead, shrouded in white cloth, have sometimes their booted feet pushing through the coarse fabric in which they are sewn. Never shall I forget the sight of one man, a great, long fellow, who seemed immense in his white shroud. A movement of the bearers struggling under his unaccustomed weight burst his winding sheet and his feet shot out as if he were making a last effort to escape from the pitiless grasp of Mother Earth extending her arms towards him in the form of a narrow trench. There was something hideous and terrible in these booted feet. One man, unnerved at the sight, gave a short cry, as if he had been struck. That is the brutal side of life—death.

There is also no room and not time to give each one a separate grave, these our dead; and so, strapped to a plank, they are lowered into the ground, a few shovelfuls of earth are hastily dropped in on top, and then another corpse is laid down. Sometimes there are three or four in a single grave, and when the grave is filled up the dead men's order is written on rough crosses. That is all.

At such burials you may see the real truth which is hidden by the mask of every-day life. Men you thought were good fellows turn out to be hearts of stone; the true hearts of gold are generally those who are devil-may-care and indifferently regarded when there is no *Sturm und Drang*. I, who have never been religious, begin to understand what such phrases mean—"*that many are called, but few are chosen.*" It is not possible that the final valuation can be that of the every-day world. Then when I think of these things, I long to get away from this imprisonment; to revalue things in a new light; to see and to understand.

But as you pass away from this torture room and this execution ground a sullen anger seizes you. Why should so many be called—why should we die thus in a hole? . . .

8

The Failure

6th July, 1900.

I have always found that there is a corrective for everything in this world. Action is the best one of all, people say. It is not always so.

The little Japanese colonel stood this morning pulling his thin moustaches very thoughtfully and looking earnestly ahead of him when I came on duty with a dozen others. In front was a great mass of ruins, concealing a couple of entrenched posts of our own men, where I was going, and farther on, half masked by the ruins, some of the enemy's advanced barricades lay.

"I think," said the colonel finally, pronouncing on the situation with inherited Japanese caution, "that it will be very difficult, but we must try."

He referred to the wretched Chinese gun belonging to the redoubtable Tung Fu-hsiang, as we had discovered from big banners pitched nearby, which had been steadily and methodically smashing in the northern front of our defence, and was fast rendering our lines untenable here. We always went on duty at these posts with little enthusiasm. We could not hit back. Another gun, a newcomer, had also been posted somewhere near the ruins of the Chinese Customs, as if encouraged by the success of the other one, and was now playing on the main-gate posts of the Su wang-fu, and rendering even these more and more dangerous for us to hold permanently.

The newcomer was, however, still, comparatively speaking, far away; it was our old friend we most dreaded. Well hidden, it pelted us with rusty but effective shells night and day. To make another sortie was highly dangerous for the ill-success of the first one in this quarter had certainly encouraged the Chinese, and this time we would have to be prepared for a very vigorous defence, which might bring on a series of counter-attacks.

Then, too, the wall-split and barricaded grounds beyond our own feeble defences meant that a single false step would lead us into an *impasse* from which we could not lightly escape. Rifle-fire would pelt us at close quarters, shells would burst right in our midst; it was not a pleasant prospect even for the biggest fire-eaters of our lines. We had, however, to remember that so long as we held firm on the outer rim of our ruins would the enormous piles of brickwork which lie around, either in the form of ruined houses or wrecked compound walls, act as traverses and make the heavy rifle and cannon fire being poured in nothing very terrible.

But as soon as we are forced to abandon our advanced lines the enemy speedily will swarm in, and then no sortie, however well planned, can dislodge him. He will make our best defences his parallels—and in a week he will be able to split us in half. These things made immediate action really advisable, and soon the word was passed round that a big sortie was to be made at once.

Once more all the morning was spent in making preparations. Marines and volunteer reserves were brought over from the British Legation to line the trenches and barricades, and cover the advance with a heavy rifle fire; the Italians, who were to co-operate by jumping down off their north-western hillock and rushing forward, were warned for duty, and had fresh ammunition served out to them; and finally volunteers were called for, and the command of the sortie handed over to a Japanese officer, Captain A——.

When everything was ready, we stood for a minute massed together while some parting instructions were given. We presented a curious and unique spectacle. There were fifteen Japanese sailors in the dirty remains of their blue uniforms, without caps or jumpers, with broken boots and begrimed faces; and alongside of them were twenty-five miscellaneous volunteers, some with bayonets to their rifles, some with none—but all determined to get home on the enemy at all costs this time. There had been sixteen days' incessant work at the trenches and barricades with next to no sleep. Mud and brickwork clung to us all with an insistence which no amount of rough dusting would remove. We were a tattered and disreputable crowd.

There was little time to reflect or to cast one's eyes around, however, for no sooner had Captain A—— received his last instructions than his bugler sounded the charge, and from the Italian lines, eight hundred feet away, which were hidden from us by walls and trees, came an answering blast. The Italians were ready. I gripped my rifle and took the flank of my detachment.

We tumbled forward in silence, forty effectives in all, with a couple dozen native converts behind us, who had been provided with some of the captured rifles and swords. As soon as we were clear, Captain A——, who was a tiny man, even among a tiny race, drew a little sword, and pointing to the enemy's barricades now looming up very close, ordered his bugler to sound the charge once more. The notes ripped out, and giving a mixed attempt at a European cheer, we quickened our pace, running as rapidly as we could over the rubbish which covered the ground and taking advantage of every piece of cover. A few stray shots pecked at us, but in this quarter, so strange that it appeared unreal, the enemy gave hardly a sign of life. Behind us, on our left, a tremendous fusillade was in progress, and the cracking of the rifles came back to us in one high-pitched roar. But the intervening trees and the ruins did not allow us to see or understand what was the cause. We had completely lost touch with the others.

Rushing round a corner, we suddenly came on the gun we had been sent to capture; it was perched high on a long, loopholed barricade, and stood quite silent and alone. We gave a shout and pitched forward in a momentary ecstasy of delight, but like a flash the scene around us changed. Dozens of soldiers jumped up around us, looking every bit like startled pheasants in their bright uniforms, and retired, firing rapidly. This, as if a preconcerted plan, was the signal for a tremendous fire on all sides, which absolutely surprised us. From every adjacent ruin and roof the enemy appeared by magic, and fired at us with ever-increasing vigour.

Now just above us the self-same gun which had demolished my outpost house a few days before loomed invitingly, and determined to have our revenge and stick the gunners like pigs if we could only get to grips, a knot of us ran on. The bugler blew a few sharp notes to rally some of those who were hanging back in confusion, and finally, riflemen in advance and the converts herded tremblingly behind by a brave Japanese Secretary of Legation in spectacles, we succeeded in climbing up on to the gun platform. The gunners, who had been lying beside their weapon, fled precipitately as soon as they saw our heads come over the barricade, but to our right and left the enemy was now swarming forward with frantic yells.

The converts, who were to drag off the gun while we covered them with our rifles and bayonets, could not be made to advance, but clung to the wall screaming piteously. We beat some of them over the head with our rifle-butts and kicked them savagely in a fever of anxiety to put some spirit in them, but nothing could move them forward. It must be always so; the Christian Chinaman face to face with his fierce, heathen countrymen is as a lamb; he cannot fight. Then before we knew it the little Japanese captain was on the ground, two or three Japanese sailors fell too, a *sauve qui peut* began, and everything was in inextricable disorder.

The Chinese commanders, seeing our plight, urged their men forward, and soon hundreds of rifles were crashing at us, and savage-looking men in brightly coloured tunics and their red trouser-covers swinging in the breeze leaped forward on us. It was a terrible sight. There was nothing to do but to retire, which we did, dragging in our wounded with brutal energy. At a ruined wall, half a dozen of us made a stand, covering the retreat, which had degenerated into a rout, and, firing steadily at a close range, we dropped man after man. Some of the Kansu soldiers rushed right up to us, and only fell a few feet from our rifles, yelling, "*Sha, Sha*,"—kill, kill, to the last moment; and one fellow, as he was beaten down, threw a sword, which stabbed one of our men in the thigh and terribly wounded him.

It must have been all over in a very few minutes, for the next thing I remember is that we were all inside our lines again, and that my knees were bleeding profusely from the scrambling over barricades and ruins. We were completely out of breath from the excitement and the running, and most of us were crimson with rage at our ill-success when we had practically had everything in our own hands. Everyone was for shooting a convert or two as an example for the rest, but in the end it came to nothing. Meanwhile the fusillade against us grew enormously in vigour. From every side bullets flicked in huge droves. The Chinese, as if incensed at our enterprise, strove to repay us by pelting us unmercifully, and awakened into action by this persistent firing, the roar of musketry and cannon soon extended to every side until it crashed with unexampled fury. Messages came from half a dozen quarters for the reserves to be sent back, and in the hurry and general confusion we could not learn what had happened to the Italians or the rest of the enterprise.

Meanwhile our wounded were lying on the ground, and the news soon spread that the Japanese surgeon had pronounced the little captain's case hopeless. I went to see him as soon as I could, and seldom have I seen a more pitiful sight. Lying on a coat thrown on the ground, with his side torn open by an iron bullet, the stricken man looked like a child who had met with a terrible accident. He could not have been more than five feet high, and his sword, which was a tiny blade, about thirty inches long, was strapped to his wrist by a cord, which he refused to have released. Beating his arms up and down in the air with that tiny sword bobbing with them, he struggled to master the pain, but the effort was too great for him, and he kept moaning in spite of himself.

A few feet from him sat a wounded Japanese sailor, who had been struck in the knee by a soft-nosed bullet. His trousers had been ripped up to put on a field dressing, and never have I before seen a more ghastly wound. The bullet had drilled into his knee-cap in a neat little hole, but the soft metal, striking the bony substance within, had splashed as it progressed through, with the result that the hole made on coming out was as big as the knee-cap itself. The sailor bore his wound with a stoicism which seemed to me superhuman. The sweat was pouring off his face in his agony, but he had stuffed a cap into his mouth so that he might not disgrace himself by crying out, and even in his agony he lay perfectly still, with staring eyes, as he waited to be carried to the operating table.

Presently the captain died with a sudden stiffening, and news came in from a number of other posts that men were falling, and we must detach some of ours to reinforce threatened points. In utter gloom the day ended, and miserably tired, we got hardly any sleep until the small hours.

9

An Interlude

8th July, 1900.

And yet in spite of such things there are plenty of interludes. For of the nine hundred and more European men, women and children besieged in the Legation lines, many are playing no part at all. There are, of course, some four hundred marines and sailors, and more than two hundred women and children. The first are naturally ranged in the fighting line; the second can be but non-combatants. But of the remainder, two hundred and more of whom are able-bodied, most are shirking. There are less than eighty taking an active part in the defence—the eighty being all young men. The others have claimed the right of sanctuary, and will do nothing. At most they have been induced to form themselves into a last reserve, which, I hope, may never be employed. If it is.... The duties of this reserve consist in mustering round the clanging bell of the Jubilee Tower in the British Legation when a general alarm is rung. When the firing becomes very heavy that bell begins clanging.

There was a general alarm the other night when I happened to be off duty, and I stopped in front of the bell-tower to see it all. The last reserve tumbled from their sleeping-places in various stages of *deshabille*, all talking excitedly. The women had too much sense to move a great deal, although the alarm might be a signal for anything. A few of them got up, too, and came out into the open; but the majority stayed where they were. Presently the commander-in chief appeared in person in his pyjamas, twirling his moustaches, and listened to the increasing fusillade and cannonade directed against the outposts. The din and roar, judged by the din and roar of every-day life, may have been nerve-breaking, but to anyone who had been so close to it for eighteen days it was nothing exceptional.

The night attack, which had been heralded after the usual manner by a fierce blowing of trumpets, simply meant thousands of rifles crashing off together, and as far as the British Legation was concerned, you might stand just as safely there as on the *Boulevard des Italiens* or in Piccadilly. There was a tremendous noise, and swarms of bullets passing overhead, but that was all. The time had not arrived for actual assaults to be delivered; there was too much open ground to be covered.

The groups of reserves stood and listened in awe, the commander-in-chief twirled his moustaches with composure, and two or three other refugee Plenipotentiaries slipped out and nervously waited the upshot of it all. It was a very curious scene. Well, the fusillade soon reached the limit of its *crescendo*, and then with delighted sighs, the *diminuendo* could plainly be divined. The Chinese riflemen, having blazed off many rounds of ammunition, and finding their rifle barrels uncomfortably warm, were plainly pulling them out of their loopholes and leaning them up against the barricades. The *diminuendo* became more and more marked, and finally, except for the usual snipers' shots, all was over. So the reserves were dismissed and went contentedly off to bed. As far as the actual defence was concerned, this comedy might have been left unplayed. In the dense gloom those men could never have been moved anywhere. Such a manoeuvre would have brought about a panic at once, for there is little mutual confidence, and nothing has been done to promote it.

At first, in the hurry and scurry and confusion of the initial attacks, when everything and everybody was unprepared and upset, this state of things escaped attention. Now all the fighting line is becoming openly discontented. There is favouritism and incompetency in everything that is being done. Two days ago a young Scotch volunteer got killed almost on purpose, because he was sick and tired of the cowardice and indecision. And now, not content with all this, there is a new folly. An alleged searchlight has been seen flickering on the skies at night, and M——, the British Minister, has in a burst of optimism declared that it is the relief under S—— signalling to us. Yet there are men who know exactly what it is—the opening of the doors of a blast-furnace in the Chinese city, which sends up a ruddy light in certain weather.

Discipline is becoming bad, too, and sailors and volunteers off duty are looting the few foreign stores enclosed in our lines. Everything is being taken, and the native Christians, finding this out, have been pouring in bands when the firing ceases and wrecking everything which they cannot carry away.

A German marine killed one, and several have been dangerously wounded. In our present condition anything is possible. Still, the fortification work is proceeding steadily, and the appearance of the base, the British Legation, has been miraculously changed. Enormous quantities of sandbags have been turned out and placed in position, and all the walls are now loopholed. With all this access of strength, we are much more secure, and yet our best contingents are being very slowly but very continuously shot to pieces. Our casualty list is now well into the second hundred, and as the line of defenders thins, the men are becoming more savage. In addition to looting, there have been a number of attempts on the native girl converts, which have been hushed up. . . . Ugly signs are everywhere, and the position becomes from day to day less enviable.

10

The Guns

10th July, 1900.
Had we a single gun how different it would be! We could parade it boldly under the enemy's nose; sweep his barricades and his advanced lines away in a cloud of dust and brick-chips; bombard his camps which we have located; make him sorry and ashamed . . . as it is we can do nothing; we have not a single piece which can be called serious artillery; and we must suffer the segment which the enemy affects in almost complete silence. Listen to our list of weapons.

First, there is the Italian one-pounder firing ballistite. It is absolutely useless. Its snapping shells are so small that you can thrust them in your pocket without noticing them. This gun is merely a plaything. And yet being the best we have, it is wheeled unendingly around and fired at the enemy from a dozen different points. It may give confidence, but that is all it can give. The other day I watched it at work on a heavy barricade being constructed by night and day by the methodical enemy. By night the Chinese soldiery work as openly as they please, for no outpost may waste its ammunition by indiscriminate shooting. But during the day, orders or no orders, it has become rash for the enemy to expose himself to our view; and even the fleeting glimpse of a moving hand is made the excuse for a hailstorm of fire. This has made excessive caution the order of the day, and you can almost believe, when no rifles are firing to disturb such a conviction, that there are only dead men round us.

Yet with nothing to be seen, countless hands are at work; in spite of the greatest vigilance barricades and barriers grow up nearer and nearer to us both night and day; we are being tied in tighter. These mysterious barricades, built in parallels, are so cunningly constructed that our fiercest sorties must in the end beat themselves to pieces against brick and stone; if the enemy can complete his plans we shall be choked silently. That is why the Italian gun is so often requisitioned.

I was saying that I watched the one-pounder at work against the enemy's brick-bound lines. Each time, as ammunition is becoming precious, the gun was more carefully sighted and fired, and each time, with a little crash, the baby shell shot through the barricades, boring a ragged hole six or eight inches in diameter. Two or three times this might always be accomplished with everything on the Chinese side silent as death. The cunning enemy! Then suddenly, as the gun was shifted a bit to continue the work of ripping up that barricade, attention would be distracted, and before you could explain it the ragged holes would be no more. Unseen hands had repaired the damage by pushing up dozens of bricks and sandbags, and before the game could be opened again, unseen rifles were rolling off in their dozens and tearing the crests of our outworks. In that storm of brick-chips, split sandbags and dented nickel, you could not move or reply. That is the Italian gun.

The next most useful weapon should be the Austrian machine-gun, which is a very modern weapon, and throws Mannlicher bullets at the rate of six hundred to the minute. Yet it, too, is practically useless. It has been tried everywhere and found to be defective. When it rattles at full speed, it has been seen that its sighting is illusory—that it throws erratically high in the air, and that ammunition is simply wasted. It cannot help us in the slightest. The value of machine-guns has been always overrated.

Then there is a Nordenfeldt belonging to the British marines, and a very small Colt, which was brought up by the Americans. The Nordenfeldt is absolutely useless and now refuses to work; the Colt is so small, being single-barrelled, that it can only do boy's work. Yet this Colt is the most satisfactory of all, and when we have dragged it out with us and played it on the enemy, it has shot true and straight. They say it has killed more men than all the rest put together....

There should be a Russian gun, too—a good Russian gun of respectable calibre. But although the shells were brought, a thousand of them, too, the gun was forgotten at the Tientsin Station! Such a thing could only happen to Russians, everybody says. But some people say it was forgotten on purpose, because De G—— had received absolute assurance from the Chinese Government that the Russian Legation would not be attacked under any circumstances, and that sailors were only brought up to keep faith with the other Powers....

This miserable list, as you will see, means that we have nothing with which to reply to the enemy's fire. We are not so proud and foolish as to wish to silence the guns ranged against us, but, at least, we should be able to make some reply. In desperation, the sailor-gunners tried to manufacture a crude piece of ordnance by lashing iron and steel together, and encasing it in wood. Fortunately it was never fired, for in the nick of time an old rusty muzzle-loader has been discovered in a blacksmith's shop within our lines, and has been made to fire the Russian ammunition by the exercise of much ingenuity. It belches forth mainly flames, and smokes and makes a terrific report. Some say this is as useful as a modern twelve-pounder....

About the Chinese guns we can find out very little, excepting that none, or very few, of the modern weapons which are in stock at Peking have been used against us. There are at most only nine or ten in constant use; perhaps the others have been dragged away down the long Tientsin road. But even these nine or ten, if they were worked together, would nearly wreck us. Our sorties have pushed some of them back.

Two of these guns are being fired at us from a staging on the palace wall—sometimes regularly and persistently, sometimes as if they had fallen under the influence of the conflicting factors which are struggling to win the day in the palace. If they bombarded us without intermission for twenty-four hours, they would render the British Legation almost untenable. Two or three more guns are on the Tartar Wall; three or four are ranged against the Su wang-fu and French lines; some are kept travelling round us searching for a weak spot. They have no system or fire-discipline. Some use shrapnel and segment; others fire solid round shot all covered with rust. Silent sometimes with a mysterious silence for days at a time, they come to life again suddenly in a blaze of activity, and wreak more ruin in a few minutes than weeks of rifle fusillade and days of firing on the fringe of outer buildings.

And yet we cannot complain. We have so many walls, so many houses, so many trees, so many obstructions of every kind, that they cannot get a clear view of anything. These singing shells, which might breach any one part, were the guns massed and their fire continuous, are sneered at by most of us already. Provided you can lie low, shell-fire soon loses even its moral effect.

11

Sniping

The siege has now become such a regular business with everyone that there are almost rules and regulations, which, if not promulgated among besieged and besiegers, are, at least, more or less understood things. Thus, for instance, after one or two in the morning the crashing of rifles around us is always quite stilled; the gunners have long ceased paying us their attentions, and a certain placid calmness comes over all. The moon may then be aloft in the skies; and if it is, the Tartar Wall stands out clear and black, while the ruined entrenchments about us are flooded in a silver light which makes the sordidness of our surroundings instantly disappear in the enchantment of night. Our little world is tired; we have all had enough; and even though they may run the risk of being court-martialled, it is always fairly certain that by three or four in the morning half the outposts and the picquets will be dead asleep. It was not like that in the beginning, for then nobody slept much night or day; and if one did, it was only to awake with a moan, the result of some weird nightmare.

Now with the weeks which have gone by since we broke off relations with the rest of the world it is quite different, and we pander to our little weakness of forty winks before a loophole, although orderly officers may stumble by all night on their rounds and curse and swear at this state of affairs. By training yourself, however, I have found that you can practically sleep like a dog, with one eye open and both ears on the alert—that light slumber which the faintest stirring immediately breaks; when you are like this you can do your duty at a loophole.

It is such dull work, too, in front of the eternal loopholes, with nothing but darkness and thick shadows around you, and the rest of a post of four or five men vigorously snoring. The first half hour goes fairly quickly, and, perhaps even the second; but the last hour is dreary, tiresome work. And when your two hours are up, and contentedly you kick your relief on the ground beside you, he only moans faintly, but does not stir. Dead with sleep is he. Then you kick him again with all that zest which comes from a sense of your own lost slumbers, and once more he moans in his fatigue, more loudly this time, but still he does not move.

Finally, in angry despair you land the butt of your rifle brutally on his chest, and he will start up with a cry or an oath.

"Time," you mutter. The relief grumblingly rises to his feet, rubbing his glued eyes violently, and asks you if there is anything. "Nothing," you answer curtly. It is always nothing, for although the enemy's barricades rear themselves perhaps not more than twenty or thirty feet from where you stand, you know that it takes a lusty stomach to rush that distance and climb your fortifications and ditches in the dark in the face of the furious fire which sooner or later would burst out. For we understand our work now. Experience is the only schoolmaster.

So with your two hours on and your four hours off the night spends itself and dawn blushes in the skies. It is in all truth weary work, those long watches of the night.... Sometimes even your four hours' sleeping time is rudely broken into by half a dozen alarms; for separated sometimes by hundreds of feet from your comrades of the next post, the instinct of self-preservation makes you line your loopholes and peer anxiously into the gloom beyond, when any one of the enemy shows that he is afoot. A single rifle-shot spitting off nearby is as often as not the cause of the alarm; for that rifle-shot cracking out discordantly and awakening the echoes may be the signal for the dread rush which would spell the beginning of the end. Once one line is broken into we know instinctively that the confusion which would follow would engulf us all. There is no confidence....

When you have time you may relieve his monotony by sniping.

In the early morning, the very early morning, is the time for this work—say, roughly, between the hours of four and six, when the soldier Chinaman beyond our lines is yawningly arousing himself from his slumbers and squats blinking and inattentive before his morning tea. Then if you are a natural hunter, are inclined to risk a good deal, and something of a quick shot, you may have splendid chances which teach you more than you could ever learn by months in front of targets. Baron von R——, the cynical commander of the Russian detachment, is the crack sniper of us all, because he has not a great deal to do in the daytime, and, also, because beyond his lines of the Russian Legation all is generally quiet with a curious and suggestive quietness.

At four in the morning R——, with his sailor's habits, generally rises, shakes himself like a dog, lights his eternal Russian cigarette, takes a few whiffs, and then sallies forth with a Mannlicher carbine and a clip of five cartridges. His sailors are duly warned to cover him if he has to retire in disorder, but so far he has met with no mishap. Cautiously pushing out beyond his barricades, he climbs a ruined wall, reaches the top and buries himself in the dust in pleasant anticipation of what will follow.

Presently he is rewarded. A Chinese brave comes out into the open, selects a corner, and sits down to smoke under cover of a barricade. The Baron pushes his clip of cartridges deliberately into the magazine, shoots one into the rifle barrel through the feed, and then very cautiously and very slowly draws a steady bead on the man. I have seen him at work. Five seconds may go by, perhaps even ten, for the Baron allows himself only one shot in each case, and then *bang*! the bullet speeds on its way, and the Chinaman rolls over bored through and through. On a good day the bag may be two or three; on a bad day the Russian commander returns with his five cartridges intact and a persistent Russian shrug, for he never fires in vain, and there are certain canons in this sport which he does not care to violate lightly.

Myself, enamoured with this game, after I had watched the Russian commander two mornings, I, too, determined that I would embark on it, although I have no such leisure in the early hours. Eleven or twelve o'clock in the bright sunlight has become my hour, when the sun beats down hotly on our heads, and everyone is drowsy with the noon-heat. Then you may also catch the Chinaman smoking and drinking his tea once again, and if you are quick a dead man is your reward. Every dead man puts another drop of caution into the attackers. It is therefore good and useful.

Yesterday I had great luck, for I got three men within very few minutes of one another; and then when I was fondly imagining that I might pick off dozens more from my coign of vantage, I was swept back into our lines under such a storm of fire as I have never experienced before. I should tell you that there are practically only two shooting-grounds where this curious sport may be had; there are only two areas of brick and ruins where by judicious manoeuvring you may steal out and get the enemy on his exposed flank where no barricades protect him from an enfilading fire. These two areas lie opposite the Russian front, and beyond the extreme Japanese western posts of the Su wang-fu. Since the Russian front is the Russian commander's own preserve, it is from the Japanese posts that I work.

On the day when I made my record bag, half-past eleven found everybody drowsy and the time propitious. Our northern Peking sun beats down pitilessly from the cloudless skies at such a time, and so I had the field completely to myself. Firing had ceased absolutely on all sides, and the Chinese had begun to sleep. Crouching low down I scurried across from the Japanese post to some ruins fifty feet off, and remained quietly squatting there, panting in the heat, to get myself bearings. Around me all was silent, and thirty or forty yards from where I lay I could see the brown face of the Japanese sailor laughing at me through a loophole. Presently bringing my glasses into play I swept the huge pile of ruined houses and streets lying huddled on all sides.

There was not a twig stirring or a shadow moving. All was dead quiet. The main Chinese camp on this side was placed in H——'s abandoned compounds—that we had discovered long ago—but the battalions there were now apparently asleep with not so much as a sentry out. So, gaining confidence, I pushed on, working parallel to Prince Su's outer walls and about fifty feet beyond them. Suddenly I stopped and dropped, quite by instinct, for although my mind had telegraphed the danger to my knees, I did not fully realise what it was until I was on the ground. Just round the corner there was a glimpse of three men stripped to the waist to be seen. Had they seen me? I waited in some suspense for a few seconds pressed my glasses back into their case, and gripped my rifle.

My anxiety was soon set at rest, for with a clatter, which seemed ten times greater than it really was, the men set quickly to work on a structure. They were building something, and now was my chance. Getting to the corner again I peered cautiously around, and there but seventy or eighty feet from where I lay three strapping fellows were raising a heavy log. They had pulled off their red and black tunics, and were only in their baggy breeches and the curious little stomach apron the Northern Chinaman affects to keep himself from catching cold.

Their brown backs glistened with sweat in the bright sunshine, and between their belts and the loose black turbans, under which their pigtails were gathered up, an ideal two-feet target presented itself.

Carefully I fired.

In a flash one broad brown back was suddenly splashed with red, a fellow sank on his knees with outstretched arms, and at last rolled over without a moan, apparently as dead as dead could be. It was brutalising.

The log the men were carrying crashed down heavily on the ground and the two remaining soldiers started back in surprise. From whence came that shot? In front of where they were working lay their advanced posts, which, facing our own, two or three hundred feet away, should completely cover them. They peered around for a few minutes, anxiously searching their front and not looking behind them. At last they apparently decided that it must have been a stray shot, for, bending down, they once more raised the log, paying no more attention to their dead companion than they would to a dead dog.

This time I let them advance towards their outposts until they were a hundred feet farther away. Then I fired again. The log came down once more with a dull thud, and both the men fell as well. But imagine my disgust when they both rose to their feet, one man merely showing the other a snipped shoulder which must be bleeding, but was evidently nothing as a wound. I cursed my government rifle, which always throws to the right. At less than a hundred yards such practice was disgraceful.

This time both the men were aroused, and, abandoning their log, they disappeared round some ruins, only to reappear with their tunics on, their *bandoliers* strapped round them, and their Mausers in their hands. They meant to have some revenge. I lost sight of them for quite ten minutes, only to have them both out again almost halfway between myself and the Japanese posts from which I had sallied forth. I was cut off! I would have to wipe those two men out or else they would do that to me.

They were in no hurry, however, for they began by beating the ground carefully and taking advantage of every piece of cover. They evidently suspected that some of our men had come out in skirmishing order and were still lying hidden; at last one saw something. He had caught sight of the Japanese sentry who was looking out anxiously to see what had become of me. So rising hurriedly, the soldier fired at the brown Japanese face. Before he had sunk on his knees again I had drilled him fair with a snapshot—in the head it must have been, because he went over with a piercing yell and with his hands plucking at his cap. The other man did not wait to see what would happen, but fled as fast as he could down a small lane that ran only twenty feet past me.

Seeing the game was played out, I rose and fired rapidly from under the crook of my arm and missed. Reloading as I scrambled after him, I drove another bullet at him, and he staggered wildly but did not fall. My blood was now up, and I was determined to get him, even if I had to follow into the Chinese camp, so I sped along too. The fellow was now yelling lustily, calling his comrades to his aid, and I seemed to be going mad in my excitement. I fired again as I ran, and must have hit him again, for he reeled still more; then he turned totteringly into a ruined doorway....

Just as I determined that I must give it up the scene changed like the flash of a lamp. My quarry stumbled and fell flat; dozens of half-stripped men came charging towards me, loading as they ran, and almost before I knew it, the ground around me was ripped with bullets.

Then in turn how I raced!

Such was the storm of fire around me that I nearly dropped my rifle so as to improve my pace, and all the moisture left my mouth. Holding grimly on I at last cleared the exposed ground, and jumped through into the Japanese barricades. In their rage the Chinese soldiery rushed into the open after me, firing angrily all along the line, and before the loopholes could be properly manned and the fusillade returned they were almost up to us. Then, as always happens, they suddenly became irresolute, and trickled away, and from behind safe cover they poured in the same long-range rifle-fire....

This, however, is only an incident—one which I provoked. Generally we are not so enterprising, but are inclined to accept events as they unroll. But this escapade proved to me that attacks are thrown against us only after special orders have been issued by the government, and that the camps of soldiery established round our lines are as much to imprison us as to slay us. They have bound us in with brickworks, and they bombard us intermittently with nine or ten guns; but each bombardment and each attack seems to be conducted quite without any relation to the general situation....

Fortunately, then, although we are ill organised and badly commanded as a whole, our units are well led, and we meet the situation as it actually is on the best plan possible for the time being. But will this last? Will not something happen which will fling our enemy against us animated by one desire —a desire to slay us one and all? It requires now but one rush of the thousands of armed men encamped about us to sweep our defence off the face of the earth like so many dried and worthless leaves.

12

The Gallant French

14th July, 1900.

The post fighting is becoming more desperate, and the French are steadily losing ground. Is it true that they are losing courage? Of course, everyone knows that they are a gallant race, and that although the Germans, by their relentless science and unending attention to detail, are rated superior in machine-like warfare, they can never be quite like the brilliant conquerors of Jena, Austerlitz, and a hundred other battles; and yet no one expected the French were going to cling to the ruins of their Legation with the bulldog desperation of which they complained in the English at Waterloo; a desperation making each house a siege in itself, and only ending with the total destruction of that house by shells or fire; were going to treat all idea of retirement with contempt, although their shabby treatment caused them two weeks ago to temporarily evacuate their lines in a fit of moroseness....

This is what has happened until now, for the French have set their teeth, and now everyone almost believes that nothing—not even mines, shells, myriads of bullets, and foolish order after order from headquarters ordering men to be sent elsewhere —will beat them back. And yet they cannot keep on this way for ever. All round them the connecting posts and blockhouses are losing more and more men, and matters are reaching a dangerous point.

It is now nearly four weeks since the first bullet flicked out the brains of the first French sailor ten minutes after the opening of hostilities at barricades far away down Customs Street, and in these twenty-five days which have elapsed the French positions have been beaten into such shapeless masses that they are quite past recognition. I had not been there for a week, and was shocked when I saw how little remains. The Chinese have, foot by foot, gained more than half of the Legation, and all that is practically left to the defenders is their main-gate blockhouse, a long barricaded trench and the remains of a few houses. These they have sworn to retain until they are too feeble to hold. Then, and then only, will they retreat into the next line behind them, the fortified Hôtel de Pékin, which has already four hundred shell holes in it.

Yesterday's losses at the French lines were five men wounded, four blown up by a mine, of whom two never have been seen again, and two men killed outright by rifle-fire. Then the last houses were set fire to by Chinese soldiers, who, able to push forward in the excitement and confusion of the mine explosions, attempted to seize and hold these strategic points, and were only driven out by repeated counter-attacks. Such events show that for some occult reason the Chinese commands are trying to carry the French lines by every possible device. . . . It has been like this for a week now.

For, from the 7th of July, the Chinese commands having prepared the ground for their attacks by a heavy cannonade lasting for sixty hours, which riddled everything above the ground level with gaping holes, started pushing forward through the breaches, and setting fire, by means of torches attached to long bamboo poles, to everything which would burn. No living men, no matter how brave, can hold a glowing mass of ruins and ashes, and the Chinese were showing devilish cunning.

Isolated combats took place along the whole French line—in a vain effort to drive off the incendiaries, little sorties of two or three men furiously attacking the persistent enemy, and each time driving him back with loss, only to find him dribbling in again like muddy water through every hole and cranny in the imperfect defences. But even this did not do much good. No one could keep an accurate record of these curious encounters during the first few days, for they have succeeded one another with such rapidity that men have become too tired, too sleepy to wish to talk. They try to act, and some of their adventures have been astonishing.

Thus a young Breton sailor, not more than seventeen years old, seeing men armed with swords collecting one night for a rush, jumped down among them from the top of an earthwork, and shot and bayoneted three or four of them before they had time to defend themselves. Then it took him half an hour to get back to safety by creeping from one hole in the ground to another and avoiding the rifle-fire. . . .

Self-preservation makes it necessary to rush out thus single handed and ease your front. Every man killed is a discouragement, which holds the enemy back a bit.

Exploits of this nature must at length have shown the Chinese soldiery that they have to face men endowed with the courage of despair in this quarter; and fearing cold steel more than anything else, they have decided that the only way of reaching their prey is by blowing them up piecemeal. That is why they have taken to mining—most audacious mining, carried on under the noses of the French defenders. If you come here at night, and remain until one of those curious lulls in the rifle-fire suddenly begins, you will distinctly hear this curious tapping of picks and shovels, which means the preparation of a gallery.

So as to save time, such mining is not begun from behind the enemy's trenches; it is audaciously commenced in the ruins which litter some of the neutral territory, which neither side holds and into which Chinese desperadoes creep as soon as it is dusk. For a few days the French did not dare to make sorties against such enterprises, but some of the younger volunteers, discovering that these sappers were only armed with their tools, have taken to creeping out and butchering in the bowels of the earth. . . . This is terribly but absolutely true.

Thus a young volunteer, named D——, found, after watching for two days, that a number of men crept into a tunnel mouth every night only twenty feet from his post, and began working on a mine right under his feet. He decided to go out himself and kill them all. . . . He told me the story. He crept out two days ago as soon as he had seen them go in, and, posting himself at the entrance, called on the men to come out, else he would block them in and kill them in the most miserable way he could think of.

They came out, crawling on their hands and knees, and as each man slipped up to the level he was bayoneted. . . . . in the end thirteen were killed like this. Three remained, but D——'s strength was not equal to it, and he had to drive them in as captives. Then they were despatched and beheaded. They say the French sailors slung back those heads far over into the advanced Chinese barricades with taunts and shouts. That stopped all work for a few hours. But it was not for long enough.

Yesterday, the 13th, the Chinese had their revenge for the loss of the hundred odd men who have been shot or bayoneted along this front during the past week. At six in the evening, when the rifle-fire all along the line had become stilled, a tremendous explosion shook every quarter of our besieged area and made everyone tremble with apprehension. Even in the most northerly part of our defences—the Hanlin posts beyond the British Legation, which are probably three or four thousand feet away—the men said it was like an earthquake. In the French lines it seemed as if the end of the world had come.

The Chinese, having successfully sapped right under one of the remaining fortified houses, had blown it up with a huge charge of black gunpowder. D——, the French commander, R——, the Austrian *Chargé d'Affaires,* the same indomitable volunteer D——, and a picket of four French sailors were in the house, and were buried in the ruins. Hardly had the echoes of the first explosion died away, when a second one blew up another house, and out of the ruins were lifted, as if the powers of darkness had taken pity on them all, the defenders who had been buried alive, excepting two. Never has such a thing been heard of before. Providence is plainly helping us. The wretched men thus cruelly treated were all the colour of death and bleeding badly when they were dragged out. The two missing French sailors must have been crushed into fragments. Only a foot has been found. . . .

That was afterwards; for the mine explosions were the signals for a terrible bombardment and rifle-fire all along the line, from which we have not yet recovered. The French, more than a little shaken, were driven into their last trench—the *tranche Bartholin,* which has just been completed. They held this to this morning and then counter-attacked. That is why I have found myself here. Reinforcements were rushed in by us at daybreak, and after a sleepless forty hours the Chinese advance has been fairly held. But for how long? If they act as earnestly during the next week we are finished!

13

The British Legation Base

15th July, 1900.

Fortunately, startling events of the sort I have just described are confined to the outposts, and the half a dozen closely threatened points. Our main base, the British Legation, is little affected, and many in it do not appear to realise or to know anything of these frantic encounters along the outer lines. They can tell from the stretcher-parties that come in at all hours of the day and night, and pass down to the hospital, what success the Chinese fire is having, but beyond this they know nothing. They secretly hope, most of them, that it will remain like this to the end; that bullets and shells may scream overhead, but that they may be left attending to minor affairs.

As I look around me, it appears more and more evident that self-preservation is the dominant, mean characteristic of modern mankind. The universal attitude is: spare me and take all my less worthy neighbours. In gaining in skin-deep civilisation we have lost in the animal-fighting capacity. We are truly mainly grotesque when our lives are in danger.

In the British Legation time has even been found to establish a model laundry, and several able-bodied men actually fought for the privilege of supervising it, they say, when the idea was mooted.

Neither have our Ministers improved by the seasoning process of the siege. Most of them have become so ridiculous, that they shun the public eye, and listen to the roar of the rifles from safe places which cannot be discovered. And yet fully half of them are able-bodied men, who might do valuable work; who might even take rifles and shoot. But it is they who give a ridiculous side, and for that, at least, one should be thankful. It is something to see P——, the French Minister, starting out with his whole staff, all armed with *fusils de chasse*, and looking *très sportsman* on a tour of inspection when everything is quiet.

Each one is well told by his tearful wife to look out for the Boxers, to be on the alert—as if Chinese *banditti* were lurking just outside the Legation base to swallow up these brave creatures!—and in a compact body they sally forth. These are the married men: marriage excuses everything when the guns begin to play. Thus the Secretary of Legation, whose name I will not divulge even with an initial, amused me immensely yesterday by calculating how much more valuable he was to the State as a father of a family than an unmarried youngster like myself. He tried to prove to me that if he died the economic value of his children would suffer—what a fool he was!—and that my own value capitalised after the manner of mathematicians was very small. I listened to him carefully, and then asked if the difference between a brave man and a coward had any economic significance. He became suddenly angry and left me. Some of the besieged are becoming truly revolting.

Even P——, who some people think ought to stay in the remains of his own Legation, is rather disgusted, and as he marches out in an embroidered nightshirt, with little birds picked out in red thread on it, he is not as absurd as I first thought. Poor man, he is attempting to do his duty after his own lights, and excepting two or three others, he has been the most creditable of all the elderly men, who think that position excuses everything.

Labouring at the making of sandbags, the women sit under shelter, and keep company with those men who have not the stomach to go out. And as shells have been falling more and more frequently in and around this safe base, and rumour has told them that the outer lines may give way, bomb-proof shelters have been dug in many quarters ready to receive all those who are willing to crouch for hours to avoid the possibility of being hit....

Otherwise, there is nothing much to note in the British Legation, for here the storm and stress of the outer lines come back oddly enough quite faintly, excepting during a general attack. The dozens of walls account for that. In the evenings the missionaries now gather and sing hymns ... sometimes Madame P——, the wife of the great Russian Bank Director, takes compassion, and gives an *aria* from some opera. She used to be a *diva* in the St. Petersburg Opera House, they say, years ago, and her voice comes like a sweet dream in such surroundings.

A week ago a strange thing happened when she was giving an *impromptu* concert. She was singing the Jewel song from *Faust* so ringingly that the Chinese snipers must have heard it, for immediately they opened a heavy "fire," which grew to a perfect tornado, and sent the listeners flying in terror. Perhaps the enemy thought it was a new war-cry, which meant their sudden damnation!

Yet we have had so much time to rectify all our mistakes that things are in much better working order. Public opinion has made the commander-in-chief distribute the British marines in many of the exposed positions and thus allow inferior fighting forces to garrison the interior lines. Twice last week, before this redistribution had been completed, there was trouble with both the Italian and the Austrian sailors and some volunteers. Posts of them retreated during the night. ... They gave as their excuse that they knew that the loose organisation would cause them to be sacrificed if the enemy began rushing. There is much to be said for them; the general command had been disgraceful, especially during the night, when only good fortune saves us from annihilation. One single determined rush is all that is needed to end this farce....

These retreats, which have not been confined to the sailors, have ended by causing great commotion and alarm among the non-combatants, and reserve trenches and barricades are being improved and manned in growing numbers. Still, the distribution is unequal. There is a force of nearly sixty rifles in what is the northern front of the British Legation—the sole front exposed to direct attack on this side of the square. With difficulty can the command be induced to withdraw a single man from here. They say it is so close to all those who have sought the shelter of the British Legation, so close to the women and children and those who are afraid, that it would be a crime to weaken this front. And yet there has been hardly a casualty among those sixty men during four weeks' siege, while elsewhere about one hundred and twenty have been killed and wounded....

The fear that fire-balls will be flung far in from here, or fire-arrows shot from the adjacent trenches, has made them institute patrols, which make a weary round all through the night to see that all's well. In the thick darkness these men can act as they please, and already the are several *sales histoires* being sold. One is very funny. The patrol in question was composed entirely of Russian students, who are not rated as effectives. Beginning at nine o'clock the day before yesterday, the patrol had got as far as the Japanese women's quarters at this northern front of the British Legation, when they were halted for a few minutes to communicate some orders. One of the volunteers, of an amorous disposition, noticed a buxom little Japanese servant at work on a wash-tub in the gloom. An appointment was made for the morrow. . . .

The next night duly came. Once more the patrol halted, and once more the young Russian told his companions to go on. The patrol moved away, and the adventurous Russian tiptoed into the Japanese quarters. Cautiously feeling his way down a corridor, he opened a door, which he thought the right one; then the tragedy occurred. Suddenly a quiet voice said to him in French out of the gloom:

Monsieur desire quelque chose? Je serai charmée de donner à Monsieur ce qu'il voudra s'il veut bien rester à la porte.

The wretched Russian student imagined he was lost; it was the wife of a minister! He hesitated a minute; then, gripping his rifle and with the perfect Russian imperturbability coming to his rescue, he replied, with a deep bow:

Merci, Madame, Merci mille fois! Je cherchais seulement de la vaseline pour mon fusil!

This phrase has become immortal among the besieged.

14

The Ever-Growing Casualty List

16th July, 1900.

And yet one is lucky if one can laugh at all. The rifle and cannon fire continues; barricades are pushing closer and closer, more of our men are falling—it is always the same monotonous chronicle. A few days ago poor T——, the Austrian cruiser captain, who aspired to be our commander-in-chief with such disastrous results, was killed in the Su wan-fu while he was encouraging his men to stand firm and not repeat some of their former performances. Today little S——, the British Minister's chief of the staff, has been mortally hit, and has just died. It was a sad affair. In the morning a party from headquarters was making a tour of inspection of the Su wang-fu posts, in order to see exactly how much battering they could stand, and how soon the Italian contention that already the hillock works were untenable would become an undeniable fact.

The Italian defences had been inspected and the little party was crossing the ornamental gardens, which are always swept by a storm of fire, when suddenly S—— fell mortally wounded, M——, the correspondent, was badly hit in the leg, the Japanese colonel alone escaping with a bullet-cut tunic. They had drawn the enemy's fire. Great was the dismay when the news became generally known; it meant that the authority of headquarters had received a cruel blow. There is no officer left who can really perform the duties of the chief of the staff, and all the outer lines will feel this loosening of a control which has really only been complimentary and nominal. Casualties among the officers of the other detachments had allowed the British marine commanders to increase their influence. Now it is finished. The only two good ones have now been struck off the list.

All day long men looked gloomily about them, and felt that gradually but surely things were progressing from bad to worse. Six of the best officers have either been killed or so badly wounded that they cannot possibly take the field again; about fifty of our most daring regulars and volunteers have been killed outright; the number of admittances to the hospital up to date is one hundred and ten; and thus of the four hundred and fifty rifles defending our lines, nearly a third have been placed out of action in less than four weeks. Excepting for a small gap across the Northern Imperial canal bridge, a continuous double, or even treble, line of the enemy's barricades now stretch unbroken from a point opposite the American positions on the Tartar Wall round in a vast irregular curve to the city wall overlooking the German Legation.

These barricades are becoming more and more powerful, and are being pushed so close to us by a system of parallels and traverses that at the Su wang-fu and the French lines only a few feet separate some of our own defences from the enemy's. Already it had twice happened that a fierce and unique deed had taken place at the same loophole between one of our men and a Chinese brave, ending in the shooting of one or the other, forcing a retirement on our part to the next line of barricades. Thus, by sheer weight of brickwork they are crushing us in, and if they have only two weeks' more uninterrupted work, it can only end in one way.

Colonel S—— has made two more frantic sorties, in both of which I took part at daybreak, with a few men, which succeeded each time in pushing back the enemy for a few days in one particular corner at the cost of casualties we cannot afford. But the work and the strain are becoming exhausting, and even the Japanese, who are being driven by little S—— like mules, are showing the effects in their lack-lustre eyes and dragging legs. The men are half drunk from lack of sleep and from bad, overheated blood, caused by a perpetual peering through loopholes and a continual alertness even when they are asleep. The strain is intolerable, I say, and pony meat is becoming nauseating, and fills me with disgust.

On top of it all the trenches are now sometimes half full of water, for the summer rains, which have held back for so long, are beginning to fall. The stenches are so bad from rotting carcases and obscene droppings that an already weakened stomach becomes so rebellious that it is hard to swallow any food at all.

In the morning it is sometimes revolting. For four days I was at a line of loopholes, with Chinese corpses swelling in the sun under my nose.... At the risk of being shot, I covered them partially by throwing handfuls of mud. Otherwise not I myself, but my rebellious stomach, could not have stood it.

Scorched by the sun by day, unable to sleep except in short snatches at night, with a never-ending rifle and cannon fire around us, we have had almost as much as we can stand, and no one wants any more. I wonder now sometimes why we have been abandoned by our own people. Reliefs and S—— are only seen in ghastly dreams....

And yet there are others near who must be faring worse than we. Far away in the north of the city, where are Monseigneur F——'s cathedral, his thousands of converts, and the forty or fifty men he so ardently desired, we hear on the quieter days a distant rumble of cannon. Sometimes when the wind bears down on us we think we can hear a confused sound of rifle-firing, far, far away. They say that Jung Lu, the *Manchu Generalissimo* of Peking, whose friendship has been assiduously cultivated by the French Bishop, is seeing to it that the Chinese attacks are not pushed home, and that a waiting policy is adopted similar to that which the Chinese have used towards us. But no matter what be the actual facts of the case, the besieged fathers must be having a terrible time....

Ponies and mules are also getting scarcer, and the original mobs, numbering at least one hundred and fifty or two hundred head, have disappeared at the rate of two or three a day as meat. Our remaining animals are now quartered in a portion of the Su wang-fu, where they are feeding on what scant grass and green vegetation they can still find in those gloomy gardens. Sometimes a humming bullet flies low and maims one of the poor animals in a vital spot. Then the butcher need not use his knife, for meat is precious, and even the sick horses that die, and whose bodies are ordered to be buried quickly, are not safe from the clutches of our half-starving Chinese refugees....

A few days ago a number of ponies, frightened at some sudden roar of battle, broke loose and escaped by jumping over in a marvellous way some low barricades fronting the canal banks. Caught between our own fire and that of the enemy, and unable to do anything but gallop up and down frantically in a frightened mob, the poor animals excited our pity for days without our being able to do a single thing towards rescuing them. Gradually one by one they were hit, and soon their festering carcases, lying swollen in the sun, added a little more to the awful stenches which now surround us. Some men volunteered to go out and bury them, and cautiously creeping out, shovel in hand, just as night fell, once more our Peking dust was requisitioned, and a coverlet of earth spread over them.

The droves of ownerless Peking dogs wandering about and creeping in and out of every hole and gap are also annoying us terribly. These pariahs, abandoned by their masters, who have fled from this ruined quarter of the city, are ravenous with hunger, and fight over the bodies of the Chinese dead, and dig up the half-buried horses; nothing will drive them away. In furious bands they rush down on us at night, sometimes alarming the outposts so much that they open a heavy fire. An order given to shoot everyone of them, so as to stop these night rushes, has been carried out, but no matter how many we kill, more push forward, frantic with hunger, and tear their dead comrades to pieces in front of our eyes. It is becoming a horrible warfare in this bricked-in battle-ground.

Inside our lines there are a number of half-starving natives, who were caught by the storm and are unable to escape. They are poor people of the coolie classes, and it is no one's business to care for them. Several times parties of them have attempted to sneak out and get away, but each time they have been seized with panic, and have fled back, willing to die with starvation sooner than be riddled by the enemy's bullets. The native troops beyond our lines shoot at everything that moves. A few days ago an old rag-picker was seen outside the Tartar Wall shambling along half dazed towards the Water-Gate, which runs in under the Great Wall into the dry canal in our centre.

The Chinese sharpshooters saw him and must have thought him a messenger. Soon their rifles crashed at him, and the old man fell hit, but remained alive. After a while he raised himself on his hands and knees and began crawling towards his countrymen like a poor, stricken dog, in the hope that they would spare him when they saw his condition. But pitilessly once more the rifles crashed out, and this time their bullets found a billet in his vital parts, for the beggar rolled over and remained motionless. There he now lies where he was shot down in the dust and dirt, and his white beard and his rotting rags seem to raise a silent and eloquent protest to high Heaven against the devilish complots which are racking Peking.

The feeding of our native Christians, an army of nearly two thousand, is still progressing, but babies are dying rapidly, and nothing further can be done.

There is only just so much rice, and the men who are doing the heavy coolie work on the fortifications must be fed better than the rest or else no food at all would be needed. . . .

The native children, with hunger gnawing savagely at their stomachs, wander about stripping the trees of their leaves until half Prince Su's grounds have leafless branches. Some of the mothers have taken all the clothes off their children on account of the heat, and their terrible water-swollen stomachs and the pitiful sticks of legs eloquently tell their own tale. Unable to find food, all are drinking enormous quantities of water to stave off the pangs of hunger. A man who has been in India says that all drink like this in famine time, which inflates the stomach to a dangerous extent, and is the forerunner of certain death.

To the babies we give all the scraps of food we can gather up after our own rough food is eaten, and to see the little disappointed faces when there is nothing is sadder than to watch the wounded being carried in. If we ever get out we have some heavy scores to settle, and some of our rifles will speak very bitterly.

Thus enclosed in our brick-bound lines, each of us is spinning out his fate. The Europeans still have as much food as they need; the Chinese are half starving; shot and shell continue; stinks abound; rotting carcases lie festering in the sun; our command is looser than ever. It is the merest luck we are still holding out. Perhaps tomorrow it will be over. In any case, the glory has long since departed, and we have nothing but brutal realities.

15

The Armistice

17th July, 1900.

The impossible has happened at the eleventh hour. Around us those hoarse-throated trumpets have been ringing out stentoriously all day. How blood-curdling they sounded! Calling fiercely and insistently to one another, this barbaric cease-fire of brass trumpets has grown to such a blood-curdling roar that attention had to be paid, and gradually but surely the rifles have been all stilled until complete and absolute silence surrounds us. At last diplomacy in the far-away outer world has made itself heard, and we who are placed in the very centre of this Middle Kingdom of China, being parleyed with by the responsible Chinese Government. It has been a long and heart-breaking wait, but it is always better late than never.

This is exactly what has happened, although I have only just learned the full details. On the 14th—that is, three days ago—a native messenger, bearing our tidings, was sent out in fear and trembling, induced to attempt to reach Tientsin by lavish promises, and by the urgency of missionary entreaties. But instead of even getting out of the city, the messenger was captured, beaten, and detained for several days at the headquarters of the Manchu commander-in-chief, Jung Lu, in the Imperial city. Then, finally, when he thought that he was being led out to be put to death, he was brought back to our barricades, presenting a very sorrowful appearance, but bearing a fateful despatch from Prince Ching and all the members of the Tsung-li Yamen.

This despatch had nothing very sensational in it, but it marked the beginning. It merely stated that soldiers and bandits had been fighting during the last few days; that the accuracy and vigour of our fire had created alarm and suspicion; and that, in consequence, our Ministers and their staffs were invited to repair at once to the Tsung-li Yamen, where they would be properly cared for. As for the rest of the thousand living and dead Europeans and the two thousand native Christians within our lines, they were not even dignified by being mentioned. Most people inferred from this that by some means even the extremists of the Chinese Government had realised that if all the foreign Ministers were killed, it would be necessary for Europe to sacrifice some members of the Imperial family.

But the despatch, although its terms were trivial and even childish, had a vast importance for us. It showed that something had happened somewhere in the vague world beyond Peking—perhaps that armies were arriving. We were reminded that we were still alive. A dignified reply was sent, and the very next day came an astonishing Washington cipher message, which has been puzzling us ever since. It was only three words: "Communicate to bearer." No one can explain what these words mean; even the American Minister has cudgelled his brains in vain, and asked everybody's opinion. But about one thing there is no doubt—that it comes straight from Washington untampered with, for these three words are in a secret cipher, which only half a dozen of the highest American officials in Washington understand, and in Peking there is no one excepting the Minister himself who has the key.

This is absolutely the first authentic sign we have had. If the reply message ever gets through, public opinion may force our rescue....

Finding that they could trust us, our own messenger has been followed by Chinese Government messengers, who, tremblingly waving white flags, march up to our barricades hand in their messages, and crouch down, waiting to be given a safe-conduct back.

There have been several such messages delivered at one point along our long front while the rifle duel was continuing elsewhere with the same monotony. Now those trumpets, gaining confidence, have brought absolute silence.

At first there was only this absolute silence. It seemed so odd and curious after weeks of rifle-fire and booming of old-fashioned cannon, that that alone was like a holiday. Then, as everyone seemed to realise that it was a truce, men began standing up on their barricades and waving white cloths to one another.

Both sides did this for some time, and as no one fired, a mutual inquisitiveness prompted men to climb over their entrenched positions and walk out boldly into the open. Still the same friendliness.

By midday friendliness and confidence had reached such a point, that half our men were over the barricades, and had met the Chinese soldiery on the neutral zone of ruins and rubbish extending between our lines. All of us left our rifles behind, and stowed revolvers into our shirts lest treachery suddenly surprised us and found us defenceless. I placed an army revolver in my trousers pocket, with a vague idea that I would attempt the prairie trick of shooting through my clothing if there was any need to resort to force. I soon found that this was unnecessary.

Boldly walking forward, we pushed right up to the Chinese barricades. Nothing surprised us so much as to see the great access of strength to the Chinese positions since the early days of the siege. Not only were we now securely hedged in by frontal trenches and barricades, but flanking such Chinese positions were great numbers of parallel defences, designed solely with the object of battering our sortie parties to pieces should we attempt to take the offensive again. Lining these barricades and improvised forts were hundreds of men, all with their faces bronzed by the sun, and with their heads encased in black cloth fighting caps. Relieving the sombre aspect of this headgear were numbers of brightly coloured tunics, betokening the various corps to which this soldiery belonged.

What a wonderful sight they made! There were Tung Fu-hsiang's artillerymen, with violet embroidered coats and blue trousers; dismounted cavalry detachments belonging to the same commander in red and black tunics and red "tiger skirts"; Jung Lu's Peking Field Force; *Manchu Bannermen*; provincial levies and many others. All these men, standing up on the top of their fortifications, made a most brilliant picture, and we looked long and eagerly. I wish some painter of genius could have been there and caught that message. For there were skulls and bones littering the ground, and representing all that remained of the dead enemy after the pariah dogs had finished with them. Broken rifles and thousands of empty brass cartridge cases added to the battered look of this fiercely contested area, and down the streets the remains of every native house had been heaped together in rude imitation of a fort, with jagged loopholes placed at intervals of eight or ten inches, allowing any number of rifles to be brought into play against us under secure cover.

The men who had manned these defences had left their rifles where they were, and by peering over we could see that the majority of these fire-pieces were tied into position by means of wooden forks so as to bear a converging fire on the exposed points of our defences. Only then did I realise how much a protracted resistance places an attacking force on the defensive. We were afraid of one another. Sauntering about, some of the enemy were willing to enter into conversation. A number of things they told filled us with surprise, and made us begin to understand the complexity of the situation around us. The Shansi levies and Tung Fu-hsiang's men—that is, all the soldiery from the provinces—had but little idea of why they were attacking us; they had been sent, they said, to prevent us from breaking into the palace and killing their Emperor.

If the foreigners had not brought so many foreign soldiers into Peking, there would have been no fighting. They did not want to fight. . . . They did not want to be killed. . . .

Somebody tried to explain to them that the Boxers had brought it all on. But to this they answered that the Boxers were finished, driven away, discredited; there were none left in Peking, and why did we not send our own soldiers away, who had been killing so many of them. Such things they repeated time without number; it was their only point of view.

The morning passed away in this wise, but there were several *contretemps* which nearly led to the spilling of blood. In one case, an English marine tried to take a watermelon from a soldier, who was very anxious to sell it; but as the latter would not give it up without immediate payment, the marine thumped his head and then knocked him over. Everyone rushed for their rifles, but some of us shouted for silence, and going over to the marine, whispered to him to keep quiet while we tied up his hands. We told him to march back into our lines, and informed our audience that he would be beaten, and that the man who had been knocked over would get a dollar. We managed by this crude acting to save an open rupture, but it was plain that the rank and file must not be allowed to mix. We managed eventually to restore a semblance of good-fellowship by purchasing at very heavy prices a great number of eggs. The women, the children, and the wounded have been long in want of eggs and fresh food, and we knew that these would do a great many people good.

Late in the afternoon, as a result of this extraordinary fraternising, a very singular thing occurred along the French front, where the bitter fighting has rebounded into a hot friendship. A French volunteer, who is as dare-devil as many of his friends, suddenly climbed over the Chinese barricades and shouted back that he was going away on a visit. They tried to make him return, but in spite of a little hesitation, he went on climbing and getting farther and farther away. Then he suddenly disappeared for good. Nobody expected to see him alive again, and everybody put it down to a manifestation of the incipient madness which is affecting a number of men. . . .

But two hours afterwards a letter came from the French volunteer. It merely said that he was in Jung Lu's camp, having an excellent time. Very late in the evening he came back himself. In spite of the foolhardiness of the whole thing his news was the most valuable we had received.

It shows us plainly that not only has something happened elsewhere, but that the Boxer plan is miscarrying in Peking itself.

The young Frenchman had been really well treated, fed with Chinese cakes and fruit, and given excellent tea to drink. Then he had been led direct to Jung Lu's headquarters, and closely questioned by the *generalissimo* himself as to our condition, our provisions, and the number of men we had lost. He had replied, he said, that we were having a charming time, and that we only needed some ice and some fruit to make us perfectly happy, even in the great summer heat. Thereupon Jung Lu had filled his pockets with peaches and ordered his servants to tie up watermelons in a piece of cloth for him to carry back. Jung Lu finally bade him goodbye, with the significant words that his own personal troops on whom he could rely would attempt to protect the Legations, but added that it was very difficult to do so as everyone was fearful for their own heads, and dare not show too much concern for the foreigner.

This makes it absolutely plain that this extraordinary armistice is the result of a whole series of events which we cannot even imagine. It is like that curious affair of the Board of Truce, but much more definite. It means . . . what the devil does it mean? After S———'s mysterious disappearance, when he was only a day's march from Peking—month ago—it is useless to attempt any speculations. How long will this last? . . . In the evening, when we had exhausted the discussion of every possible theory, somebody remarked on the silence. I will always remember how, for some inexplicable reason, that remark annoyed me immensely—made me nervous and angry. Perhaps it was that after weeks of rifle-fire and cannon booming, the colourless monotone of complete silence was nerve-destroying. Yes, it must have been that; a perpetual, aggravating, insolent silence is worse than noise. . . . But this will mean nothing to you; experience alone teaches.

16

The Resumption of a Semi-Diplomatic Life

20th July, 1900.

The third phase continues unabated, with nothing even to enliven it. Despatches in Chinese from nowhere in particular continue to drop in from the Tsung-li Yamen; pen had been put to paper, and the despatches have been duly answered, leaving the position unchanged. I have been even requisitioned, rebelliously, I will confess, to turn my hand to despatch writing; but my fingers, so long accustomed only to rifle-bolts and triggers, and a clumsy wielding of entrenching tools, produce such a hideous calligraphic result, that I have been coldly excused from further attempts. It is incredible that one should so easily forget how to write properly, but it is nevertheless true—eight weeks in the trenches will break the best hand in the world. An ordinary man would think that what I write now is in a secret cipher!

But of diplomatic life. All these despatches which come in are in the same monotonous tone; they are entreaties and appeals to evacuate the Legations and place ourselves under the benevolent care of the Tsung-li Yamen, to come speedily before it is too late. Of course, not even our ministers will go.

But there is more news, although it is not quite cheering or definite. On the 18th the Japanese received a message direct from Tientsin, giving information to the effect that thirty thousand troops were assembling there for a general advance on Peking. They say that ten days or a fortnight may see us relieved, but somehow the Japanese are not very hopeful.

On this same date came a secretary from the Tsung-li Yamen in person, accompanied by a trembling *t'ingoh'ai*, or card-bearer, frantically waving the white flag of truce. They must been very frightened, for never have I seen such convulsiveness. The secretary, walking quickly with spasmodic steps, held tight to the arm of his official servant, and made him wave, wave, wave that white flag of truce until it became pitiful.

Thus preceded, the Tsung-li Yamen secretary advanced to the main-gate blockhouse of the British Legation, where he was curtly stopped, given a chair, and told to await the arrival of the Ministers, or such as proposed to see him. Seated just outside this evil-smelling dungeon—for the blockhouse, encased in huge sandbags, is full of dirt and ruins and has many smells—the feelings of this representative of the Chinese Government must have been charmingly mixed. Nearby were grimy and work-worn men, in all manner of attire, with their rifles; in the dry canal alongside were rude structures of brick and overturned. Peking carts, line upon line, thrown down and heaped up to block the enemy's long-expected charges; and on all sides were such stenches and refuse—all the flotsam and jetsam cast up by our sea of troubles.

Until then I did not realise how many carcases, fragments of broken weapons, empty cartridge cases, broken bottles, torn clothing, and a hundred other things were lying about. It was a sordid picture. Presently the British Minister, in his capacity of commander-in-chief and protector of the other ministers, came out and took his seat by the side of his guest, an interpreter standing beside him to help the interview. Then the French Minister approached and insinuated himself into the droll council of peace; the Spanish Minister, as *doyen*, also appeared, and one or two others. But those ministers who are without Legations, who so uncomfortably resemble their colleagues at home—those without portfolios—formed a group in the middle distance, humble as men only are who have to rely upon bounty. I saw the Belgian Minister and the Italian *Chargé* for the first time for several weeks. My own chief was also there, rubbing his hands, trying to seem natural. The interview proceeded apace, and as far as we could judge there were no noticeable results.

There were assurances on both sides, regrets, the crocodile tears of diplomacy, and vague threats. All our Ministers seemed comforted to feel that diplomacy still existed—that there was still a world in which protocols were binding. And yet nothing definite could be learned from this Yamen secretary. He said that everyone would be protected, but that the "bandits" were still very strong. After this official interview, other private interviews took place. Buglers and orderlies from the Chinese generals around us trooped in on us for unknown reasons. Three came over the German barricades, and were led blindfolded to the British Legation to be cross-questioned and examined.

One trumpeter said that his general wished for an interview with one of our generals at the great Ha-ta Gate, where were his headquarters. He wished to discuss military matters. Other men came in a big deputation to the little Japanese colonel, and said they wanted an interview too. It means the temporary resumption of a species of diplomatic life. I suppose it is in the air, and everybody likes the change. Yesterday, too, came another despatch from Prince Ching and others—as these letters are now always curiously signed, the lesser men hiding their identity in this way—asking the ministers once more to do something impossible; and once more a despatch has gone back, saying that we are perfectly happy to remain where we are, only we would like some vegetables and fruit. . . . And so, today, four cartloads of melons and cabbages have actually come with the Empress Dowager's own compliments. The melons looked beautifully red and ripe, and the cabbages of perfect green after this drab-coloured life.

But many people would not eat of this Imperial gift; they feared being poisoned. More despatches from Europe have also been transmitted—notably a cipher one to the French Minister, saying that fifteen thousand French troops have left France. Evidently a change has taken place somewhere.

But while these *pourparlers* are proceeding, some of us are not at all quieted. Fortification of the inner lines is going on harder than ever. The entire British Legation has now walls of immense strength, with miniature blockhouses at regular intervals, and a system of trenches. If our advanced posts have to fall back they may be able to hold this Legation for a few days in spite of the artillery fire. French digging, in the form of very narrow and very deep cuts designed to stop the enemy's possible mining, is being planned and carried out everywhere, and soon the general asylum will be even more secure than it has been since the beginning.

Undoubtedly we are just marking time—stamping audibly with our diplomatic feet to reassure ourselves, and to show that we are still alive. For in spite of all this apparent friendliness, which was heralded with such an outburst of shaking hands and smiling faces, there have already been a number of little acts of treachery along the lines, showing that the old spirit lurks underneath just as strong.

In the Northern Hanlin posts which skirt the British Legation, a black-faced Bannerman held up a green melon in one hand, and signalled with the other to one of our men to advance and receive this gift. Our man dropped his rifle, and was sliding a leg over his barricade, when with a swish a bullet went through the folds of his shirt—the nearest shave he had ever had. The volunteer dropped back to his side, and then, after, a while, waved an empty tin in his hand as a notice that he desired a resumption of friendly relations. The Chinese brave cautiously put his head up, and once again, with a crack, the compliment was returned, and the soldier was slightly wounded, and now we only peer through our loopholes and are careful of our heads. The novelty of the armistice is wearing off, and we feel that we are only gaining time.

Still, we are improving our position. There is a more friendly feeling among the commands in our lines, and the various contingents are being redistributed. By bribing the Yamen messenger, copies of the *Peking Gazette* have been obtained, and from these it is evident that something has happened. For all the decreeing and counter-decreeing of the early Boxer days have begun again, and the all-powerful Boxers with their boasted powers are being rudely treated. It is evident that they are no longer believed in; that the situation in and around Peking is changing from day to day. The Boxers, having shown themselves incompetent, are reaping the whirlwind. They must soon entirely disappear.

It is even two weeks since the last one was shot outside the Japanese lines at night, and now there is nothing but regular soldiery encamped around us. This last Boxer was a mere boy of fifteen, who had stripped stark naked and smeared himself all over with oil after the manner of Chinese thieves, so that if he came into our clutches no hands would be able to hold him tight. The most daring ones have always been boys. He had crept fearlessly right up to the Japanese posts armed only with matches and a stone bottle of kerosene, with which he purposed to set buildings on fire and thus destroy a link in our defences. This is always the Boxer policy. But the Japanese, as usual, were on the alert. They let the youthful Boxer approach to within a few feet of their rifles—a thin shadow of a boy faintly stirring in the thick gloom. Then flames of fire spurted out, and a thud told the sentries that their bullets had gone home.

When morning came we went out and inspected the corpse, and marvelled at the terrible muzzle velocity of the modern rifle. One bullet had gone through the chest, and tiny pin-heads of blood near the breast-bone and between the shoulders was all the trace that had been left. But the second pencil of nickel-plated lead had struck the fanatic on the forearm, and instead of boring through, had knocked out a clean wedge of flesh, half an inch thick and three inches deep, just as you would chip out a piece of wood from a plank. There was nothing unseemly in it all, death had come so suddenly. The blows had been so tremendous, and death so instantaneous, that there had been no bleeding.

It was extraordinary.

Meanwhile, from the Pei-t'ang we can still plainly hear a distant cannonade sullenly booming in the hot air. We have breathing space, but they, poor devils are still being thundered at. No one can understand how they have held out so long.

Our losses, now that we have time to go round and find out accurately, seem appalling. The French have lost forty-two killed and wounded out of a force of fifty sailors and sixteen volunteers; the Japanese, forty-five out of a band of sixty sailors and Japanese and miscellaneous volunteers; the Germans have thirty killed and wounded out of fifty-four; and in all there have been one hundred and seventy casualties of all classes. Many of the slightly wounded have returned already to their posts, but these men have nothing like the spirit they had before they were shot.

The shell holes and number of shells fired are also being counted up. The little Hotel de Pékin, standing high up just behind the French lines, has been the most struck. It is simply torn to pieces and has hundreds of holes in it. Altogether some three thousand shells have been thrown at us and found a lodgement. The wreckage round the outer fringe is appalling, and in this present calm scarcely believable. Another three thousand shells will bring everything flat to the ground.

17

Diplomacy Continues

24th July, 1900.

The situation is practically unchanged, and there is devilish little to write about. During the last two or three days no Chinese soldiers have been coming in to parley with us, except in one or two isolated instances. Cautious reconnaissances of two or three men creeping out at a time, pushing out as far as possible, have discovered that the enemy is nothing like as numerous as he was at the beginning of this armistice.

Some of his barricades seem even abandoned, and stand lonely and quite silent without any of the gaudily clothed soldiery to enliven them by occasionally standing up and waving us their doubtful greetings. But, curious contradiction, although some barricades have been practically abandoned, others are being erected very cautiously, very quietly, and without any ostentation, as if the enemy were preparing for eventualities which he knows must inevitably occur. Sometimes, too, there is even a little crackle of musketry in some remote corner, which remains quite unexplained. A secret traffic in eggs and ammunition is still going on with renegade soldiery from Tung Fu-hsiang's camp; but no longer can these things be purchased openly, for a Chinese commander has beheaded several men for this treachery, and threatens to resume fighting if his soldiers are tampered with.

But there is another piece of curious news. A spy has come in and offered to report the movements of the European army of relief, which he alleges has already left Tientsin and is pushing back dense bodies of Chinese troops. This offer has been accepted, and the man has been given a sackful of dollars from Prince Su's treasure-rooms. He is to report every day, and to be paid as richly as he cares if he gives us the truth. Some people say he can only be a liar, who will trim his sails to whatever breezes he meets. But the Japanese, who have arranged with him, are not so sceptical; they think that something of importance may be learned.

Down near the Water-Gate, which runs under the Tartar Wall, the miserable natives imprisoned by our warfare are in a terrible state of starvation. Their bones are cracking through their skin; their eyes have an insane look; yet nothing is being done for them. They are afraid to attempt escape even in this quiet, as the Water-Gate is watched on the outside night and day by Chinese sharpshooters. It is the last gap leading to the outer world which is still left open. Tortured by the sight of these starving wretches, who moan and mutter night and day, the posts nearby shoot down dogs and cows and drag them there. They say everything is devoured raw with cannibal-like cries. . . The position is therefore unchanged. We have had a week's quiet, and some letters from the Tsung-li Yamen, which assures us of their distinguished consideration, yet we are just as isolated and as uneasy as we were before. This solitude is becoming killing.

18

The Unrest Grows and Diplomacy Continues

27th July, 1900.

It is not so peaceful as it was. Trumpet calls have been blaring outside; troops have been seen moving in big bodies with great banners in their van; the Imperial world of Peking is in great tumult; the soldier-spy alleges new storms must be brewing.

In spite of this, however, the Tsung-li Yamen messengers now come and go with a certain regularity. This curious diplomatic correspondence must be piling up. Even the messengers, who at first suffered such agonies of doubt as they approached our lines, frantically waving their flags of truce and fearing our rifles, are now quite accustomed to their work, and are becoming communicative in a cautious, curious Chinese way which hints at rather than boldly states. They tell us that our barricades can only be approached with some sense of safety from the eastern side—that is, the Franco-German quarter; in other quarters they may be fired on and killed by their own people.

The Peking troops, who can be still controlled by Prince Ching and the Tsung-li Yamen, are on the eastern side of the enclosing squares of barricades; elsewhere there are field forces from other provinces—men who cannot be trusted, and who would massacre the messengers as soon as they would us, although they are clad in official dress and represent the highest authority in the Empire. This position is very strange.

But more ominous than all the trumpet calls and the large movements of troops which have been spied from the top of the lofty Tartar Wall, are the tappings and curious little noises underground. Everywhere these little noises are being heard, always along the outskirts of our defence. It must be that the mining of the French Legation is looked upon as so successful, that the Chinese feel that could they but reach every point of our outworks with black powder placed in narrow subterranean passages, they would speedily blow us into an ever narrower ring, until there was only that left of us which could be calmly destroyed by shells.

We now occupy such an extended area, and are so well entrenched, that shelling, although nerve-wracking, has lost almost all its power and terror. Were Chinese commanders united in their purpose and their men faithful to them, a few determined rushes would pierce our loose formation. As it is, it is our salvation. In the quiet of the night all the outposts hear this curious tapping. It is heard along the French lines, along the German lines, along the Japanese lines, and all round the north of the British Legation. Were we to remain quiescent the armistice might be suddenly broken some day by all our fighting men being hoisted into the air. Our counter-action has, however, already commenced.

For while the enemy is pushing his lines cunningly and rapidly under our walls and outworks, we are running out counter-mines under his—at least, we are attempting this by plunging a great depth into the earth, and only beginning to drive horizontally many feet below the surface line. Hundreds of men are on this work, but the Peking soil is not generous; it is, indeed, a cursed soil. On top there are thick layers of dust—that terrible Peking dust which is so rapidly converted into such clinging slush by a few minutes' rain. Then immediately below, for eight feet or so, there is a curious soil full of stones and *débris*, which must mean something geologically, but which no one can explain. Finally, at about a fathom and a half there is a sea of despond—the real and solid substratum, thick, tightly bound clay, which has to be pared off in thin slices just as you would do with very old cheese. This is work which breaks your hands and your back. Somebody must do it, however; the same men who do everything help this along as well....

With all this mining going on many curious finds are being made, which give something to talk about. In one place, ten feet below the surface, hundreds and hundreds of ancient stone cannon-balls have been found which must go back very many centuries. Some say they are six hundred years and more old, because the Mongol conqueror, Kublai Khan, who built the Tartar City of Peking, lived in the thirteenth century, and these cannon-balls lie beneath where tilled fields must then have been. Are they traces of a forgotten siege? In other places splendid drains have been bared—drains four feet high and three broad, which run everywhere. Once, when Marco Polo was young, Peking must have been a fit and proper place, and the magnificent streets magnificently clean. Now ...!

Today the soldier-spy has brought in news that the Court is preparing to flee, because of the approach of our avenging armies, and that the moving troops and the hundreds of carts which can be seen picking their way through the burned and ruined Ch'ien Men great street in the Chinese city will all be engaged in this flight. Our troops are advancing steadily, he says, driving everything before them. Still no one believes these stories very much. We have had six weeks of it now and several distinct phases. Somehow it seems impossible that the whole tragedy should end in this unfinished way—that thousands of European troops should march in unmolested and find us as we are... There is practically no day duty now and very easy work at night. One can have a good sleep now, but even this seems strange and out of place.

19

The First Real News

28th July, 1900.

Something has again happened, something of the highest importance. A courier from Tientsin has arrived at last—a courier who slipped into our lines, delivered his quill of a message which had been rolled up and plaited into his hair for many days, and is now sitting and fanning himself—a thin slip of a native boy, who has travelled all the way down that long Tientsin road and all the way back again for a very small earthly reward. A curious figure this messenger bringing news from the outside world made as he sat calmly fanning himself with the stoicism of his race. Nobody hurried him or questioned him much after he had delivered his paper; he was left to rest himself, and when he was cool he began to speak. I wish you could have heard him; it seemed to me at once a message and a sermon—a sermon for those who are so afraid.

The little pictures this boy dropped out in jerks showed us that there were worse terrors than being sealed in by brickwork. He had been twenty-four days travelling up and down the eighty miles of the Tientsin road, and four times he had been caught, beaten, and threatened with death. Everywhere there were marauding bands of Boxers; every village was hung with red cloth and pasted with Boxer legends; and each time he had been captured he had been cruelly beaten, because he had no excuse. Once he was tied up and made to work for days at a village inn. Then he escaped at night, and went on quickly, travelling by night across the fields. Somehow, by stealing food, he finally reached Tientsin.

The native city was full of Chinese troops and armed Boxers; beyond were the Europeans. There was nothing but fighting and disorder and a firing of big guns. By moving slowly he had broken into the country again, and gained an outpost of European troops, who captured him and took him into the camps. Then he had delivered his message, and received the one he had brought back. That is all; it had taken twenty-four days. This he repeated many times, for everybody came and wished to hear. It was plain that many felt secretly ashamed, and wished that there would be time to redeem their reputations. There would be that!

For about then someone came out from headquarters and posted the translation of that quill of a cipher message, and a dense crowd gathered to see when the relief would march in. March in! The message from an English Consul ran:

"Your letter of the 4th July received. Twenty-four thousand troops landed and 19,000 at Tientsin. General Gaselee expected at Taku tomorrow; Russians at Pei-tsang. Tientsin city under foreign government. Boxer power exploded here. Plenty of troops on the way if you can keep yourselves in food. Almost all the ladies have left Tientsin."

I suppose it was cruel to laugh, but laugh I did with a few others. Never has a man been so abused as was that luckless English Consul who penned such a fatuous message. The spy had already marched our troops half way and more; even the pessimistic allowed that they must have started; an authentic message showed clearly that it was folly and imagination. We would have to have weeks more of it, perhaps even a whole month. The people wept and stormed, and soon lost all enthusiasm for the poor messenger boy who had been so brave.

Two hours afterwards I found him still fanning himself and cooling himself. He was quite alone; most people had rather he had never come. Yet the message has been heeded. The significant phrase is that we must keep ourselves in food. Ponies are running short; there is only sufficient grain for three weeks' rations; so if there is another month, it will be a fair chance that a great many die for lack of food. Lists are therefore being made of everything eatable there is, and all private supplies are to be commandeered in a few days. People are, of course, making false lists and hiding away a few things. If there is another month of it there will be some very unpleasant scenes—yes, some very unpleasant scenes.

20

The Third Phase Continues

30th July, 1900.

From the north that dull booming of guns ever continues. The Pei-t'ang is still closely besieged, and no news comes as to how long Monseigneur F——, with his few sailors and his many converts, can hold out, or why they are exempted from this strange armistice, which protects us temporarily. Nothing can be learned about them.

And yet our own armistice, in spite of Tsung-li Yamen despatches and the mutual diplomatic assurances, cannot continue forever. Barricade building and mining prove that. Today the last openings have been closed in on us for some curious reason, and the stretch of street which runs along under the pink Palace walls and across the Northern canal bridge has been securely fortified with a very powerful barricade. Outside the Water-Gate the Chinese sharpshooters have dug also a trench....

This last barricade was not built without some attempt on our part to stop such a menacing step, for we tried with all our might, by directing a heavy rifle-fire, and at last dragging the Italian gun and a machine-gun into position, to make the barricade-builders' task impossible. But it was all in vain, and now we are neatly encased in a vast circle of bricks and timber; we are absolutely enclosed and shut in, and we can never break through.

Of course this has been a violation of the armistice, for it was mutually agreed that neither side should continue offensive fortification work, or push closer, and that violation would entail a reopening of rifle and gun fire. We reopened our fire for a short interval, but little good that did us. We lost two men in the operation, for an Italian gunner was shot through the hand and made useless for weeks, and a volunteer was pinked in both shoulders, and may have to lose one arm. After that we stopped firing, for those bleeding men showed us how soon our defence would have melted away had we not even this questionable armistice.

Very soon there was a partial explanation of why this immense barricade had been built. Late in the afternoon Chinese troops began to stream past at a trot under cover of the structure. First there were only infantrymen, whose rifles and banners could just be seen from some of our lookout posts on the highest roofs. But presently came artillery and cavalry. Everybody could see those, although the men bent low. Unendingly they streamed past, until the alarm became general. Even in Peking, quite close to us, there were thousands of soldiery. When the others were driven in off the Tientsin road it would be our doom.

From the top of the Tartar Wall came the same reports. Our outposts saw nothing but moving troops picking their way through the ruins of the Ch'ien Men great street—troops moving both in and out, and accompanied by long tails of carts bearing their impedimenta. Yet it was impossible to trace the movements of the corps streaming past under cover of the newly built barricade. The flitting glimpses we got of them as they swarmed past were not sufficient to allow any identification. Perhaps they were passing out of the city; perhaps they were being massed in the palace; perhaps. . . . Anything was possible, and, as one thought, imperceptibly the atmosphere seemed to become more stifled, as if a storm was about to break on us, and we knew our feebleness. Yet we are strong as we can ever be. The fortification work has gone on without a break. It has become unending. . . .

21

More Diplomacy

31st July, 1900.

More despatches have been sent by our diplomats to the Tsung-li Yamen, complaining about all the ominous signs we see around us, and asking for explanations. Explanations—they are so easy to give! Every question has been promptly answered, even though the Yamen itself is probably only just managing to keep its head above the muddy waters of revolution which surge around. Listen to the replies. The sound of heavy guns we hear in the north of the city are due to the government's orders to exterminate the Boxers and rebels, who have been attacking the Pei-t'ang Cathedral and harassing the converts. The great barricade across the Northern canal bridge was built solely to protect the Chinese soldiery from the accuracy of our fire, which is greatly feared. As for the mining, our ears must have played us false. None is going on.

Such was the gist of the answers which have been promptly sent in. These answers and this correspondence give our diplomats satisfaction, I suppose, but most people think that they are making themselves more undignified than they have been ever since this storm broke on us. The Yamen can in any case do nothing; it is merely a consultative or deliberative body of no importance. Probably exactly the same type of despatches are being sent to the commanders of the relieving columns at Tientsin.

There being so little for the rank and file to do or talk about at the present moment, there is endless gossip and scandal going on. The subject of eggs is one of the most burning ones! Great numbers of eggs are being obtained by the payment of heavy sums to some of the more friendly soldiery around us, who steal in with baskets and sacks, and receive in return rolls of dollars, and these eggs are being distributed by a committee. Some people are getting more than others.

Everybody professes tremendous rage because a certain lady with blue-black hair is supposed to have used a whole dozen in the washing of her hair! She is one of those who have not been seen or heard of since the rifles began to speak. There are lots of that sort, all well nourished and timorous, while dozens of poor missionary women are suffering great hardships. Several people who had relations in Paris thirty years ago tell me it was the same thing then, and that it will always be the same thing. This story of the eggs, however, has had one immediate result. People are hiding away more provisions and marking them off on their lists as eaten. What is the use of depriving one's self for the common good later on under such circumstances? What, indeed!

There is another sign which is not pleasing any one. An official diary is being now written up under orders of the headquarters. It will be full of our Peking diplomatic half-truths. But, worst of all, our only correspondent, M——, who was shot the other day and is getting convalescent, has been taken under the wing of our commander-in-chief, and his lips will be sealed by the time we get out—if ever we get out. With an official history and a discreet independent version, no one will ever understand what bungling there has been, and what culpability. It is our chicken-hearted chiefs, and they alone, who should be discredited. With a few exceptions, they are more afraid than the women, and never venture beyond the British Legation. Everything is left to the younger men, whose economic value is smaller! I hope I may live to see the official accounts. . . .

22

The World Beyond Our Bricks

2nd August, 1900.

A new month has dawned, and with it have come shoals of letters bringing us exact tidings from the outer world. Yesterday one messenger slipped in bearing three letters. Today another has arrived with six missives—making nine letters in all for those who have had nothing at all except a couple of cipher messages for two entire months. Those nine letters meant as much to us as a winter's mail by the overland route in the old days. ...

For as each one confirms and adds to the news of the others, we can now form a complete and well-connected story of almost everything that has taken place. We even begin to understand why S—— and his two thousand sailors never reached us. There have been so many things doing.

But all minor details are forgotten in the fact that there is absolute and definite news of the relief columns—news which is repeated and confirmed nine times over and cannot be false this time. The columns were forming for a general advance as the letters were sent off. The advance guard was leaving immediately, the main body following two days later; and the whole of the international forces would arrive before the middle of the month of August. That is what the letters said. Also, the American Minister's cipher message had got through, and was now known to the entire world. Everybody's eyes were fixed on Peking. There was nothing else spoken of. That made us stronger than anything else. Poor human nature—we are so egotistical!

But there were other items of news. For the first time we learned that Tientsin has had a siege and bombardment of its own; that all Manchuria is in flames; that the Yangtse Valley has been trembling on the brink of rebellion; that Tientsin city has at last been captured by

European troops and a provisional government firmly established; and that many of the high Chinese officials have committed suicide in many parts of China. It is curious what a shock all this news gave, and how many people behaved almost as if their minds had become unhinged. But then we have had two months of it, and in two months you can travel far. In the hospital it was noticed, too, that all the wounded became more sick.... It has been decided that any further news must be only gradually divulged, and that despatches which give absolute details can no longer be posted on the Bell-tower....

A network of ruined houses around the old Mongol market have just been seized and occupied by a volunteer force. This is the last weak spot there is—a half-closed gap, which could be rushed by bodies of men coming in from the Ch'ien Men Gate and ordered to attack us. This new angle of native houses are being sandbagged and loopholed. Both sides, defenders and attacking forces, are now as ready as possible. What is going to happen? I am mightily tired of speculating and of writing.

23

Trifles

4th August, 1900.

There is now, and has been for the best part of the last forty-eight hours, outpost shooting on all sides, which remains quite unexplained. Listen how it happens.

You are sitting at a loophole, half asleep, perhaps, during the day-time, when *crack!* a bullet sends a shower of brick chips and a powder-puff of dust over your head. You swear, maybe, and quietly continue dozing. Then come two or three rifle reports and more dust. This time the thing seems more serious, it may mean something; so you reach for your glasses and carefully survey the scene beyond through your loophole. To remain absolutely hidden is the order of the day. So there is nothing much to be seen. Far away, and very near, lie the enemy's barricades, some running almost up to your own, but quite peaceful and silent, others standing up frowningly hundreds of yards off, monuments erected weeks ago.

These latter are so distant that they are unknown quantities. Then just as you are about to give it up as a bad job, you see the top of a rifle barrel glistening in the sun. You. . . . *bang!* perilously near your glasses another bullet has struck. So you pull up your rifle by the strap, open out your loophole a little by removing some of the bricks, and carefully and slowly you send the answering message at the enemy's head. If you have great luck a faint groan or a distant shout of pain may reward your efforts; but you can never be quite sure whether you have got home on your rival or not. Loophole shooting is very tricky, and the very best shots fire by the hour in vain. I have seen that often. . . .

Yesterday I directly disobeyed orders by opening the ball myself. I had been posted in the early morning very close to one of the enemy's banners—perhaps not more than forty feet away—and this gaudy flag, defiantly flapping so near the end of my nose, must have incensed me; for almost before I had realised what I was doing I was very slowly and very carefully aiming at the bamboo staff so as to split it in two and bring down the banner with a run. I fired three shots in ten minutes and missed in an exasperating fashion. It is the devil's own job to do really accurate work with an untested government rifle. But my fourth shot was more successful; it snapped the staff neatly enough, and the banner floated to the ground just outside the barricade.

This Chinese outpost must have been but feebly manned, as, indeed, all the outposts have been since the armistice, for it was fully ten minutes before anything occurred. Then an arm came suddenly over and pecked vainly at the banner. I snapped rapidly, missed, and the arm flicked back. Another five minutes passed, and then a piece of curved bamboo moved over the barricade and hunted about. It was no use, however, the arm had to come, too. I waited until the brown hand clasping the bamboo was low and then pumped a quick shot at it. A yell of pain answered me; the bamboo was dropped, the arm disappeared. I had drawn blood.

Nothing now occurred for a quarter of an hour, and I heard not a sound. Then suddenly half a dozen arms clasping bamboos appeared at different points, and as soon as I had fired six heads swooped out and directed this bamboo fishing. In a trice they had harpooned the flag, and before I could fire again it was back in their camp. I had been beaten! Then, as a revenge, I was steadily pelted with lead for more than half an hour and had to lie very low. They searched for me with their missiles with devilish ingenuity. This firing became so persistent that one of our patrols at last appeared and crept forward to me from the line of main works behind. Only by ingenious lying did I escape from being reported. . . .

Probably incidents like this account for the outpost duels which are hourly proceeding, in spite of all the Tsung-li Yamen despatches and the unending mutual assurances. Many of our men shoot immediately they see a Chinese rifle or a Chinese head in the hopes of adding another scalp to their tale. In any case, this does no harm. It seems to me that only the resolution of the outposts, acting independently, and sometimes even in defiance to orders from headquarters, has kept the enemy so long at bay. The rifle distrusts diplomacy.

This diplomatic correspondence with the Yamen is rapidly accumulating. Many documents are now coming through from European Foreign Offices in the form of cipher telegrams, that are copied out by the native telegraphists in the usual way. No one is being told what is in these documents; we can only guess. The Yamen covers each message with a formal despatch in Chinese, generally begging the Ministers to commit themselves to the care of the government. They now even propose that everyone should be escorted to Tientsin—at once. And yet we have learned from copies of the *Peking Gazette* that two members of the Yamen were executed exactly seven days ago for recommending a mild policy and making an immediate end of the Boxer *régime*. It is thus impossible to see how it will end. Our fate must ultimately be decided by a number of factors, concerning which we know nothing.

This breathing space is giving time, however, which is not being entirely wasted on our part. At several points we have managed to enter into secret relations with some of the Chinese commands, and to induce traitors to begin a secret traffic in ammunition and food supplies....

It is curious how it is done. By tunnelling through walls and houses in neglected corners, protected ways have been made into some of the nests of half-ruined native houses. And by spending many bags of dollars, friendship has first been bought and then supplies.

The Japanese have been the most successful. Instead of killing the soldier-spy, who had been selling them false news, they pardoned him and enlisted him in this new cause. He has been very useful, and arranged matters with the enemy....

The other night I crept out through the secret way to the Japanese supply house to see how it was done. There were only two little Japanese in there squatting on the ground, with several revolvers lying ready. A shaded candle just allowed you to distinguish the torn roof, the wrecked wooden furniture. Nobody spoke a word, and we all listened intently.

A full hour must have passed before a very faint noise was heard, and then I caught a discreet scratching. It was the signal. One of the little men got up and crawled forward to the door like a dog on his hands and knees. Then I heard a revolver click—a short pause, and the noise of a door being opened. Then there was a tap—tap—tap, like the Morse code being quietly played, and the revolver clicked down again. It was the right man. He, too, crawled in like a dog; got up painfully, as if he were very stiff, and silently began unloading. Then I understood why he was so stiff; he was loaded from top to bottom with cartridges.

It took a quarter of an hour for everything to be taken out and stacked on the floor. He had carried in close on six hundred rounds of Mauser ammunition, and for every hundred he received the same weight in silver. This man was a military cook, who crept round and robbed his comrades as they lay asleep, not a hundred yards from here. Of course, he will be discovered one day and torn to pieces, but I have just learned that by marvellous ingenuity and with the aid of a few of his fellows thousands of eggs have been brought in by him. It is a curious business, and adds yet another strange element to this strangest of lives.

24

Diplomatic Confidences

6th August, 1900.

Firing has been more persistent and more general during the last two days, although the armistice ostensibly still continues in the same way as before. A number of our men have been wounded, and two or three even killed during the past week. It is an extraordinary state of affairs, but better than a general attack all along the line. We have no right to complain. The day before yesterday several Russians were badly wounded; yesterday a Frenchman was killed outright and a couple of other men wounded; today three more have been hit. In spite of the discharges from the hospitals, the numbers *hors de combat* remain the same.

Today, too, trumpets are again blaring fiercely, and more and more troops can be seen moving if one looks down from the Tartar Wall. Up on the wall itself, however, all is dead quiet. It has been like that for weeks. No men have been lost there.

Neither is there any news of the thick relief columns which should be advancing from Tientsin. In spite of the shoals of letters I have duly recorded, assuring us of their immediate departure, the majority of us have again become rather incredulous about our approaching relief. It has become such a regular thing, this siege life, and all other kinds of life are somehow so far away and so impossible after what we have gone through, that we look upon the outer world as something mythical. . . . Some men have their minds a little unhinged; two are absolutely mad.

One, a poor devil of a Norwegian missionary, who has been living in misery for years in a vain effort to make converts, became so dangerous long ago that he had to be locked up, and even bound. But one night he managed to escape, climb our defences and deliver himself up to the Chinese soldiery. They led him also to the Manchu Generalissimo, Jung Lu, half suspecting that he was crazy. Jung Lu questioned him closely as to our condition, and the Norwegian divulged everything he knew. He said the Chinese fire had been too high to do us very much harm; that they should drive low at us, and remember the flat trajectory of modern weapons. After keeping him for some hours and learning all he could, Jung Lu sent him back. The poor devil, when he lurched in again, vacantly told the people in the British Legation what he had said, and a number demanded that he be shot for treason. If they once began doing that an end would never be reached....

Some go mad, too, during the fighting. It is always those who have too much imagination. Thus, during a lull in the attacks against the French lines, a Russian volunteer, with rifle and bandolier across his back and a bottle of spirits in his hand, charged furiously at the Chinese barriers with insane cries. No effort could be made to save him, because hundreds of Chinese riflemen were merely waiting for an opportunity to pick off our men. So the doomed Russian reached the first Chinese barricade unmolested, put a leg over, and then fell back with a terrible cry as a dozen rifles were emptied into his body. By a miracle he picked himself up even in his dying condition, and made another frantic effort to climb the obstacle. But more rifles were then discharged, and finally the wretched man fell back quite lifeless. Then over his body a fierce duel took place. Chinese commanders having placed a price on European heads, these riflemen were determined not to lose their reward. Man after man attempted to drag in that dead body; but each time our men were too quick for them, and a Chinese brave rolled over. In the end they hooked the corpse in with long poles and it was seen no more.

A yet more blood-curdling case is that of a British marine, who has been hopelessly mad for weeks now. He shot and bayoneted a man in the early part of the siege, and the details must have horrified him. They say he first drove his bayonet in right up to the hilt through a soldier's chest; and then, without withdrawing, emptied the whole of the contents of his magazine into his victim, muttering all the time. Now he lies repeating hour after hour, "How it splashes! how it splashes!" and at night he shrieks and cries.... In that miserable Chancery hospital, swept by rifle-fire and full of such cries and groans, the nights have become dreaded, until it is a wonder the wounded still live....

Still, with all this, the Yamen messengers continue to come and go with clockwork regularity. Yesterday the Chinese Government excelled itself, and made some who have still a sense of humour left laugh cynically. In an original official despatch—that is, not a mere covering despatch—it politely informed the Italian *Chargé d'Affaires* that King Humbert had been assassinated by a lunatic, and it begged to convey the news with its most profound condolences! Perhaps, however, there was a wish to point a moral—a subtle moral such as Chinese scholars love. Yes, on second thoughts that was rather a clever despatch; in diplomacy the Chinese have nothing to learn. . . .

25

The Plot Again Thickens

8th August, 1900.

Some strange deity is helping the Chinese Government. There is always something appropriate to write about. Yesterday the Duke of Edinburgh died. We were officially informed to that effect, after the King Humbert manner, and the condolences were great. Yesterday, also, during the evening, shelling suddenly commenced and the cannon-mouths that have been leering at us from a distance in dull curiosity at their inactivity have barked themselves hoarsely to life again. Thus, while diplomacy still continues, shrapnel and segment are plunging about. At times it really seems as if the Chinese Government had succeeded in dividing us up into two distinct categories. It has tried to save the diplomats from shells and bullets; since they remain with the others they must share their fate.

We listened to this cannonade with tightly pressed lips last night for an hour and more, and, lying low, watched the splinters fly; and then, just as the clamour appeared to be growing, it ceased as suddenly as it had commenced, and the uproarious trumpets, that we know so well, once more called off the attacking forces with their stentorian voices. It seems as if an internecine warfare had begun outside our lines—that the loosely jointed Chinese Government is also struggling with itself. Thus legs and arms thrash around for a while and cause chaos; then the brain reasserts its sway, and the limbs become quieted and reposeful for a time. Never will there be such a siege again. I am beginning to understand something of all its vast complexity, to know that everybody is at once guilty and innocent, and that a strange deity decrees that it must be so....

For while we are beginning to be attacked fitfully, other strange things have been observed from the Tartar Wall. There has been some fighting and shooting in the burned and ruined Ch'ien Men great street down below, and Chinese cavalry have been seen chasing and cutting down red-coated men. A species of Communism may in the end rise from the ashes of the ruined capital, or a new dynasty be proclaimed, or nothing may happen at all, excepting that we shall die of starvation in a few weeks. . . .

The native Christians in the Su wang-fu are already getting ravenous with hunger, and are robbing us of every scrap of food they can garner up. Their provisioning has almost broken down, in spite of every effort, and the missionary committees and sub-committees charged with their feeding are beginning to discriminate, they say. These vaunted committees cannot but be a failure except in those things which immediately concern the welfare of the committees themselves. The feeble authority of headquarters, now that puny diplomacy has been so busy, has become more feeble than it was in the first days, and, like the Chinese Government, we, too, shall soon fall to pieces by an ungumming process.

Native children are now dying rapidly, and two weeks more will see a veritable famine. The trees are even now all stripped of their leaves; cats and dogs are hunted down and rudely beaten to death with stones, so that their carcases may be devoured. Many of the men and women cling to life with a desperation which seems wonderful, for some are getting hardly any food at all, and their ribs are cracking through their skin. There is something wrong somewhere, for while so many are half starving, the crowds of able-bodied converts used in the fortification work are fairly well fed. Nobody seems to wish to pay much attention to the question, although many reports have been sent in.

Perhaps, from one point of view, it is without significance whether these useless people die or not. Hardly any of the many non-combatant Europeans stir beyond the limits of the British Legation, even with this lull. All sit there talking—talking eternally and praying for relief, calculating our chances of holding out for another two or three weeks, but never acting. A roll, indeed, has been made at last, with every able-bodied man's name set down, and a distribution table drawn up. But beyond that no action has been taken, and the hundred and more men who might be added to our active forces are allowed to do nothing.

This might be all right were there not certain ominous signs around us, which show that a change must soon come. For the enemy has planted new banners on all sides of us, bearing the names of new

Chinese generals unknown to us. Audaciously driven into the ground but twenty or thirty feet from our outposts, these gaudy flags of black and yellow, and many other colours, flaunt us and mock us with the protection assured by the Tsung-li Yamen. Still, those despatches continue to come in, but the first interpreter of the French Legation, who sees some of them in the original, says that their tone is becoming more surly and imperative.

It is ominous, too, that the Chinese commands, which have been so reinforced and are now of great strength, are so close to our outer line that they heave over heavy stones in order to maim and hurt our outposts without firing. All the outer barricades and trenches are being hurriedly roofed in to protect us from this new danger. One of our men, struck on the head with a twenty-pound stone, has been unconscious ever since, and a great many many others are badly hurt in other ways. The Chinese can be very ingenious devils if they wish, and the score against them is piling up more and more.

26

More Messengers

10th August, 1900.

At last some great news! Messengers from the relief columns have actually arrived, and the columns themselves are only a few days' march from Peking. What excitement there has been among the non-combatant community; what handshaking; what embracing; what fervent delight! This unique life is to end; we are to become reasonably clean and quite ordinary mortals again, lost among the world's population of fifteen hundred millions—undistinguished, unknown—that is, if the relief gets in....

The messengers came to us apparently from nowhere, walking in after the Chinese manner, which is quite nonchalantly, and with the sublime calm of the East. One of the first slid in and out of the enemy's barricades with immense effrontery at dawn, and then climbed the Japanese defences, and produced a little ball of tissue paper from his left ear. Fateful news contained so long in that left ear! It was a cipher despatch from General Fukishima, chief of the staff of the relieving Japanese columns. It said that the advance guard would reach the outskirts of Peking on the 13th or 14th, if all went well. Heavens, we all said, as we calculated aloud, that meant only three or four days more....

This news was soon duplicated, for hardly had the first excitement subsided when the news spread that a second messenger from the British General of the relieving forces had managed to force his way through. It was a confirmation, was his message; three or four days more.... But the messenger, when he spoke, had other things to say. He had been sent out by us a week before by being lowered by ropes from the Tartar Wall. Forty miles from Peking he had met Black cavalry and Russian cavalry miles in advance of the other soldiery. They had charged at him and captured him, and led him before generals and officers. . . . The roads leading to Peking were littered with wounded and disbanded Chinese soldiery; there had been much fighting, but the natives could not withstand the foreigner—that is what their compatriot said. Everybody was terrified by the Black soldiery from India; they had come in the same way forty years before. . . .

So the relieving armies are truly rolling up on Peking. It seems incredible and unreal, but it is undoubtedly true, and it must be accepted as true. . . .

As if goaded by the terrors conjured up by these avenging armies, which are now so close, the Tsung-li Yamen, in some last despatches, has informed our Plenipotentiaries that it is decapitating wholesale the soldiery that have been firing on us—that it wishes for personal interviews with all our Ministers to arrange everything, so that there may be no more misunderstandings later on. Vain hope! Numbers of documents are coming in, and every Minister wishes to write something in return—to show that with the return of normal conditions there will be a return of importance. Somehow it seems to me that not one of them can become important again in Peking. They have been too ridiculous—politically, they are already all dead.

27

The Attacks Resumed

12th August, 1900.

All thoughts of relief have been pushed into the middle distance—and even beyond—by the urgent business we have now on hand. For the attacks have been suddenly resumed, and have been continuous, well sustained, and far worse than anything we have ever experienced before, even in the first furious days of the siege. What stupendous quantities of ammunition have been loosed off on us during the past forty-eight hours—what tons of lead and nickel! Some of our barricades have been so eaten away by this fire, that there is but little left, and we are forced to lie prone on the ground hour after hour, not daring to move and not daring to send reliefs at the appointed intervals. So intense has the rifle-fire been around the Su Wang-fu and the French Legation lines, that high above the deafening roar of battle a distinct and ominous snake-like hissing can be heard—a hiss, hiss, hiss, that never ceases.

It is the high-velocity nickel-nosed bullet tearing through the air at lightning speed, and spitting with rage at its ill success in driving home on some unfortunate wretch. They hiss, hiss, hiss, hour after hour, without stopping; and as undertone to that brutal hiss there is the roll of the rifles themselves, crackling at us by the thousand like dry fagots. At first this storm of sound paralyses you a little; then a lust for battle gains you, and you steadily drive bullets through the Chinese loopholes in the hope of finding a Chinese face. Whenever they bunch and press forward we wither them to pieces. . . . But men are falling on our side more rapidly than we care to think—one rolled over on top of me two hours ago drilled through and through—and if anything should happen to the relieving columns and delay their arrival for only two or three days, this tornado of fire will have swept all our defenders into the hospitals.

The Chinese guns are also booming again, and shrapnel and segment are tearing down trees and outhouses, bursting through walls, splintering roofs, and wrecking our strongest defences more and more. Just now one of our few remaining ponies was struck, and it was a pitiable sight, giving a bloody illustration of the deadly force of shell-fragments. The piece that struck this poor animal was not very big, but still it simply tore into his flank, and seemed to burst him in two. With his entrails hanging out and his agonised eyes mutely protesting, the pony staggered and fell. Then we despatched him with our rifles.

Our casualty list has now passed the two hundred mark, they say. In a few days more, fifty *per cent*. of the total force of active combatants will have been either killed or wounded.

During the lulls which occur between the attacks, when the Chinese soldiery are probably coolly refreshing themselves with tea and pipes and hauling away those who have succumbed, we hear from the north of the city the same dull booming of big guns, continuous, relentless, and never-tiring. It is the sound of the Chinese artillery ranged against the great fortified Roman Catholic Cathedral. When we have a few moments we can well picture to ourselves this valiant Bishop F——, with cross in hand, like some old-time warrior-priest, pointing to the enemy, and urging his spear-armed flocks to stand firm along the outer rim. We can also see, in the smoke and dust, the thin fringe of sailors who must be forming the mainstay of the defence. Perhaps, sprinkled along the compound walls, with harsh-speaking rifles in their hands, they are a sort of human incense, exorcising by their mere presence the devils in pagan hearts. . . .

Scant time for thoughts; none for recording, as each hour shows more clearly what we may expect. Scarcely has the fire been stilled in one quarter than it breaks out with even greater violence in another, and we are hurried in small reinforcements from point to point. And from the positions on the Tartar Wall, which are now also dusted by a continually growing fire that would sweep our men off in a cloud of sandbags and brick-chips, the enemy's attacks can be best understood. The growing number of rifles being brought to bear on us; the violence and increasing audacity; the building of new barricades that press closer and closer to our own, and are now so near that they almost crush in our chests—are all clear from the reports sent down.

The relief columns on the Tientsin road are driving in unwieldy Chinese forces on top of us, and this native soldiery is falling back on the capital to be remarshalled after a fashion—placed on the city walls or flung against us in a despairing attempt to kill us all, and remove the Thing which is making the relieving columns advance so quickly. Crazy with fear, and with ghosts of the chastisement of 1860 etched on every column of dust raised by their retreating soldiery, the Chinese Government is acting like one possessed.

Today I saw it all beautifully, with the aid of the best glasses we have got. First came bodies of infantry trotting hurriedly in their sandals and glancing about them. In the dust and the distance they seemed to have lost all formation—to be mere broken fragments. But once a man stopped, looked up at us, a mere dot in the ruined streets hundreds and hundreds of yards away, and then savagely discharged his rifle at us. He knew we were on the Tartar Wall, and so sent his impotent curses at us through a three-foot steel tube.... Behind such men were long country carts laden with wounded and broken men, and driven by savage-looking drivers, powdered with our cursed dust and driving standing up with voice and whip alone.

The teams of ponies were all mud-stained and tired, and moved very slowly away; and their great iron-hooped wheels clanked discordantly over the stone-paved ways. Sometimes a body of cavalry, with gaudy banners in the van and the men flogging on their steeds with short whips, have also ridden by escaping from the rout. Infantry and horsemen, wounded in carts and wounded on foot, flow back into the city through the deserted and terror-stricken streets, and it is we who shall suffer. So much of this has been understood by everybody, that an order has been privately given that no one is to be allowed on the Tartar Wall, excepting the regular reliefs. There is in any case no time for most of us to creep up there and look on the city below; we are tied to the barricades and trenches down in the flat among the ruins, chained to our posts by a never-ending rifle-fire.

28

The Thirteenth

13th August, 1900.

It is the 13th, that fateful number, and there are some who are divided between hope and fear. Is it good to hope on a 13th, or is it mere foolishness to thing about such things? Who knows?—for we have become unnatural and abnormal—subject to atavistic tendencies in thought and action. . . . . Most people are keeping their thoughts to themselves, but actions cannot be hidden. You would not believe some of the things. . . .

There has not been a sign or a word from the relief column for many hours. The fleeing Chinese soldiery we witnessed in such numbers yesterday entering the city have stopped rushing in, and now from the Tartar Wall the streets below in the outer city seem quite silent and deserted. Last night, too, it was seen that the line of the enemy's rifles packed against us was so continuous, and the spacing so close, that one continuous flame of fire ripped round from side to side and deluged us with metal. So heavy was this firing, so crushing, that it was paralysing. Any part broken into would have been irretrievably lost. The bullets and shells struck our walls and defences in great swarms sometimes several hundred projectiles swishing down at a time. There must have been ten or twelve thousand infantry firing at us and fifteen guns.

Where I lay, with a post of sixteen men, there were more than five hundred riflemen facing us, at distances varying from forty feet to four hundred yards. Every ruined house outside the fringe of our defence has now been converted into a blockhouse by the persistent enemy. Every barricade we have built has a dozen other barricades opposing it in parallels, in chessboards, in every kind of formation; and from these barricades the fire poured in since the 10th—that is, for sixty long hours—has only ceased at rare intervals. Our stretcher-parties have been very busy, but how many men we have lost since the armistice was deliberately broken no one knows. Yesterday a French captain, a gallant officer, who feared nothing, was shot dead through the head, making the ninth officer killed or severely wounded since the beginning.

Yesterday, also, the new Mongol market defences trembled on the brink hour after hour, and with them the fate of three thousand heads. New Chinese troops armed with Mannlicher carbines, the handiest weapons for barricade fighting, had been pushed up behind a veil of light entrenchments to within twenty feet of the Mongol market posts, and their fire was so tremendous that it drove right through our bricks and sandbags. God willed that just as the final rush was coming a Chinese barricade gave way; our men emptied their magazines with the rapidity of despair into the swarms of Chinese riflemen disclosed; dozens of them fell killed and wounded, and the rest were driven back in disorder.

Ten seconds more would have made them masters of our positions. The closeness of this final agony was such that squads of reserves, who had not fired a shot during the siege, voluntarily went forward to the threatened points and lay there the whole night. At last it has been driven home on all that our fate hangs in the balance, and has hung in the balance for weeks. But it is too late now. If a single link in our chain is broken there will be a *sauve qui pent* which no heroism can stop.

29

The Night of the Thirteenth

14th August, 1900.

All yesterday the fire hardly diminished in violence, and more and more of our men were hit. . . . The Chinese commanders, having learned of the loss of a Chinese general and a great number of his men at the Mongol market, have been having their revenge by giving us not a minute's rest. Up to six o'clock yesterday evening I had been continually on duty for forty-eight hours, with a few minutes' sleep during the lulls. At six in the evening I stretched out. At half-past eight the pandemonium had risen to such a pitch that sleep without opiates was impossible. All round our lines roared and barked Mausers, Mannlichers, *jingals*, and Tower muskets, every gun that could be brought to bear on us firing as fast and as fiercely as possible in a last wild effort. The sound was so immense, so terrifying, that many could hardly breathe. Against the barricades, through half-blocked loopholes, and on to the very ground, myriads of projectiles beat their way, hissing and crashing, ricocheting and slashing, until it seemed impossible any living thing could exist in such a storm.

It was the night of the 13th. Not a word had been heard of the relief columns, not a message, not a courier had come in. But could anything have dared to move to us? Even the Tsung-li Yamen, affrighted anew at this storm of fire which it can no longer control, had not dared or attempted to communicate with us. We were abandoned to our own resources. At best we would have to work out our own salvation. Was it to be the last night of this insane Boxerism, or merely the beginning of a still more terrible series of attacks with massed assaults pushed right home on us?

In any case, there was but one course—not to cede one inch until the last man had been hit. All the isolated post-commanders—I had risen to be one—decided that on us hinged the fate of all. The very idea of a supreme command watching intelligently and overseeing every spot of ground was impossible. It had been a war of post-commanders and their men from the beginning; it would remain so to the bitter end. A siege teaches you that this is always so.

By ten o'clock every sleeping man had been pulled up and pushed against the barricades. Privately all the doubtful men were told that if they moved they would be shot as they fell back. Everywhere we had been discovering that in the pitch dark many could hardly be held in place. By eleven o'clock the fire had grown to its maximum pitch. It was impossible that it could become heavier, for the enemy was manning every coign of vantage along the entire line, and blazing so fiercely and pushing in so close that many of the riflemen must have fallen from their own fire.

From the great Tartar Wall to the palace enclosure, and then round in a vast jagged circle, thousands of jets of fire spurted at us; and as these jets pushed closer and closer, we gave orders to reply steadily and slowly. Twice black bunches of men crept quickly in front of me, but were melted to pieces. By twelve o'clock the exhaustion of the attackers became suddenly marked. The rifles, heated to a burning pitch, were no longer deemed safe even by Chinese fatalists; and any men who had ventured out into the open had been so severely handled by our fire that they had no stomach for a massed charge. Trumpet calls now broke out along the line and echoed pealingly far and near. The riflemen were being called off.

But hardly had the fire dropped for ten or fifteen minutes than it broke out again with renewed vigour. Fresh troops lying in reserve had evidently been called up, and by one o'clock the tornado was fiercer than ever. Our men became intoxicated by this terrible clamour, and many of them, infuriated by splinters of brick and stone that broke off in clouds from the barricades and stung us from head to foot, sometimes even inflicting cruel wounds, could no longer be held in check. By two o'clock every rifle that could be brought in line was replying to the enemy's fire. If this continued, in a couple of hours our ammunition would be exhausted, and we would have only our bayonets to rely on. I passed down my line, and furiously attempted to stop this firing, but it was in vain. In two places the Chinese had pushed so close, that hand-to-hand fighting had taken place. This gives a lust that is uncontrollable.... Everything was being taken out of our hands....

Suddenly above the clamour of rifle-fire a distant boom to the far east broke on my ears, as I was shouting madly at my men. I held my breath and tried to think, but before I could decide, *boom!* came an answering big gun miles away. I dug my teeth into my lips to keep myself calm, but icy shivers ran down my back. They came faster and faster, those shivers.... You will never know that feeling. Then, *boom!* before I had calmed myself came a third shock; and then ten seconds afterwards, three booms, one, two, three, properly spaced. I understood, although the sounds only shivered in the air. It was a battery of six guns coming into action somewhere very far off. It must be true! I rose to my feet and shook myself. Then, in answer to the heavy guns, came such an immense rolling of machine-gun fire, that it sounded faintly, but distinctly, above the storm around us. Great forces must be engaged in the open....

I had been so ardently listening to these sounds that the enemy's fire had imperceptibly faded away in front of me unnoticed, until it had become almost completely stilled. Single rifles now alone cracked off; all the other men must be listening too—listening and wondering what this distant rumble meant. Far away the Chinese fire still continued to rage as fiercely—but near us, by some strange chance, these distant echoes had claimed attention.

Again the booming dully shook the air. Again the machine-guns beat their replying rataplan. Now every rifle nearby suddenly was stilled, and a Chinese stretcher-party behind me murmured, "*Ta ping lai tao liao*"—"the armies arrived." Somebody took this up, and then we began shouting it across in Chinese to our enemy, shouting it louder and louder in a sort of ecstasy, and heaving heavy stones to attract their attention. We must have become quite crazy, for my throat suddenly gave out, and I could only speak in an absurd whisper.... Oh, what a night!...

Behind the barricades facing us we could now distinctly hear the Chinese soldiery moving uneasily and muttering excitedly to one another. They had understood that it must be the last night of Boxerism, so we threw more stones and shouted more taunts. Then, as if accepting the challenge, a rifle cracked off, a second one joined it, a third, a fourth, and soon the long lines blazed flames and ear-splitting sounds again. But it was the last night—this did not matter—assuredly it was the last night, and from our posts we despatched the first news to headquarters to report that heavy guns had been heard to the east...

Presently, going back during a lull to see ammunition brought up, I found that inside our lines the women and children had all risen, and were craning their necks to catch the distant sounds which had been so long in coming. All night long the buildings in the Su wang-fu, which are packed with native Christians, had been filled with the sound of praying. The elders appointed to watch over this vast flock had been warned that perhaps they would all have to retreat to the base at the last minute, and that all must remain ready during the night and none sleep.

As soon as it was possible, they were told that the relief was coming—that the end was near. . . . What a sight it was to see them all grouped together, for they had scrupulously obeyed orders! In one great hall five hundred Roman Catholic women and children in sober blue gowns were sitting patiently and silently, with their hands folded—had been sitting so all the long night, waiting to hear any news or orders that might be brought to them. Relief or retreat, massacre or deliverance—all must be taken with the stoicism of the East. A single lamp cast its dim rays over these people; and a hundred feet farther on were other halls and buildings, all filled to overflowing with these waiting miserables. A word would have sent them surging back across the dry Imperial Canal—to seek safety for a few hours in our base. Would it have been safety? An immense flood of feeling overwhelmed me. . . .

So the night passed uneasily away, but no more distant sounds were heard, and in the end we began to wonder whether our ears after this strain of weeks had not played us false.

30

How I Saw the Relief

14th August, 1900.

Day broke, after that tremendous night, in a somewhat shambling and odd fashion. Exhausted by so much vigilance and such a strain, we merely posted a scattered line of picquets and threw ourselves on the ground. It was then nearly five o'clock, and with the growing light everything seemed unreal and untrue. There was not a sound around us; there was going to be no relief, and we had been only dreaming horrid dreams—that was the verdict of our eyes and looks. There was but scant time, however, for thinking, even if one could have thought with any sense or logic. The skies were blushing rosier and rosier; a solitary crow, that had lived through all that storm, came from somewhere and began calling hoarsely to its lost mates. We were dead with sleep; we would sleep, or else....

I awoke at eleven in the morning sick as a beaten dog. The sun beating hotly down, and a fierce ray had found its way through the branches of my protecting tree and had been burning the back of my neck. The Eastern sun is a brute; when it strikes you long in a tender spot, it can make you sicker than anything I know of. Arousing ourselves, we got up all of us gruntingly; reposted the sentries; drank some black tea; made a faint pretence at washing; and finding all dead quiet and not a trace of the enemy, sauntered off for news. Not a word anywhere, not a sound, not a message. Everybody was standing about in uneasy groups, from the French and German lines to the northern outposts of the British Legation. Where the devil were our relieving columns?

From the Tartar Wall we scanned the horizon with our glasses. Not a soul afoot—nothing. Was all the world still asleep, tired from the night's debauch, or was it merely the end of everything? As time went on, and the silence around us was uninterrupted, we became more and more nervous. In place of the storm of fire which had been raging for so many hours this unbroken calm was terrible; for far worse than all the tortures in the world is the one of a solitary silent confinement.

At one o'clock I could stand it no longer. Getting leave to take out a skirmishing party, I called for volunteer and got six men and two Chinese scouts. At half-past one we slid over the Eastern Su wang-fu barricades—near where the messengers are sent from—and scurried forward into the contested territory beyond. Working cautiously in a long line, we beat the ground thoroughly; approached the enemy's flanking barricades; peered over in some trepidation, and found the Chinese riflemen gone. Every soul had fled. Something had most certainly happened somewhere. This quiet was becoming more and more eloquent....

We abandoned our cover, and boldly taking to the brick-littered street, climbed over fortifications which had shut us in for so long. Not a sound or a living thing. On the ground, however, there were many grim evidences of the struggle which had been so long proceeding. Skulls picked clean by crows and dogs and the dead bodies of the scavenger-dogs themselves dotted the ground; in other places were pathetic wisps of pigtails half covered with rubbish, broken rifles, rusted swords, heaps of brass cartridges—all proclaiming the bitterness with which the warfare had been waged in this small corner alone. Eagerly gazing about us, we slowly pushed on, drinking in all these details with eager eyes. How sweet it is to be an escaped prisoner even for a few short minutes!

In a quarter of an hour we had cleared the ground intervening between our defences and the long-abandoned Customs Street— perhaps a couple of hundred yards; and peering about us, we at last jumped over the French barricade, where our first man had been shot dead two months ago. Two months—it might have been two years! Still there was not a sound. Nothing but acres of ruins. Forward.

Splitting into two sections, we began working down Customs Street towards the Austrian Legation, tightly hugging the walls and expecting a surprise every moment. Suddenly, as we were going along in this cautious manner, a tall, gaunt Chinaman started up only twenty feet from us, where he had been lying buried in the ruins. Our rifles went up with a leap, and "Master," cried the man, running towards me with outstretched arms, "master, save me; I am a carter of the foreign Legations, and have only just escaped."

He pulled up his blue tunic, this strange apparition, and showed me underneath his *scapula*. He was of Roman Catholic family; there was no time to investigate; he was all right. Telling him to join us, we marched on. We progressed another fifty yards, and then there was a scuffle. I looked round, and our Catholic had disappeared. Were we trapped? Just as I was calling out, he reappeared; this time he was bearing a rifle and a bandolier. This was disconcerting.

"I saw the man," he began calmly, "and with my hands I killed him by pulling on the throat—thus." He made a horrid pantomime with his hands. Behind a wall we found the red and black tunic of a Chinese soldier, the sash and the boots, but of a corpse there was no sign. I was glad I understood.

"What do you mean by deceiving me?" I sternly asked the carter. "These are yours, and it was you who were fighting against us." The man fell on his knees, and confessed then and there without subterfuge. He had been captured, he said and imprisoned weeks ago by a Chinese commander, who had threatened to break the bones of his legs unless he enlisted against us. So he had joined and had been fighting for a month. Last night, as soon as the big guns had been heard, he deserted, and had lain where we found him for fifteen hours, waiting for our advances, and may his legs be broken if he lied. I paused in doubt for a minute; then I made up my mind—we let him follow! The odds were in any case against him.

As we moved stealthily forward we came on more and more fortifications. A formidable blockhouse had been constructed by dragging out big steel safes, looted from the various European offices in this abandoned area, and building them into a thick half-moon of stone and brick, making a shell-proof defence. On the ground brass cartridge-cases and broken straps and weapons were littered more and more thickly, but of any sign of life there was absolutely none. Absolute stillness reigned around us. We might have been in a city abandoned for dozens of years....

Past this blockhouse we crept more and more cautiously, beating the ground thoroughly, and wasting many minutes to make sure that no riflemen lurked in the ruins which covered the ground. Our new recruit had shown us how easily we could be trapped. Loopholes squinted at us from countless low-lying barricades roughly made by heaping bricks and charred timbers together. They had feared our sorties evidently as much as we had their rushes, had these Chinese soldiers. Their fortified lines were hundreds of feet deep.

We were now down near the abandoned Austrian Legation, and, rapidly trotting forward in Indian file under cover of the high encircling wall, we at last reached the main entrance. This was debatable ground. I looked round the corner with one cautious eye, and even as I did so, a shadow rushed along the ground.... Instantly I snapped off my rifle from my hip, the others followed suit, and a howl of canine rage answered us. We had rolled over a wolfish dog searching for dead bodies. Before we had time to realise much, the savage animal was up again and rushing at us—to escape through the gate.

As it passed, we clubbed and bayoneted him with neatness, for we have now some art in close-quarter work, and with a last howl the animal's life flickered out. Dogs are highly dangerous, as we knew to our cost; they give the alarm in a way which no living man, even in these civilised days, can fail to understand. We waited in some anguish to see whether this scuffle had been heard; we were a quarter of a mile away from our own lines by the circuitous route we had been forced to take, and if we were ambuscaded, no one would probably go back to tell the tale....

Still not a sound, not a word. A little encouraged, we crept more valiantly into the Austrian Legation, and stood amazed at the spectacle. Rank-growing weeds covered the ground two or three feet high; all the houses and residences had been gutted by fire, everything combustible burned, leaving a terrible litter. But the brickwork and stonework stood almost intact, and the tall Corinthian pillars with which it had been the architect's fancy to adorn this mission of His Most Catholic Majesty, stood up white and chaste in all this scene of devastation and ruin; they might have dated from centuries ago. Broken weapons, thousands more of brass cartridges, and sometimes even a soldier's bloodstained tunic could be seen among the weeds. This must have been the site of another camp of Chinese soldiery. Abandoned straw matting showed where rough huts had once been built line upon line. But all these hosts had flown.

We now held a council of war. What should we do—push on or go back? It seemed highly dangerous, but suddenly making up my mind, I cut short all deliberations and ordered an advance. To feel for the enemy, to get in touch with the enemy at all costs, and to scratch him if possible, is evidently the scout's duty, even when the scout is but a siege amateur, with broken trousers, a mud-stained shirt and a battered rifle. But we must make ourselves secure. We bolted the big gates behind us; we sweatily piled up sufficient bricks to make its opening a matter of minutes for an enemy's hand, and then we once again trotted forward. This time we were irrevocably inside the Legation, and separated, perhaps, for good and all from our own people....

We rapidly covered the ground until we reached the extreme eastern corner of the vast enclosing Legation wall. Very recently there had been someone just here for a fire was still smouldering on the ground, and in some earthenware bowls there was some cold rice. We must see what was beyond....

The big recruit lent me his broad shoulder, and with some struggling I caught the edge of an outhouse roof and hitched myself astride of the main wall. Still nothing to be seen except ruined and battered houses; again not a soul, not a dog, not a vestige of life. The others came up, too, and we rapidly improvised a ladder to get down the other side and back again if necessary.

We were busily at work completing these preparations when suddenly the big recruit grabbed me unceremoniously by the shoulder and uttered a single word in a hoarse tone of excitement. "Look," he said; "look!" I looked, and far down the street below us towards where lay the palace and the Imperial city, I saw a figure rapidly moving. A pair of binoculars were pulled out and brought to bear. It was a Chinese soldier!

We flattened ourselves on the top of the wall like so many crawling snails, pushed out our rifles in front of us, and at four hundred yards we most foolishly opened on the man. By instinct and experience, we had all learned much in two months; yet in a moment of excitement everything was being rapidly unlearned....

It takes some shooting to get home on a flickering figure, dodging along a street with irregular lines, at that range, and I confess we drew no blood. But still loophole shooting must spoil open-air work, otherwise at that range.... The man had paused irresolutely as the stream of bullets had hissed past him, and had then run violently into a doorway. Presently, as we intently watched, his head emerged, then his whole body; and, finally dodging quickly in and out, he gained a cross-road and disappeared. What did this mean?

It did not take long to learn, for just as we had finished swearing at our ill luck, other figures began to appear in the same direction, and as they ran we could see that they were throwing down their things. It seemed plain now; these must be deserters slipping out of the Imperial city and the palace enclosures and fleeing rapidly to escape some fate. Something must have certainly happened somewhere, although there was still nothing to be heard, except perhaps a distant movement in the air, which might mean the rattle of musketry. Sometimes we could hear that faint suggestion of sound, sometimes we could not; it was impossible to say what it was.

Running gives Dutch courage, so we dropped from our wall, and we, too, began running—towards the deserters. Most foolish scouts were we becoming. The first band of fugitives saw us and bolted to the north, one man loosing off his rifle at us as he ran, and his bullet making an ugly swish in the air just above our heads. It was that Chinese hip-shot which is practised with *jingal* and matchlock in the native hunting, and which these Northern Chinese can with difficulty unlearn. As that swish reached us we pressed forward even more eagerly, and soon had debouched once more on the long Customs Street—this time many hundreds of yards higher up than we had ever been before. Flattening ourselves on the ground, and barricading our heads with bricks, we waited in silence for more of the enemy to appear. We were now admirably and safely posted.

It was some time before any more of them were to be seen, but at last, in twos and threes, other soldiers appeared, running hurriedly, and looking quickly about them, as if they expected to be shot down. This time they were men of many corps, whose uniforms we could almost make out at this short distance, and as they ran many of them threw off their tunics and loosened their leggings. This meant open and flagrant desertion. Just as I was about to give the order to fire a volley, a dense mass of men, in close formation, came out of a great building leaning up against the pink palace walls and started marching rapidly towards us. Then as soon as they reached a cross-road five hundred yards away, they bent quickly due north and disappeared in a cloud of dust. What did this fleeing to the north of the city and this ominous quiet mean? What in the name of all that is extraordinary was happening to cause these strange doings?

There was little time for reflection, however, for like some theatre of the gods new scenes began to unroll. Soon other bodies of troops appeared and disappeared, always heading away there towards the north, always marching rapidly with hurried looks cast around them. Now safe in the knowledge that a general retreat was taking place from this quarter, we started volleying savagely. Bunched together in twos and threes, the enemy offered an easy mark, and with a callousness born of long privations we dropped at least fifteen or twenty men in very few minutes. Lying flat on the ground our angles soon grew fixed on to our rifle-sights, and at one house-corner four hundred yards away, six times I made the same shot and dropped a deserter. But this heavy firing must have attracted attention, for lead began to pelt at us from hidden places, and soon this little action became very warm. It was a curious experience. . . .

It was now three in the afternoon, and, excepting for this unexplained movement of Chinese troops, we had not discovered any sign of our relief. Our volleying was becoming nonsensical, for having picked up numbers of Chinese Mauser cartridges, we amused ourselves firing away almost all the ammunition we carried. This could not continue indefinitely. So once more I drew my men together, and once again we scurried away, changing our direction to due east towards the great Ha-ta Gate. We were becoming callous, now that we knew there was small possibility of our being cut off, and half a mile from home meant nothing to us.

We had almost reached the Ha-ta great street, and were beginning to feel that by some strange chance we had half the city to ourselves, when a furious galloping gave us a timely signal, and made us shrink into a native house, the doorway of which had been beaten in by marauders. We were just in time, for no sooner had we disappeared than a body of Manchu cavalry came rapidly past, flogging their ponies, and shouting excitedly to one another as they passed. At their head were a number of high officials, and our new recruit whispered in a hoarse voice that an old man was no other than Jung Lu, the *Manchu Generalissimo*, who had command of everything. But whether this was actually so or not, there could be no doubt about the soldiery. They were *ch'in ping*, or bodyguard troops, in sky-blue tunics, and this retirement was the most significant of all. There was now not a shadow of doubt.

We waited patiently in some trepidation, until the sound of these galloping hoofs had died away completely and then peering out and finding the coast clear, we ran for it as hard as we could leg. Faster and faster we spun along; we were not as safe as we thought, Three minutes brought us back again on Customs Street, and, panting sorely from this unaccustomed exertion, we looked around. Here there was now not a single sound, not the sight of a single man.

For many minutes nothing again occurred, but at length more Chinese troops began to appear, all running rapidly in long flights, and a troop of cavalry came out of a side street not more than two hundred yards away from where we lay, and headed away at a furious gallop. Everybody was obviously making for the north of the city; what was going on in the other quarters to cause this exodus? The cavalry, as they moved in close formation, were so tempting, that without hesitation once more our rifles rang out in a well-knit volley. That caused a terrible commotion, for cavalry are an easy mark.

Ponies broke away and galloped frantically into side streets; there was a waving and a mix-up which blurred everything, and yet before we had time to realise it, bullets were hissing all round us and kicking up little spurts of dust a few inches from our bodies; a resolute commander was in front of us. This firing became so violent that we were driven to take shelter, and as we ran and were seen the bullets hissed quicker and quicker. Then as suddenly as it had commenced this pelting ceased; we saw our cavalrymen flicker away in the distance, and once more everything was absolutely quiet. It was obvious that something so urgent was taking place, that no one had any time to lose in pranks.

Many minutes elapsed before we noticed any fresh signs of life, and we remained spread across the street on our stomachs, earnestly searching in vain for some explanation. At last, when I was becoming tired of it, figures began to move on the long street again—little indecisive blue dots that jerked forward, halted, appeared and disappeared in a most curious way. They were also coming towards us—jerking about like people possessed. Climbing a wall, I brought my glasses to bear; they were ordinary townspeople, there was not a shadow of doubt about that, men, women, and children, running violently, waving and calling to one another, and apparently much distressed.

I remained on this wall-top idly gazing until my vision began to become blurred, and I could no longer see. Then something made me close my eyes for a second to regain command over them again; and when I opened them and looked again through that powerful Leiss, my jaw dropped. This time, with a vengeance, it was something new. Dense bodies of men in white tunics and dark trousers were debouching into the street, thousands of yards away, and were then marching due east—that is, towards the palace. They came on and on, until it seemed they would never cease. What were these newcomers? Were they white troops at last—were they Bannermen of the white Banners? . . .

They might be anything—anything in the world—but they might be. . . .

Yes, without a doubt they might be ordinary Russian infantry of the line. Russian infantry of the line! It was imperative to learn.

I clambered off the wall and decided at once on a grim test. All of us pushed up our flaps to the extreme range and gave four sharp volleys—the eight rifles crashing off jarringly together. As we were preparing to give them the last cartridge on the clips, the white specks we could just see with the naked eye stopped and flickered away. Then as we waited there was a moment's silence; a little vapour spurted up far away, and *bang!* a shell whizzed, and burst two hundred yards to our rear. That was an immense surprise! But now we had no doubts; these were European troops; the relief must have come; it was all over, we must communicate the news. . . .

Before our ideas had grouped themselves coherently, we found ourselves bolting home—bolting like madmen. We charged clear down the middle of the streets, with a disregard for everything; we headed straight as arrows for the French lines, right through the heart of the most formidable Chinese works, where but twelve hours before furious attacks had been developed. We tore through hundreds of feet of trenches, barricades, saps, half-opened tunnels, where everything was scored and beaten by the riotous passage of nickel and lead. We vaguely saw, as we rushed, lines of mat huts, broken walls, charred timbers, countless brass cartridge cases, gaping holes—all the wreckage left by these weeks of insane warfare. But of living things there was not a trace.

Beating our way rapidly forward, we at length passed through those death-strewn French Legation lines, and reached our own last barricades, where the defence had been driven. Supposing that our men were still behind them, we violently shouted that we were friends. Nobody answered us.

Curiously alarmed, we clambered forward more and more quickly, and at last near the fortified little Hôtel de Pékin a confused sound of voices arose from a stoutly fortified quadrangle. Then as we drew nearer the voices grew, until they framed themselves into half-suppressed cheers—a multitude of men uneasily greeting and calling to one another. At least, we had not been abandoned I put my leg up to swarm over a wall, and suddenly a thick smell greeted my nostrils, a smell I knew, because I had smelt it before, and yet a smell which belonged to another world. . . . With tremendous heart-beating, I looked over. It was the smell of India!

Into this quadrangle beyond hundreds of native troops were filing and piling arms. They were Rajputs, all talking together, and greeting some of our sailors and men, and demanding immediately *pane, pane, pane* all the time in a monotonous chorus. I could not understand that word. The relief had come; this must be some sections of an advance guard which had been flung forward, and had burst in unopposed.. . .

We hurried forward in a sort of daze and looked for officers, to ask them how they had come, and whether it was all right. We found a knot of them standing-together, wiping the sweat from their streaming faces, and calling for water. They wanted to go to the British Legation; not to this place—what was it; where was the British Legation? In the heat and smell and excitement those continuous questions made one confused and angry. This advance guard which had rushed in could not understand our all-split area; yet it had been the saving of us. I told them where the British Legation was. I told them to follow me; I was going to run.

I ran on, once more choking a little, and with a curious desire to weep or shout or make uncouth noises. I was now terribly excited. I remember I kicked my way through barricades with such energy that once for my foolishness I came crashing down, my rifle loosing off of its own account and the bullet passing through my hat. I did not care; the relief had come. It was an immense occasion and I had not been there to see it.

Along the dry canal-bed, as I ran out of the Legation Street, I noted without amazement that tall Sikhs were picking their way in little groups, looking dog-tired. But they were very excited, too, and waved their hands to me as I ran, and called and cried with curious intonations. Pioneers, smaller men, in different turbans, were already smashing down our barricades, and clearing a road, and from the west, the palace side, a tremendous rifle and machine-gun fire was dusting endlessly. I rushed into the British Legation through the canal open-cut, and here they were, piles and piles of Indian troops, standing and lying about and waving and talking. A British general and his staff were seated at a little table that had been dragged out, and were now drinking as if they, too, had been burned dry with thirst.

Around all our people were crowding a confused mass of marines, sailors, volunteers, ministers—everyone. Many of the women were crying and patting the sweating soldiery that never ceased streaming in. People you had not seen for weeks, who might have, indeed, been dead a hundred times without your being any the wiser, appeared now for the first time from the rooms in which they had been hidden and acted hysterically. They were pleased to rush about and fetch water and begin to tell their experiences. All that day, I was told, these hidden ones had taken a sudden interest in the hospital; had roused themselves from their lethargy and fright, because the end was coming. Now....

As we stood about, twisting our fingers and cheering, and trying to find something sensible to say or to do, there was a rush of people towards the lines connecting with the American Legation and the Tartar Wall This caused another tremendous outburst of cheering and counter-cheering, and led by C——, the American Minister, columns of American infantry in khaki suits and slouch hats came pressing in. In they came—more and more men, until the open squares were choking with them. These men were more dog-tired than the Indian troops, and their uniforms were stained and clotted with the dust and sweat flung on them by the rapid advance. Soon there was such confusion and excitement that all order was lost, until the Americans began filing out again, and the native troops were pushed to the northern line of defences.

In the turmoil and delight everything had been temporarily forgotten, but the growing roar of rifles had at length called attention to the fact that there might be more fierce fighting. Every minute added to the din, and soon the ceaseless patter of sound showed machine-guns were firing like fury. Somebody called out to me that there was a fine sight to be seen from the Tartar Wall, for those who did not mind a few more bullets; and, enticed by the storm of sound that rose ever higher and higher, I ran hastily through our lines towards the city bastions.

Every street and lane from the Ch'ien Men Gate was now choked with troops of the relieving column, all British and American, as far as I could see, and already the pioneers attached to each battalion were levelling our rude defences to the ground in order to facilitate the passage of the guns and transport waggons.... Strange cries smote one's ears—all the cursing of armed men, whose discipline has been loosened by days of strain and the impossibility of manoeuvring. One word struck me and clung to me again; everybody among the Indian troops was crying it: "*Chullo, chullo, chullo*," they were calling.

The general advance, which had been from the outer city, as soon as the news had been brought through that a way to the Legations had been opened, had thrown the various units into an immense confusion. Infantry, cavalry, artillery, and the fighting trains, were all mixed in a terrible tangle. Some had come forward so rapidly, in their eagerness not to be left out of it all, that they had passed in under the walls as soon as the gates had been burst open, and had now got jammed into our narrow streets and were unable to move. Just under the ramp of the Tartar Wall I came on some Indian cavalry—about thirty or forty troopers covered with mud and dirt, and led by a single British officer. As soon as the latter caught sight of me, he shouted an angry question as to what all this firing meant, and how in h—— he could get out of this into the open.... He rained his questions at me like the others had done, never waiting for an answer.

The firing, in all truth, had increased enormously, and now rang out with a most tremendous roar. It always came from over there to the northwest, round about the palace entrances. Evidently Chinese troops were holding all the palace gates in great force, and for some reason wished to keep the relief columns at bay at all costs until nightfall. I yelled something of this to my disconsolate cavalry officer, and suggested that he should follow me up the wall and see for himself. I knew nothing. "Cavalry can't climb a wall," he furiously replied as I rushed up above, and as I climbed higher that voice followed me in gusts which became fainter and fainter, "Cavalry can't climb a wall! cavalry can't climb a wall!" Then the road blotted him and his voice completely out and a swelling scene was before me.

For up there I soon understood. A mass of Indian infantry, with some machine-guns, had established themselves for hundreds of yards along this commanding height, among the old Chinese barricades, and were now firing as fast as they could down into the distant Palace enclosures. Overhead bullets were passing in continuous streams, and crouching low in an angle of the buttresses lay a number of wounded men. Of the enemy, however, there was no sign to be seen; that he was firing back more and more quickly and desperately was certain. All these bullets....

As I stood and looked, suddenly the horrid bark of the modern high-velocity field-gun began down below in our lines, and the word passed along that a British battery had succeeded in getting through the jam, and was opening on the enemy from just outside the Legations. The barking went on very rapidly for a few minutes, and then ceased as suddenly as it had begun. The cause was not long to seek; an infantry advance had followed, for without any warning swarms of Chinese riflemen began running out from the nests of ruined Chinese houses a few hundred yards to the rear of our old lines. They came out in rapid rushes just as flights of startled sparrows dart over the ground, and, although very distant, from the commanding height of the Tartar Wall they offered a splendid mark.

The rifles rattled at them as hard as possible, but the practice was as poor as ever. Of the first batch a dozen fell and began crawling and staggering away; but the next lot, although they ran and halted at first like dazed men under the sleet of nickel, rapidly became more cunning. All fell as if by some sudden signal on the ground, and crawling and jumping forward, they soon managed to push through without losing a single man, and immediately after this there was a droll incident such as only occurs at such times as these.

These bunches of men had ceased falling back in their sudden rout, and the firing of our men was being concentrated on some distant walls flanking the Palace enclosures, when a solitary Chinese rifleman, who had evidently been forgotten in the turmoil, trotted peacefully out. Then, seeing he was almost in the hands of his enemies, he ran like a hunted deer straight across a vast open, which lies directly in front of the Dynastic Gate—never seeking cover, but running like a madman in the open. It was wonderful.

A roar went up from our whole line when he was seen, but the infantry did not attempt to bring him down. A single machine-gun started rapping at him.... The man ran faster and faster as the swish of bullets hurtled around him, until his legs were twinkling so rapidly that he seemed to be fairly flying. The machine-gun went on rapping and clanging ever quicker as it followed him up, and it seemed at length impossible that he should get through. With a natural impulse, everybody's attention became concentrated on this fugitive: would he reach cover in safety?

The answer came almost before one had thought the question, for with sudden disgust the machine-gun stopped dead; the man ran a few seconds longer, and then with a last bound he had disappeared—a tiny dot of blue and red flicking vaguely away behind some wall. Instinctively, then, someone began laughing; the next man took it up, and soon a roar of hoarse-throated laughter came from the hundreds of Indian soldiery who had witnessed the scene. It was like a scene in a theatre from that height, and I remember that this laughter of free men resounded in my ears for a long time—the laughter of free men who have never been enslaved in bricks. It came from straight off the chest, without any nervous nasal twanging or sudden stopping....

Soon after this the firing dropped and dwindled away to nothing, as if by common consent. Everybody was dog-tired, and as night fell both sides felt that nothing could be gained or materially changed until another day had dawned. I wandered round for the last time. Our lines, so carefully and painfully built up during those long neverending weeks, had crumbled to pieces in half as many hours. The barricades and trenches obstructing the streets had been thrown all in a lump and sent to join the huge litter which surrounded them. There was hardly a sentry or a picquet to be seen, only a hundred of little camp-fires twinkling and twinkling everywhere.

Such battalions and units as had pushed in had bivouacked exactly where they had halted. Far away under the Tartar Wall, on the long, sandy stretches, there were little wood fires blazing at regular intervals, with countless dots moving around. From a hundred other places there came that confused murmur which, speaks of masses of men and animals. There were faint cries, hoarse calls, and orders, with always a vague undercurrent trembling in the air. For the time being, they were only British and American troops—not a soldier of a single other nationality had been seen. As the hours went, other people, whose troops had not come in, began making excuses, and pretending that their generals were very wise in acting as they had done. There were all sorts of theories. Some said that they were securing all the gates of the city, and capturing the Court, and seeing to very important things.

It was the political situation of three months ago being suddenly reborn, reincarnated, by all these people, before we had even breathed the air of freedom. It was for this that we had been rescued by the main body of the troops: merely because had we been all killed and all recent Peking history made an utter blank, there would have been a terrible gulf which no protocols could bridge. It would have meant an end, an absolute end, such as governments and their distinguished servants do not really love. We were mere puppets, whose rescue would set everything merrily dancing again—marionettes made the sport of mad events. We had merely saved diplomacy from an impossible situation. . . .

As I stood there in the night, thinking of these things, and trying to escape from people with theories, a faint cheering arose, a hurrahing which somehow had but little vigour. I knew what it meant; the ground was being noisily cleared right up to the palace walls, to make sure that none of the enemy were lurking in the ruins, and that the play could begin merrily on the morrow. After that cheering came a few dull explosions, the blowing-up of a few unnecessary walls, and then all was dead quiet again, excepting for the faint stirring of the soldiery encamped around us, which never ceased. There was not a volley, not a shot. It was all over, this siege, everything was finished.

With a growing blackness and distress in my heart, which I could not explain, and sought in vain to disguise, I wandered about. I wanted some more movement—some fresh distraction to tear my attention away from gloomy thoughts.

Near the battered Hôtel de Pékin officers who had strayed from their commands and who were hungry had already gathered, and were paying in gold for anything they could buy. Luckily, there were a few cases of champagne left and a few tins of potted things, which could now be tranquilly sold. I found some French uniforms. Some officers had at last come in from the French commander, saying that at daylight the French columns would march in. At present they were too exhausted to move.

All these men, seated at the tables, were noisily discussing the relief. I learned how it had been effected and the moves of the few preceding days. They said that the Russians had attempted to steal a march on the Japanese on the night of the 13th, in order to force the Eastern gates, and reach the Imperial city and the Empress Dowager before anyone else. That had upset the whole plan of attack, and there had then simply been a mad rush, everyone going as hard as possible, and trusting to Providence to pull them through.

Most of the officers at the tables soon became highly elated. That is the way when your stomach has been fed on hard rations and you have had fourteen days of the sun. They then all began shouting and singing and not talking so much. But still they were all devilishly keen to know about the siege, and who had fought best, and who had been killed.

I left them in what remains of a little barricaded and fortified hotel disputing away in rather a foolish fashion, because they were more or less inebriate and the sun had burned them badly. And speeding to my *cache*, I drew out my two blankets and my waterproof. While I had been forgetting other things, I had learned two new things—how to sleep and how to shoot—and now since there was no more need to practise the one, I would do the other.

PART 3-THE SACK

1

The Palace

16th August, 1900.
The next morning (which was only yesterday!) I awoke in much the same strange despondency. Around me, as the grey light stole softly into my lean-to, everything was absolutely quiet. It was the same in every way as it had been the morning after the last terrible night; and yet that was already so long ago! Almost mechanically, I searched the breast pocket of my soil-worn shirt for the previous day's orders, so as to see about picquet posting; then I remembered suddenly, with a curious heart-sinking, that it was all over, finished, completed. . . . It was so strange that it should be so—that everything should have come so suddenly to an end.

After all those experiences, to be lying on the ground like some tramp in Europe, without a thing to one's name, was to be merely grotesque and incongruous. Yet it was necessary to become accustomed immediately to the idea that one belonged to the ordinary world, where one would not be distinguished from one's fellow; where everything was quiet and orderly. . . . And I was separated from this by such a mighty gulf. I knew so many things now. What! was I no longer to experience that supreme delight of shooting and being shot at—of that unending excitement? Oh! was it really over? . . .

I got up, and shook myself disconsolately, retied what remained of a neckcloth, and then looked in disgust at my boots. My boots! Two and a half months' work and sleep in them—my only pair—had not improved their appearance. Yet I had not even suspected that before; the evil fruit of relief had made my nakedness clear. . . .

Alongside the whole post of ten men was still peacefully slumbering—regulars and volunteers heaped impartially together. Poor devils! Each one, after the enormous excitement of the relief, had come back mechanically to his accustomed place, because this strange life of ours, imposed by the discipline of events, has become a second nature, which we scarcely know how to shake off. Like tired dogs, we still creep into our holes. The youngest were moaning and tossing, as they have done every night for weeks past—shaking off sleep like a harmful narcotic, because the poison of fighting is too strong for most blood in these degenerate days. What sounds have I not heard during the past two months—what sighs, what gasps, what groans, what muttered protests! When men lie asleep, their imaginations betray their secret thoughts. . . .

Day had not broken properly before the murmur and movements of the night before rose again. This time, as I looked around me, they were more marked—as if the relieving forces had become half accustomed to their strange surroundings, and were acting with the freedom of familiarity. There were bugle-calls and trumpet-calls, the neighing and whinnying of horses, the rumble of heavy waggons, calls and cries. . . . But hidden by the high walls and the barricades, nothing could be seen. We got something to eat, and, wishing to explore, I marched down to the dry canal-bed, jumped in, and made for the Water-Gate, through which the first men had come. In a few steps I was outside the Tartar Wall, for the first time for nearly three long months.

At last there was something to be seen. Far along here, there were nothing but bivouacs of soldiery moving uneasily like ants suddenly disturbed, and as I tramped through the sand towards the great Ch'ien Men Gate I could see columns of other men, already in movement, though day had just come, winding in and out from the outer Chinese city. Thick pillars of smoke, that hung dully in the morning air, were rising in the distance as if fire had been set to many buildings; but apart from these marching troops there was not a living soul to be seen. The ruins and the houses had become mere landmarks and the city a veritable desert.

I wandered about listlessly and exchanged small talk disconsolately with numbers of people. Nobody knew what was going to happen, but everybody was trying to learn from somebody else. The wildest rumours were circulating. The Russians and Japanese had disappeared through the Eastern Gates of the city, and the gossip was that each, in trying to steal a march on the other, had knocked up against large bodies of Chinese troops, who, still retaining their discipline, had stood their ground and inflicted heavy losses on the rivals. But whether this was true or not, there was, for the time being, no means of knowing. I thought of my last rifle-shots of the siege at those endless white and black dots, which had suddenly debouched on that long, dusty street, and held my tongue. Idly we waited to see what was going to happen. After so many climaxes one's imagination totally failed.

It was still very early in the morning when, without any warning, gallopers came suddenly from the American headquarters and set all the soldiery in motion. I remember that it seemed only a few minutes before the American infantry had become massed all round the southern entrances to the Palace, while with a quickness which came as an odd surprise to me after the deliberation of the siege field-guns suddenly opened on the Imperial Gates. A number of shells were pitched against the huge iron-clamped entrances at a range of a few hundred yards with a horrid coughing, and presently, yielding to this bombardment, with a crash the first line had been beaten to the ground.

I understood then why the powerful American Gatlings had been kept playing on the fringe of walls and roofs beyond; for as the infantry charged forward in some confusion, with their cheering and bugling filling the air, the dusting Chinese fire, which we knew so well, rang out with an unending rattle and hissing. Thousands of riflemen had been silently lying inside the Palace enclosures ever since the previous afternoon waiting for this opportunity. It was the last act. Well, it had come. . . .

The Chinese fire was partially effective, for as I ran forward through the burst and bent gates, panting as if my heart would break, a trickle of wounded American soldiers came slowly filing out. Some were hobbling, unsupported, with pale faces, and some were being carried quite motionless. On the ground of this first vast enclosure, which was hundreds and hundreds of yards long and entirely paved with stone, were a number of Chinese dead—men of some resolution, who had met the charge in the open and died like soldiers. That, indeed, had been our own experience. Even with the ambiguous orders which must have been given in every command ranged against us, there were always men who could not be restrained, but charged right up to our bayonets. . . . Now as I ran forward firing was going on just as heavily, and the ugly rush and swish of bullets filled the air with war's rude music. It seemed curious to me that everyone should be out in the open with no cover; after a siege one has queer ideas.

The bursting of this first set of gates meant very little, as I personally knew full well, for immediately beyond was a far more powerful line, with immense pink walls heaving straight up into the air. The Tartar conquerors, who had designed this Palace, had with good purpose made their Imperial residence a last citadel in the huge city of Peking—a citadel which could be easily defended to the death in the old days even when the enemy had seized all the outer walls, for without powerful cannon the place was impregnable.

On the sky-line of this great outer wall Chinese riflemen, with immense audacity, still remained, and as I ran for cover rifles were quickly and furiously discharged at me.... Presently the American guns came rapidly forward, but their commanders were wary, and did not seem to like to risk them too close. There was a short lull, while immense scaling ladders, made by the Americans for attacking the city walls in case the relief had failed to get in any other way, were rushed up. The idea was evidently to storm the walls and batter in the gates, line upon line, until the Imperial residences were reached and the inmost square taken. It might take many hours if there was much resistance. The area to be covered was immense.

To the north a faint booming proclaimed that other forces, perhaps the Russians and the Japanese still in rivalry, were at work on this huge Forbidden City, racing once more to see that neither got the advantage of the other.... All this meant slow work without startling developments. Everybody was moving very deliberately, as if time was of no value. A new idea came into my head. It was impossible to cover such distances continually on foot without becoming exhausted. Already I was tired out. I must seize a mount somewhere before it was too late. I must go back.

Trotting quickly, I reached the Legation area to find that the scene had changed. The ruined streets were once again filled with troops. The transport and fighting trains of a number of Indian regiments, which had spent the night somewhere in the outer Chinese city, had evidently been hurriedly pushed forward at daylight to be ready for any eventualities. Ambulance corps and some very heavy artillery were mixed with all these moving men and kicking animals in hopeless confusion, and rude shouts and curses filled the air as all tried to push forward. Among these countless animals and their jostling drivers it was almost impossible to fight one's way; but with a struggle I reached the dry canal, and, once more jumping down, I had a road to myself. I went straight along it.

Under the Tartar Wall, as I climbed again to the ground-level, I met the head of fresh columns of men. This time they were white troops—

French *Infanterie Coloniale*, in dusty blue suits of torn and discoloured *nankeen*. There must have been thousands of them, for after some delay they got into movement, and, enveloped in thick clouds of dust, these solid companies of blue uniforms, crowned with dirty-white helmets, started filing past me in an endless stream. The officers were riding up and down the line, calling on the men to exert themselves, and to hurry, hurry, hurry.

But the rank and file were pitifully exhausted, and their white, drawn faces spoke only of the fever-haunted swamps of Tonkin, whence they had been summoned to participate in this frantic march on the capital. They had always been behind, I heard, and had only been hurried up by constant forced marching, which left the men mutinous and valueless. Once again they were being hurried not to be too late....

I only lost these troops to find myself crushed in by long lines of mountain artillery carried on mules, and led by strange-looking Annamites. In a thin line they stretched away until I could only divine how many there were. These batteries, however, were not going forward, and to my surprise I found the guns being suddenly loaded and hauled to the top of the Tartar Wall up one of the ramparts which had been our salvation. This was a new development, and in my interest, forgetting my pony, I ran up, too.

Up there I found a mass of people, mostly comprising those who had been spectators rather than actors in the siege. I remember being seized with strange feelings when I saw their little air of derision and their sneers as they looked down towards the palace in pleasurable anticipation. They imagined, these self-satisfied people who had done so little to defend themselves, that a day of reckoning had at last come when they would be able to do as they liked towards this detestable Palace, which had given them so many unhappy hours. It would all be destroyed, burned. Little did they know!

Soon enough these small French batteries of light guns came into action, and sent a stream of little shells into the Palace enclosures a couple of thousand yards away. The majority pitched on the gaudy roofs of Imperial pavilions far inside the Palace grounds, bursting into pretty little fleecy clouds, and starting small smouldering fires that suddenly died down before they had done much damage. But a number fell short, and swept enclosures where I knew American soldiery had already penetrated. I drew my breath, but said nothing....

The view from here was perfect. The sun had risen and was shining brightly. Directly below lay the ruined Legations, with their rude fortifications and thousands of surrounding native houses levelled flat to the ground; but beyond, for many miles, stretched the vast city of Peking, dead silent, excepting for these now accustomed sounds of war, and half hidden by myriads of trees, which did not allow one to see clearly what was taking place.

The palace, with its immense walls, its yellow roofs, and its vast open places, lay mysteriously quiet, too, while this punishment was meted out on it. You could not understand what was going on. To the very far north a heavy cloud, which had already attracted my attention, now rose blacker and blacker, until it spread like a pall on the bright sky. *Cossacks* or Japanese, who by this time had swept over the entire ground, must have met with resistance; they were burning and sacking, and a huge conflagration had been started.

For a quarter of an hour and more I watched in an idle, tired curiosity, which I could not explain, those little French shells bursting far away and falling short, and presently, as I expected, the inevitable happened. A young American officer rode up and began shouting angrily up to the wall. I knew exactly what he meant, but everybody was so interested that he remained unnoticed. And so, presently, more furious than ever, he dismounted and rushed up red with rage. He was so angry that he was funny. He wanted to know if the commander of these d—— pop-guns knew what he was firing at, and whether he could not see the United States army in full occupation of the bombarded points.

He swore and he cursed and he gesticulated, until finally cease fire was sounded and the guns were ordered down. All the Frenchmen were furious, and I saw P——, the minster, go down in company with the gaunt-looking Spanish *doyen*, vowing vengeance and declaiming loudly that if they were stopped everybody must be stopped too. There must be no favouring; that they would not have. I understood, then, why the mountain guns had come so quickly into action; they were gaining time for that exhausted colonial infantry to get round to some convenient spot and begin a separate attack. It was each one for himself.

Somehow I understood now that it was a useless time for ceremony, and that one must act just as one wished. So, finding some ponies tethered to a post below, without a word I mounted one and rode rapidly back to the palace. For an instant, as I passed the great Ch'ien Men Gate, I could see Indian troops filing out in their hundreds, and forcing a path through the press of incoming transport and guns. Evidently the British commanders considered that the thing was over; that it was no use going on. Already they had had enough of our Peking methods....

I must have ridden nearly a mile straight through the vast enclosures of the palace, past lines and lines of American infantry lying on the ground, with the reserve artillery trains halted under cover of high walls, before I saw ahead of me a set of gates which were still unbroken. General firing had quite ceased now, and excepting for an occasional shot coming from some distant corner, there was no sound. The bulk of the American infantry had not even been advanced as far as I had come. A skirmishing line, evidently formed only a short time before my arrival, was still lying on the ground; but the men were laughing and smoking, and the officers had withdrawn out of the heat of the sun into a side building, where they were examining a map. The scaling-ladders were left behind.

I was soon told that orders had come direct from headquarters to stop the attack absolutely, and not to advance an inch further on any consideration. The inner courts of the palace and the residences of the Emperor and the Empress Dowager could not be approached until concerted action had been taken up by all the Allies. I laughed—it was the hydra-headed diplomacy of Peking raising its head defiantly less than eighteen hours after the first soldiers had rushed in. . . .

The massive set of gates in front of me were those just without a most beautiful marble courtyard. That I knew from the rude Chinese maps of the Forbidden City which are everywhere sold; if this boundary were passed the Imperial Palaces, with all their treasures, would be reached. I thought, with my mouth watering a little, although I had no actual desire for riches, of General Montauban, created Comte de Palikao, because in the 1860 expedition, when the famous Summer Palace was so ruthlessly sacked, he had taken all the most splendid black pearls he could find and had carried them back to the Empress Eugénie as a little offering. If one could only get past this boundary and the protocol had not stepped in!

Moved a little by such thoughts, I advanced on the central gate, and peered through a chink near which an infantryman was standing alert, rifle in hand. There were the marble courtyards, the beautiful yellow decorated roofs. I could see them clearly, and then . . . a rifle from the other side was discharged almost in my ear; a bullet hissed past a few inches from my head, too; and I had a flitting vision of a

Chinese soldier in the sky-blue tunic of the Palace Guards darting back on the other side. There must still be numbers of soldiery waiting sullenly beyond for the expected advance; they would only fall back in rapid flight as our men rushed in, just as they had been doing from the beginning. I discharged my own revolver rather aimlessly through the chink in the hope that something would happen, but all became quiet again. Everything was finished here.

But although the advance down this grand approach to the inner halls and palaces had been stayed, nothing had been said about piercing through the great outer enclosures to the right and left; and, catching my pony, I rode round a corner where a broad avenue led to another set of entrances. Perhaps here would be something. All along I found a sprinkling of American infantrymen, in their sweaty and dust-covered khaki suits, lying down and fanning themselves with anything that came handy, and sending rude jests at one another. Old-fashioned Chinese *jingals*, gaudy banners, and even Manchu long-bows, were scattered on the ground in enormous confusion.

The Palace Guards belonging to the old Manchu levies had evidently been surprised here by the advance of the main body of American troops through the Dynastic Gate, and had fled panic-stricken, abandoning their antiquated arms and accoutrements as they ran. The soldiery who had been doing all the fighting and firing must have been the more modern field forces engaged in the last attacks on the Legations, or those driven in on Peking by the rout on the Tientsin road. Still, there was nothing worth seeing, and the miniature Tartar towers crowning the angles of the great pink walls looked down in contempt, as if conscious that no enemy could hurt them. I must push along.

I trotted quickly, exchanging chaff with the Americans, who called out to me with curious oaths that they had had no breakfast, and wanted to know why in h—— this fun was being stopped, and that they were being left there. Alas! I could give them no news. I only swore back in the same playful way. At the end of an immense wall I came on the last of this soldiery—a corporal's guard, squatting round a small wicket-gate and looking very tired. They told me that they were still being shot at from somewhere on the inside; and even as I paused and looked a curious *pot-pourri* of missiles grounded angrily against the gate-top. There were modern bullets, old iron shot, and two arrows—a strange assortment.

Somehow those quivering arrows, shot from over the immense

pink walls, and attempting to vent their old-fashioned wrath on the insolent invaders who had penetrated where never before an enemy's foot had trod, made us all stare and remain amazed. It seemed so curious and impossible—so out of date. Then one of the Americans ran into a guard-house, bringing out with him a huge Manchu bow, which he had secreted there as his plunder. He plucked with difficulty the arrows out of the woodwork in which they had been plunged, and with an immense twanging of catgut sent them high into the air, until they were suddenly lost to our sight in the far beyond.

An answer was not long in coming. In less than half a minute a crackle of firearms broke harshly on the air, and a fresh covey of bullets whistled high overhead. The enemy was plainly still on the alert inside the last enclosures, where no one might penetrate. What a pity it had been stopped....

I rode off, bearing away some flags and swords, and, making due east, as last reached some broad avenues near the Eastern Gates of this Forbidden City.... Fresh masses of moving men now appeared. The main body of French infantry I had seen a couple of hours before were being marched in here, while smaller bodies were tramping off to the north, and sappers were blowing down walls to clear their way. As I ambled along, seeking a way out, a couple of officers galloped up to me, and, touching their helmets, begged me in the name of goodness to tell them what was being done. What were the general orders, they wanted to know. I explained to them that nobody knew anything; that as far as I could see, the Americans had stopped attacking for good; that the Indian troops were already marching out into the Chinese city; and that nothing more was to be done, as the other columns had been completely lost touch with.

"*Toujours cette confusion, toujours pas d'ordres,*" the French officers angrily commented, and in a few words they told me rapidly how from the very start at Tientsin it had been like this, each column racing against the others, while they openly pretended to co-operate; with everyone jealous and discontented. Where were the Russians, the Italians, and the Germans? I answered that I had not the slightest idea, and that nobody knew, or appeared to care at all. I personally was going on; I had had enough of it....

To my surprise, as I turned to go, I found that the men of the *Infanterie Coloniale*, in their dirty-blue suits, had pushed up as close as possible to overhear what was being said, and now surrounded us. One private indeed boldly asked the officers whether they were going to be able to enter the palace at once; and when he got an angry negative, he and his comrades took to such cursing and swearing, that it seemed incredible that this was a disciplined army. The men wanted to know why they had been dragged forward like animals in this burning heat and stifling dust, day after day, until they could walk no longer, if they were to have no reward—if there was to be nothing to take in this cursed country. In the hot air the sullen complaints of these sweating men rang out brutally. They wanted to loot; to break through all locked doors and work their wills on everything. Otherwise, why had they been brought? These men knew the history of 1860.

I turned in disgust, and went slowly back the way I had come, only to find all unchanged. . . . Everything had obviously been stopped by explicit orders; there was no doubt about that now; diplomacy, afraid to allow anyone to enter the inner palaces for fear of what would follow, and how much one Power might triumph over another, had called an absolute halt. But no one was taking any chances, or placing too much confidence in the assurances of the dear Allies. That was plain! For, even as I had almost finished trotting up to the Dynastic Gate, I came on a large body of Italian sailors, who had evidently just entered Peking, and who, marching with the quick step of the *Bersaglieri*, were being led by C——, the lank Secretary of Legation, right up to the last line of gates.

They were in an enormous hurry, and looked about them with eager eyes. C—— and some others called out to me as I passed, and wanted to know whether it was true that the Americans and the French had already got in, and had sacked half the place, and whether fire had been set to the buildings. I answered with no compunction that it appeared to be so, and that the Russians and the Japanese had burst in also through the north, and had actually fired on the others coming from the south, thinking they were Manchu soldiery. . . . I told them that they were too late; that every point of importance had already been seized. That set them moving faster than ever. It was truly comical and ridiculous. Beyond this there were more troops of other nationalities that had just arrived, and were now looking about them in bewilderment. No wonder. With no orders and no maps, and surrounded by these immense ruins, and still more immense squares, they could not understand it at all. What confusion!

As I paused, debating what I should do, once again something else speedily attracted my attention. This time big groups of American soldiery, whom I had not observed before, were gathering like swarms of flies at the door of one of the Chinese guard-houses, which line the enclosing walls of the palace. They were evidently much excited by some discovery. Wishing to learn what it was, I dismounted and pushed in.

Grovelling on the ground lay an elderly Chinese, whose peculiar aspect and general demeanour made it clear what he was. He was a palace eunuch, left here by some strange luck. The man was in a paroxysm of fear, and, pointing into the guard-house behind him, he was beseeching the soldiery with words and gestures not to treat him as those inside had been handled. Through the open door I could see a confused mass of dead bodies—men who had been bayoneted to death in the early morning—and from a rafter hung a miserable wretch, who had destroyed himself in his agony to escape the terror of cold steel.

As the details became clear, the scene was hideous. Never, indeed, shall I forget that horrid little *vignette* of war—those dozens upon dozens of curious soldier faces framed in slouch hats only half understanding; the imploring eunuch on the ground, the huddled mass of slaughtered men swimming in their blood in the shadow behind; that thick smell of murder and sudden death rising and stinking in the hot air; and the last cruel note of that Chinese figure, with a shriek of agony and fear petrified on the features, swinging in long, loose clothes from the rafter above. In the bright sunlight and the sudden silence which had come over everything, there was a peculiar menace in all this which chilled one....

Perhaps the eunuch had divined from my different dress that he would be better understood by me than by these rough crowds of rank and file who crushed him in; for, as I gazed, he had thrown himself at my feet, with muttered words and a constant begging and imploring. I noticed then that the unfortunate man could not walk, could only drag himself like a beaten dog. The reason soon transpired: both his legs had been broken by some mad jump which he must have essayed in his agony to escape. I quieted the man's fears as best I could, and, tearing a sheet from a note-book, wrote a description of him, so that a field hospital would dress him.

Then, anxious to learn something concrete with this vapour of haziness and confusion blinding us all, I began questioning him quickly about the palace, the numbers of soldiery within, the strength of the inner enclosures, and the residences of the Emperor and the Empress Dowager. The man answered me willingly enough, but suddenly said it was all no use, that we were too late. The Emperor, the Empress Dowager, indeed, the whole Court, had disappeared—had fled, was gone....

Gone!

On my life, I could scarcely believe my ears. After all these weeks of confusion and plotting, had the Empress Dowager and her whole Court fled at the very last moment, and, by so doing, escaped all possibility of vengeance? Was it really so? One might have known that this loose-jointed relief expedition could accomplish nothing, would do everything wrong; and still we were acting as if everything was in our hands. Then, suddenly, I fined down my questions, and imperatively asked when the Court had fled; exactly at what hour and in what direction.

At first I could get no reliable answer, but, pushing my questions and assuming a threatening attitude, the shattered eunuch at length collapsed, and whiningly informed me that the flight had taken place at nine o'clock exactly the previous night, and had been carried out by way of the Northern Gates of the city. They had left five hours after the relief had come in! I calculated quickly. That meant twenty hours' start at four miles an hour—for they would travel frantically night and day—eighty miles! It was hopeless; they were safe through the first mountain-passes, and if they had soldiery with them, as was more than certain, these had most certainly been dropped at the formidable barriers which nature has interposed just forty miles beyond Peking. The mountain-passes would protect them. There could be no vengeance exacted; no retribution could overtake the real authors of this *débâcle*. Nothing. It was a strange end....

Disconsolately I turned and rode back into the Legation lines, feeling as if an immense misfortune had come. Here I met finally some Japanese cavalry and some *cossacks*. After being actually in Peking twenty-four hours, they had at length formed junction with their Legations. The cavalrymen were trotting up and down, and trying to discover their own people. Neither did they understand it all.

I communicated the news I had learned speedily enough to all people of importance whom I could find, told it to them all frantically; but it aroused no interest, even hardly any comment. Once or twice there was a start of surprise, and then the old attitude of indifference. A species of torpor seems to have come over everyone as a crushing anti-climax after the various climaxes of the terrible weeks. No one cares, excepting that the siege is finished. C——, of the British Legation, who has practically directed its policy for years (indeed, ever since it has been in the present hands), told me that when the British commander had come in, he had simply placed himself at the disposal of the Legation, and had said that his orders were concerned only with the relief. He was not to attempt anything else; to do nothing more, absolutely nothing. . . .

Later in the afternoon, at a Ministerial meeting, convened in haste, the ministers decided that as they did not know what was going to happen to them or what policy their governments proposed to adopt, in the absence of instructions they could take no steps about anything. Of course, everyone of importance will be transferred elsewhere, and probably be sent to South America, or the Balkan States, or possibly Athens. The confirmation of the news that the Empress Dowager and the Court had fled concerned them less than the dread possibilities which the field telegraphs bring. The wires have already been stretched into Peking, and messages would have to come through soon. . . .

That evening, as dusk fell, and I was idly watching some English sappers blowing an entrance from the canal street through the pink Palace walls, so that a private right of way into this precious area could be had right where the twin-cannon were fired at us for so many weeks, a sound of a rude French song being chanted made me turn round. I saw then that it was a soldier of the *Infanterie Coloniale* in his faded blue suit of *nankeen*, staggering along with his rifle slung across his back and a big gunny-sack on his shoulder. He approached, singing lustily in a drunken sort of way, and reeling more and more, until, as he tried to step over the ruins of a brick barricade, he at last tripped and fell heavily to the ground. The English sappers watched him curiously for a few moments as he lay moving drunkenly on the ground, unable to rise, but no one offered to help him, or even stepped forward, until one soldier, who had been looking fixedly at something on the ground, said suddenly to his mates in a hoarse whisper, "Silver! Silver!" He spoke in an extraordinary way.

I stepped forward at these words to see. It was true. The sack had been split open by the fall, and on the ground now scattered about lay big half-moons of silver-*sycee*, as it is called. The sappers took a cautious look around, saw that all was quiet and only myself there; and then the six of them, seized with the same idea, went quietly forward and plundered the fallen Frenchman of his loot as he lay. Each man stuffed as many of those lumps as he could carry into his shirt or tunic. Then they helped the fallen drunkard to his feet, handed him the fraction of his treasure which remained, and pushed him roughly away. The last I noticed of this curious scene was this marauder staggering into the night, and calling faintly at intervals, as he realised his loss, "*Sacrés voleurs! Sacrés voleurs anglais!*" Then I made off too. It was the first open looting I had seen. I shall always remember absolutely how curiously it impressed me. It seemed very strange.

2

The Sack

18th August, 1900.

After these events and the curious entry of our relieving troops, nothing came as a surprise to me. I can still remember as if it had only occurred ten seconds ago how, after witnessing those English sappers calmly strip that drunken French marauder of his gains, I came back into the broken Legation Street to find that a whole company of savage-looking Indian troops—*Baluchis* they were—had found their way in the dark into a compound filled with women-converts who had gone through the siege with us, and that these black soldiery were engaged, amidst cries and protests, in plucking from their victims' very heads any small silver hair-pins and ornaments which the women possessed. Trying to shield them as best she could was a lady missionary. She wielded at intervals a thick stick, and tried to beat the marauders away.

But these rough Indian soldiers, immense fellows, with great heads of hair which escaped beneath their turbans, merely laughed, and carelessly warding off this rain of impotent blows, went calmly on with their trifling plundering. Some also tried to caress the women and drag them away..... Then the lady missionary began to weep in a quiet and hopeless way, because she was really courageous and only entirely over-strung. At this a curious spasm of rage suddenly seized me, and taking out my revolver, I pushed it into one fellow's face, and told him in plain English, which he did not understand, that if he did not disgorge I would blow out his brains on the spot. I remember I pushed my short barrel right into his face, and held it there grimly, with my finger on the trigger. That at least he understood.

There was a moment of suspense, during which I had ample time to realise that I would be bayoneted and shot to pieces by the others if I carried out my threat. It was ugly; I did not like it. At the last moment, fortunately, my fellow relented, and throwing sullenly what he had taken to the ground, he shouldered his rifle and left the place. The others followed with mutterings and grumbles, and the women being now safe, began barricading the entrance of their house against other marauders. They were green-white with fear. They feared these Indian troops. . . .

That same night, very late, a transport corps, composed of Japanese coolies, in figured blue coats, belonging to some British regiment, came in hauling a multitude of little carts; and within a few minutes these men were offering for sale hundreds of rolls of splendid silks, which they had gathered on their way through the city. You could get them for nothing. Someone who had some gold in his pocket got an enormous mass for a hundred *francs*. The next day he was offered ten times the amount he had paid. In the dark he had purchased priceless fabrics from the Hangchow looms, which fetch anything in Europe. Great quantities of things were offered for sale after that as quickly as they could be dragged from haversacks and knapsacks. Everybody had things for sale.

We heard then that everything had been looted by the troops from the sea right up to Peking; that all the men had got badly out of hand in the Tientsin native city, which had been picked as clean as a bone; and that hundreds of terrible outrages had come to light. Every village on the line of march from Tientsin had been treated in the same way. Perhaps it was because there had been so little fighting that there had been so much looting.

The very next morning a decision was arrived at to send away all non-combatants in the Legation lines as quickly as possible from such scenes—to let them breathe an air uncontaminated by such ruin and devastation and rotting corpses—to escape from this cursed bondage of brick lines. There would be a caravan formed down to Tungchow, which is fifteen miles away, and then river transport. To provide conveyances for these fifteen miles of road, people would have to sally forth and help themselves; near the Legations there was absolutely nothing left. We must hustle for ourselves. . . . The same men who have done all the work would have to do this.

I shall never forget the renewed sense of freedom when I went out the next morning with my men and some others I picked up, this time boldly striking into the rich quarter in the eastern suburbs of the Tartar city and leaving the garrisoned area far behind. It was something to ride out without having to take cover at every turning....The first part of our route was the same as that of my scouting expedition made so few days before. But this time we went forward so quickly to the main streets beyond the white ruins of the Austrian Legation that it seemed incredible that we should have wasted so much time covering the ground before. That shows what danger means. I alone was mounted, riding the old pony I had commandeered the day before; my men were on foot and ran pantingly alongside. We were so keen!

For half a mile or so we met occasional detachments of European troops, an odd enough *pot-pourri* of armed men such as few people ever witness. They made a curious picture, did this soldiery in the deserted streets, for every detachment was loaded with pickings from Chinese houses, and some German mounted infantry, in addition to the great bundles strapped to their saddles, were driving in front of them a mixed herd of cattle, sheep and extra ponies which they had collected on the way.

The men were in excellent humour, and jested and cursed as they hastened along, and in a thick cloud of dust raised by all these hoofs they finally disappeared round a corner. It was only when they were gone that I realised how silent and deserted the streets had become. Not a soul afoot, not a door ajar, not a dog—nothing. It might have been a city of the dead. After all the roar of rifle and cannon which had dulled the hearing of one's ears for so many days there was something awesome, unearthly and disconcerting in this terrified silence. What had happened to all the inhabitants?

I had ridden forward slowly for a quarter of an hour or so, glancing keenly at the barred entrances which frowned on the great street, when suddenly I missed my men. My pony had carried me along the raised highway—the riding and driving road, which is separated from the sidewalks by huge open drains. My men had been across these drains, keeping close to the houses so that they could soon discover some sign of life. Then they had disappeared. That is all I could remember.

I rode back, rather alarmed and shouting lustily. My voice raised echoes in the deserted thoroughfare, which brought vague flickers of faces to unexpected chinks and cracks in the doors, telling me that this desert of a city was really inhabited by a race made panic-stricken prisoners in their own houses by the sudden entry of avenging European troops. There were really hosts of people watching and listening in fear, and ready to flee over back walls as soon as any danger became evident. That explained to me a great deal. I began to understand. Then suddenly, as I looked, there were several rifle shots, a scuffle and some shouting, and as I galloped back in a sweat of apprehension I saw one of my men emerge from the huge *porte-cochère* of a native inn mounted on a black mule.

My men were coolly at work. They were providing themselves with a necessary convenience for moving about freely over the immense distances. In the courtyard of the inn two dead men lay, one with his head half blown off, the second with a gaping wound in his chest. My remaining servants were harnessing mules to carts, and each, in addition, had a pony, ready saddled to receive him, tied to an iron ring in the wall. I angrily questioned them about the shots, and pointed to the ghastly remains on the ground; but they, nothing abashed, as angrily answered me, saying that the men had resisted and had to be killed. Then, as I was not satisfied, and continued muttering at them and fiercely threatening punishment, one of them went to the door of a gate-house, and flinging it back, bade me look in.

That was a sight! It was full of great masses of arms and all sorts of soldiers' and Boxers' clothing; and tied up in bundles of blue cloth were stacks of booty, consisting of furs and silks, all made ready to be carried away. This was evidently one of the many district headquarters which the Boxers had established everywhere. My men had known it, because these things become speedily known to natives. They had acted. After all, this was a vengeance which was overtaking everybody. What could I do?...

I said nothing then, and somewhat gloomily watched them proceed. With utmost coolness they finished harnessing the carts; drove them with curses to a point near the gate-house, and silently loaded all those bundles of booty into them, strapping the swords and rifles on in stacks behind. It was evidently to be a clean sweep, with nothing left. Then, when they had made everything ready, one of them disappeared for a short time into a back courtyard, and after some fresh scuffling, reappeared, driving in front of him three men in torn clothing and with dishevelled hair, who had been hiding all the while, and were trembling like aspen leaves now that they had been caught.

My men, without undue explanations, told them that they had to drive, one to each cart, and that if one tried to escape all would be shot down. With protestations, the captives swore that they would obey; only let them escape with their lives; they were innocent.... Then in a body we sallied forth, this time a fully-equipped and well-mounted body of marauders. It was a fate from which it was impossible to escape—my men had such decision left when every person in authority was already drifting. . . .

Fitted out in this wise, we now rattled along the streets with faster speed, and the clanking cart-wheels, awaking louder and louder echoes which sounded curiously indiscreet in these deserted streets, made heads bob from doorways and windows with greater and greater frequency. Down in the side alleys, now that we were a mile or two away from our lines, people might be even seen standing in frightened groups, as if debating what was going to happen; these melted silently away as soon as we were spied. But finding that they were disregarded, and that no rifles cracked off at them as they half expected, forthwith the groups formed again, and men even came out into the main street and followed us a little way, calling half-heartedly to the drivers to know if there was any news. . . . The terrible quiet which had spread over the city after the Allies had burst in from two or three quarters seemed indeed inexplicable; such troops as had passed had gone hurriedly westwards towards the palace. This quarter could scarcely have been touched. . . .

Our little cavalcade was clattering along midst these strange surroundings, when my attention was attracted by the similarity of the occupation which now appeared to be engaging numbers of people on the side streets. The occupation was plainly a doubtful one, since as soon as we were seen everyone fled indoors. All had been standing scraping away at the door-posts with any instruments which came handy; and one could hear this scratching and screeching distinctly in the distance as one approached. It was extraordinary. Determined to solve this new mystery, on an inspiration I suddenly drove my old pony full tilt up an alleyway before the rest of my men had come in view, and, dashing quickly forward, secured one old man before he could escape.

Once again I understood: all these people had been scraping off little diamond-shaped pieces of red paper pasted on their door-posts; and on these papers were written a number of characters, which proclaimed the adherence of all the inmates to the tenets of the Boxers. In their few weeks' reign, this Chinese *sans-culottism* had succeeded in imposing its will on all. Everyone was implicated; the whole city had been in their hands; it had been an enormous plot. . . .

Inside the house I had singled out, we found only old women and young boys—the rest had all fled. Spread on the ground were pieces of white cloth on which flags were being rudely fashioned—Japanese, English, French and some others. They were changing their colours, all these people, as fast as they could—that is what they were doing; and farther on, as we came to more remote quarters, we found these protecting insignia already flying boldly from every house. Everybody wished to be friends. But my men exhorted me to proceed quickly and to escape from these districts, which, they alleged, were still full of Boxers and disbanded soldiery; and yielding to their entreaties, we again dashed onwards quicker and quicker. For half an hour and more we had, indeed, lost sight of every friendly face.

The succession of streets we passed was endless. There were nothing but these deserted main thoroughfares, and the scuttling people on the side alleys, and in absolute silence we reached an immense street running due north and south. To my surprise, although everything was now quite quiet, dead Chinese soldiers lay around here in some numbers. There were both infantry and cavalry flung headlong on the ground as they had fled. One big fellow, carrying a banner, had been toppled over, pony and all, as he rode away, and now lay in picturesque confusion, half thrown down the steep slope of the raised driving road, with his tragedy painted clearly as a picture.

In the bright sunshine, with all absolutely quiet and peaceful around, it seemed impossible that these men should have met with a violent death such a short while ago amid a roar of sound. It was funny, curious, inexplicable. . . For my men, however, there were no such thoughts; they climbed off their ponies, and, whipping out knives or bayonets, they slit the *bandoliers* and pouches from every dead soldier and threw them into the carts. They had become in this short time good campaigners; you can never have too much ammunition.

The big Shantung recruit, whom I had come across so oddly only three days before, was now once again plainly excited and smelled quarry. I remembered, then, that there was nothing very strange in the decisive actions of all my followers; they were being led by this man and told exactly what to do. He had, after all, been outside all the time, and knew what had been going on and where now to strike hard! Quickly, without speaking a word, he pushed ahead, and arriving at the big gates of another inn, loudly called on someone inside to open. He could not have got any very satisfactory answer, for the next thing I saw was that he had sprung like lightning from his stolen pony, had thrown his rifle to the ground, and was attacking a latticed window with an old bayonet he had been carrying in his hand.

With half a dozen furious blows he sent the woodwork into splinters, and, springing up with a lithe, tiger-like jump, he clambered through the gap, big man as he was, with surprising agility. Then there was a dead silence for a few seconds and we waited in suspense. But presently oaths and protests came from far back and drew nearer and nearer, until I knew that the someone who had refused to answer had been duly secured. The gates themselves were finally flung open, and I saw that an oldish man of immense stature had been driven to do this work—a man who, so far from being afraid, was only held in check by a loaded revolver being kept steadily against his back. The Shantung man's face had become devilish with rage, and I could see that he was slowly working himself up into that Chinese frenzy which is such madness and bodes no good to anyone. I was at a loss to understand this scene.

Our captured carts were driven in and the gates securely shut; and then, driving his captive still in front of him, my man led us, with a rapidity which showed that he knew every inch of his ground, to a big building at the side. Then it was my turn to understand and to stare. Within the building a big altar had been clumsily made of wooden boards and draped with blood-red cloth; and lining the wall behind it was a row of hideously-painted wooden Buddhas. There were sticks of incense, too, with inscriptions written in the same manner as those we had seen being scraped so feverishly from the door-posts a few minutes ago. Red sashes and rusty swords lay on the ground also. Here there could be absolutely no mistake; it was a headquarters of that evil cult which had brought such ruin and destruction in its train. The Boxers had been in full force here.

The Shantung man, for reasons I could not yet unravel and did not care to learn, had become absolutely livid with rage now, and the others, who were all Catholics, shared his fury. They said that here converts had been tortured to death—killed by being slit into small pieces and then burned. Everybody knew it. With spasmodic gestures they called on the captive to fling to the ground the whole altar, to smash his idols into a thousand pieces, to destroy everything. But the man, resolute even in captivity, sullenly refused. Then, with a movement of uncontrollable rage, one man seized a long pole, and in a dozen blows had broken everything to atoms. Idols, red cloth, incense sticks, bowls of sacrificial rice and swords lay in a shapeless heap. And with ugly kicks my men ground the ruin into yet smaller pieces. Somehow it made me wince. It was a brutal sight; to treat gods, even if they be false, in this wise....

As I looked and wondered, scarcely daring to interfere, the Shantung man had pushed his face, after the native manner, close into that of his enemy and was muttering taunts at him, which were hissed like the fury of a snake in anger. This could not last—my man was carrying it too far. It was so. With a cry his victim suddenly closed on him, seized him insanely by the throat and hair, tried to tear him to the ground. I remember I had just a vision of those brown wrestling bodies half-bared by the fury of their clutches, and I could hear the quickly drawn pants which came at a supreme moment, when there was a sharp report, which sounded a little muffled, a piece of plaster flew out of the wall behind the two, and some biting smoke bit one's nostrils.

Before I realised what had been done, the giant Boxer was staggering back; then he tottered and fell on his knees, talking strangely to himself, with his voice sliding up and down as if it now refused control. Some blood welled up to his lips and trickled out; he shook a bit, and then he crashed finally down. There he lay among the ruins of his faith—dead, stone-dead, killed outright. The Shantung man stood over him with a smoking revolver in his hand. I remembered then that he had never taken his hand from the weapon. He had been waiting for this—it was an old score, properly paid....

I had had enough, however, of this mode of settling up under cover of my protection, and angrily I intimated that if there was any more shooting I should draw too, and pistol every man. I was proceeding to add to these remarks, and was even becoming eloquent as my righteous feelings welled up, when a thunder of blows suddenly resounded on the outer gates, and made me realise with a start that this was no place for abstract morality. Strayed so far from safety, we had taken our lives into our own hands; at any moment we might have to fight once more desperately against superior numbers. Perhaps in the end we would totter over in the same way as the unfortunate who had strayed across our path.... Indeed, it was no time for morality....

The thunder on the gates continued, and then with a crash they came open suddenly, and a party of French soldiers, with fixed bayonets and their uniforms in great disorder, rushed in on us. They did not see me at first, and, charging down on our captured carters, merely yelled violently to them, "*Rendez-vous! Rendez-vous!*" Before we could move or disclose ourselves, they had seized some of the carts and were making preparations to drive them off without a second's delay.

But then I made up my mind in a flash, too, and becoming desperate, I threw down the gauntlet. The contagion had caught me. Running at them with my drawn revolver, I, too, shouted, "*Rendez-vous! Rendez-vous!*" and with my men following me, we interposed ourselves between the marauders and their only line of retreat. There was no time for thinking or for explanations; somebody would have to give way or else there would be shooting. In a second, a fresh desperate situation had arisen.

The marauders, astonished at my sudden appearance and the manner in which their *razzia* had been interrupted, stood debating in loud voices what they should do, and calling me names. Twice they turned as if they would shoot me down; then one of them made up the minds of the others by declaring that their object was not to fight, but to pillage—these few carts did not matter. With lowering faces they speedily withdrew, cursing me with calm insolence as they reached the gates. Outside we saw that they had a number of other carts and mules, all loaded up with huge bundles; and reeling round these captured things were other drunken soldiers, whose disordered clothing and leering faces proclaimed that they had given themselves solely up to the wildest orgies. Today there would be no quarter....

We waited until the clamour of these men had died away in the distance, and then, with a strange double grin, the big Shantung man turned silently back into an inner courtyard, and pointed me out another building. I did not understand, for the very stables were empty and deserted here, as if everything had been already looted or carried away into safety. There appeared to be not a cart, not a piece of harness, not a stick of furniture, nothing left at all. The big Shantung man still grinned, however, and quickly made for the building he had pointed out.

The door was open, as if there was nothing to conceal, and only enormous bins made of bamboo matting half blocked the entrance. But with a few rough efforts my men sent these soon flying; then there was a mighty stamping and neighing of alarm, and as I looked in I laughed from sheer surprise. The house was full of ponies, mules, and even donkeys, which had been driven in and tethered together tightly behind barricades of tables and chairs. Now seeing us, they stood there all eyes and ears, and with prolonged whinnies and gruntings plainly welcomed this diversion. With glee we drove them out and counted them up—ten more animals!

It was with disgust, however, that I remembered that there was neither harness nor carts; but to my surprise, now that the animals had been discovered, my men were running busily around searching every likely hiding-place of the huge straggling courtyards. Like rats, they ran into every corner, turned over everything, pulled up loose floorings, and presently the body of a cart was found hidden in a loft in the most cunning way. But it was only the body of a cart; there were no wheels. And yet the wheels could not be far off.

Five more minutes' search had discovered them suspended down a well, under a bucket, which itself contained a mass of harness; and then in every impossible place we discovered the inn property cleverly stored away. In the end, we had all the animals hitched up, and the carts themselves full of fodder. Then, by employing the same tactics as before, just outside drivers were discovered and induced to follow us, and now, with a heavy caravan to protect against all comers, we sallied forth. This time we would have our work cut out.

An hour and more had elapsed since we had been on the open streets, and it being near midday, and everything still quiet, we were surprised to see people of the lower classes moving cautiously about on the main streets, but disappearing quickly at the mere sight of other people whose business they could not divine. That, too, was soon explained; for, seeing one rapscallion trying to run away with a sack over his back, we discharged a rifle at him. Straightway the man stopped running, fell on his knees, and whiningly said that he had been permitted to take what he was carrying by honourable foreign soldiery whom he had been allowed to assist. The bundle contained only silks and clothes; with a kick we let him go.

Plainly the plot was thickening on all sides, and it was becoming more and more dangerous to be abroad. Seized with a new thought, I stopped the whole caravan, and giving orders to that effect, we soon had every driver we had so summarily impressed securely strapped to his cart with heavy rope. At least, if we had to cut our way back I had secured that our carts could not be stampeded with ease. The drivers would make them go on; it would be easier to run forward than to turn back.

Then, as if we realised the danger of the road, we began driving frantically. We wished to carry the carts into safety. It was not long before we saw in the distance many groups of people clustering round a big building surrounded by high walls. That made me nervous, for the groups formed and dissolved continually, as if they were in doubt, and seeking to gain something which was bent on resisting. But no sooner had they seen this than my men began laughing coarsely, and exclaimed in the vernacular that it was a pawn-shop which the common people were trying to loot. Of course, it was certain that every pawn-shop would go sooner or later; but the sight of an actual attack in progress seemed strange while the populace was still so terror-stricken. To our further surprise, on coming up we found that a number of marauders and stragglers belonging to a variety of European corps had been halted by this sight; and as we drew nearer we found a private of the French *Infanterie Coloniale* groaning on the ground, with a ghastly wound in his leg.

No one was attending to him—they were too busy with their own business, and had we not tied him roughly with some cloth and rope, he might have lain there bleeding to death. We carried the man to the carts and decided we would take him to safety. But as we made preparations to start a warning shout in French bade us not to pass in front of the pawn-shop gates, and, looking up, I found that several other French soldiers, together with some Indians and Annamites, had climbed the roofs of adjacent houses, and with their rifles thrown out in front of them, were attempting to get a shot at people inside. The place was evidently securely held and refused to surrender. Grouped all round, and armed with choppers, bars of iron and long poles, the crowd of native rapscallions waited in a grim silence for the *dénouement*. It was an extraordinary scene. Everything and everyone was so silent. I decided to stop and see it through. Such things never happen twice in a lifetime.

A shot fired from the gate at an incautious man, who darted across the street, showed that the defenders were both vigilant and desperate, and knew what to expect at the hands of the foreign soldiery and the populace once they poured in. Spurred by this sound, the French soldiers on the roofs pushed down cautiously nearer and nearer to their prey; but presently, when I thought that they had almost won their way, a shower of bricks and heavy stones was sent at them by unseen hands with such savageness and skill that another man was placed *hors-de-combat,* and came down groaning with his head split. His, however, was only a scalp wound, and, discovering that a bandage left him practically none the worse, he took his place with savage curses at a corner just beyond the main gate, fixing his bayonet in grim preparation for the end. Decidedly there would be no quarter when that end came.

But there appeared to be, nevertheless, no means of bringing about the desired climax. The defenders showed their alertness by occasional shots that grated harshly on the still air, and the attack could make no progress. I wondered what would happen. Yet it did not last long, for Providence was at work. Two *cossacks* came cantering along the street, bearing some message from a Russian command; and although warning shouts were sent at them, too, as they approached, they paid no heed, but rode carelessly by.

As they came abreast of the main gate a sudden volley, which made their mounts swerve so badly that less adept horsemen would have been flung heavily to the ground, greeted them and sent them careering wildly for a few yards. But here were men who understood this kind of warfare. First, it is true, they were a little angry as they pulled up, unslung their carbines and shot home cartridges as if they would act like the rest.... But then, when they saw how things were, they grinned in some delight, and finally dismounting and driving their beasts with shouts off the road, they prepared to join the fray. With renewed interest I watched them go to work.

A little inspection showed the newcomers that the pawn-shop was too difficult to capture by direct assault unless special means were adopted, for such places being constructed with a view to resisting the attacks of robbers even in peaceful times, are nearly always little citadels in themselves. They are the people's banks. For some time the two new arrivals walked stealthily around, with their carbines in their hands, peering here and there, and trying to find a weak spot. Then one man said something to the other, and they disappeared into a neighbouring house, only to emerge almost immediately with some bundles of straw and some wood.

To their minds it was evidently the only thing to be done; they were going to set fire! Before there was time to protest, the *cossacks* had piled their fuel against an angle of the gate-house, just where they could not be shot at, and with a puff the whole thing was soon ablaze. The scattered groups of native rapscallions on the street, when they saw what had been done, gave a subdued howl of despair, and cried aloud that the whole block of buildings would catch fire, and that everything in them would be destroyed. These confident looters had already imagined that the pawn-shop was theirs to dispose of—after the honourable foreign soldiery had had their fill!

The *cossacks*, however, were men of many ideas, and paid not the slightest attention to all this tumult beyond striking two or three of the nearest men. They watched the blaze with cunning little eyes, and as the short flames shot across the gate, driven by the wind, and raised blinding clouds of smoke, one of them said it was all right and that we would be soon inside. On the roofs the French soldiers and their companions lay silently watching in amazement the antics of the two dismounted horsemen, and from the shouts and curses which now came from the pawn-shop compound itself, it was plain that this method of attack would be productive of some result. It was becoming more and more interesting.

My attention was distracted for an instant by seeing one of the *cossacks* climb up beside two French soldiers and explain to them gravely, with a violent pantomime of his hands, what they should do in a moment or two. When I turned, it was to find that the second had driven with boot-kicks and some swinging blows from his loaded carbine a number of the street people towards some of those long poles which can always be found stacked on the Peking main streets. My own men, understanding now what was to be done, ran forward, too, to help, and in the twinkling of an eye two long poles had been borne forward and laid in position across the highway. In spite of all modern progress, much the same ways of attack have still to be adopted in siege work.

Then, with some further pantomime explaining how it would be impossible to see or hurt them under cover of that smoke, the *cossacks* induced the crowd to raise the poles again. This time everybody's blood was up, and, urging one another on with short *staccato* shouts, dozens of willing men, stripped to the waist, jumped forward, and the timbers were driven with a tremendous impetus against the gates. As they crashed against the wood, and half splintered the stout entrances, a succession of shots rang out from the roofs, and I saw the French marauders sliding rapidly down and fall out of sight into the compound. The defence had been broken down—at least, at this point. It seemed quite over.

It was the work of a moment to hack the gates aside, and through the choking fumes and charred remains the whole infuriated crowd now poured. The little blaze, having met with much brick and stone, was smouldering out, and so long as it was not kindled anew there was no danger of the fire spreading.

Like a rush of muddy waters, the sweating, brown-backed men, now mad with a lust for pillage, tore through the first courtyard. I was born along with them perforce like a piece of flotsam on a raging flood-tide; there was no turning back. Besides, such things do not happen every day....

The Frenchmen and their companions had already disappeared

inside, and on the ground lay two of the pawn-shop men, dead or dying, swimming silently in their own blood. Beyond this there was a first hall, empty and devoid of furniture, excepting for immensely long wooden counters; and as I jumped through to the warehouses beyond, I saw dimly in the darkened room those dozens of city rapscallions whom we had unleashed hurl themselves on to the counters and literally tear them to pieces. They knew! Thousands of strings of cash were laid bare by this action, and with the quickness of lightning hundreds of furious hands tore and snatched, while hot voices smote the air in snarls and gasps. They wanted this money—would lose their lives for it. In an instant the pawn-shop hall had been turned into a sulphurous saturnalia horrid to witness. That gave you a grim idea of mob violence. I rushed to escape it. . . .

In the warehouses beyond I found the Frenchmen and the first *cossack*, who had directed the carrying of the place by assault, breaking open with rude jests chests and boxes, and flinging to the ground the contents of countless shelves. They cared nothing for the things they found; they were hunting for treasure. With curses as their disappointment deepened, and always hurling more and more shelves and cupboards to the ground, they soon reduced room after room to a confusion such as I have never before witnessed. Rich silks and costly furs, boxes of trinkets, embroideries, women's head-dresses, and hundreds of other things were flung to the ground and trampled underfoot into shapeless masses in a few moments, raising a choking dust which cut one's breathing. They wanted only treasure, these men, gold if possible, something which possessed an instant value for them—something whose very touch spelled fortune. Nothing else.

In some amazement I watched this frantic scene. From the outer courtyards came the same roar of excitement as the street crowd fought with one another for possession of all that wealth in cash; separated from one another by only a few yards, European marauders and Chinese vagabonds, I reflected, were acting in much the same way. I followed the Frenchmen and their companions into the last great rooms, all dust-laden and filled with boxes without number, which were carefully ticketed and stacked one upon another. Some were prized open with bayonets; some had their pigskin covers beaten through by butt-end blows; but whatever their treatment, there were always the same furs and silks. There was no treasure.

My men had now fought their way through the outer crowd, and rapidly flinging out coat after coat, suggested that sables were at least worth the taking and the keeping. They selected two or three score of these coats of precious skins, beautiful long Chinese robes reaching to the feet, and tumbling them into emptied trunks, we went out as soon as possible. We had had enough. The explanation of why the crowd had not rushed through was in front of us. The remaining *cossack* had seated himself, carbine in hand, on the stone ledge at the entrance to the inner courtyards and held everyone in check; just beyond hundreds and hundreds of men stripped to the waist, glistening in their sweat and trembling in their excitement, were waiting for the signal which would let them go. I noticed that now there were old women, too. The whole quarter was coming as fast as it could. . . .

The *cossack* grinned when he saw me appear, and looked with a shrug of his shoulders at the sables. To him these were not priceless. Then he explained his unconcerned attitude in a single gesture. He pushed a hand down into his rough riding boots and pulled out one of those Chinese gold bars which look for all the world like the conventional yellow finger-biscuits which one eats with ice-cream. The rascal had elsewhere come across some rich preserve and had his feet loaded with gold—for he pulled out other bars to show me—and he did not care for this petty pilfering.

Then the Frenchmen began coming out, with the Annamites and the Indians, each man with a bundle on his back, and the *cossack*, esteeming his watch ended, got up and stepped back. Once again, like bloodhounds, the crowd rushed in, an endless stream of men, women, and even children, all summoned by the news that the pawn-shop, which was their natural enemy, had fallen. They roared past us, striking and tearing at one another with insane gestures as if each one feared that he would be too late. Inside the scene must have baffled description, for a clamour soon rose which showed that it was a battle to the death to secure loot at any price.

Shrill cries and awful groans rose high above the storm of sound, as the *desperadoes* of the city, who were mixed with the more innocent common people, struck out with choppers and bar iron and mercilessly felled to the ground all who stood in their way. With conflicting feelings we struggled outside, and as I mounted my pony, a wretched man covered with blood rushed forward, and flinging himself at my feet, cried to me sobbingly to save him. He was the last of the pawn-shop defenders and was bleeding in a dozen places. Him, too, we roughly tied up and saved, and telling him to mount a cart and to lie concealed inside, at last we moved on again. We were gathering odd cargo.

The day was now waning, for the time had flown swiftly with such strange scenes, and people began to slink out from side alleys more and more frequently, as if they had been waiting for this dusk. Several times we passed bands of men armed with swords and knives—Boxers, without a doubt—who calmly watched us approach, as if they were debating whether they should attack us or not. Once, too, a roll of musketry suddenly rang out sharp and clear but a few hundred feet away from the high road, only to be succeeded by an icy silence—more speaking than any sound. We did not dare to stray away to inquire what it might be; the high road was our only safety. Even that was doubtful. Curious isolated encounters were taking place all over the vast city of Peking; it was now everyone for himself, and not even the devil taking care of the hindmost. It was no place for innocents.

At last, by vigorous riding and driving, which caused a great clatter and drew forth many leering faces from darkened doorways, we debouched into that long main street down which I had shot so few days before in such an agony of doubt. Hurrying homeward in the same direction, we now met bands of our siege converts in groups of forty and fifty strong. These men, who had come so near to starving during the siege, were having their own revenge. They had sallied forth with such arms as they could lay their hands on, and had been plundering all day within easy reach of the Legations. They had done what they could, and had gathered every manner of thing in which they stood most in need.

Each man had immense bundles tied to his back—it was the revenge for all they had suffered. They had given no quarter either, and before many more hours had gone by they would have made up for those long weeks.... We soon left these groups behind, and with the whole cavalcade now going at a hand-gallop, it dawned on our companions and beasts which we had so curiously gathered during the day that we were nearing our destination.

But here the roadway was absolutely deserted, and in the dusk I realised that had we been farther from home we would almost certainly be ambuscaded by some of the many ruffians Boxerism had unloosed on the city. Here was a sort of neutral belt. At every turning I half expected a volley to greet us; at every door-creak I thought there would be some rush of armed men which would have been impossible for us to meet without losing half the convoy. Yet these fancies were not justified, for to my immense surprise, at a cross-road I saw numbers of women in their curious Manchu head-dress standing at a big gateway, all dressed in their best clothes.

As we passed they caught sight of me, and, nothing abashed, began immediately calling to me and waving with their arms. This was extraordinary and unlocked for. At first I thought that they were only courtesans, who had been deprived for so long of all custom that they had been rendered desperate, and were seeking to inveigle me *faute de mieux*; but remembering that such women are confined to the outer city, I reined in my mount, halted the whole caravan, and went slowly towards them, half fearing, I confess, some ruse. Yet the women greeted me with fresh cries and words. There were a full dozen of them of the best class, and they explained to me that they had been left, absolutely abandoned, two nights before by all the men of the household, who, fearing the worst and hearing that the way out through the north of the city was still open, had seized all the draft and riding animals and ridden rapidly away, saying that the women would be spared by the foreign soldiery, but that probably every man of rank would be killed.

No one had molested them so far, because this house lay so close to the foreign troops, but with so many armed men on the streets, and with the pillaging and the murder that was going on, they did not know how long they would be spared. They told me this quickly in gasps. I paused in doubt to know what to answer; it was everyone for himself, and the devil not even looking after the hindmost, as I have just said. But women. . . . I must propose something.

They saw my hesitation, and women-like, renewed their pleading in chorus. I noticed, also, that two or three of the older ones grouped themselves close together, and, putting down their heads, began rapidly discussing in loud whispers, which showed their trepidation. Then they called a tall, splendidly built woman, and, telling her something in an undertone, pushed her forward towards me. Unabashed, she advanced on me with a firm step, and laying a white-skinned hand—for the Manchus can be very white—on my arm, she begged me to stop here myself—to make this my house for the time being—to do as I pleased with all of them. . . . After all those weeks of privation, that constant rifle-fire, that stench of earth-soiled men, this woman so close seemed strange. . . . I answered, in greater confusion, that I could not yet say whether it was possible for me to stay so far away; that there might be trouble; that I would see and let them know before the night was far advanced. . . .

Not wholly satisfied and half doubting, they let me draw off with their pleadings renewed. Then, as I thought something might happen before I could let them know, I gave them two rifles from the store we had collected, and telling them to bar and bolt their gate, showed them how a shot or two would probably drive off an attack. We clattered on and lost them in the gloom....

It was almost dark as we re-entered the ruined Legation lines and picked our way slowly though the *débris* which still stood stacked on the streets. Fatigue parties of many corps were finishing their work of attempting to restore some order and cleanliness, and clouds of murky dust hung heavily in the air. All round these narrow streets there was an atmosphere of exhaustion and disorder, crushed on top of one another, which oppressed one so much after the open streets, that an immense nostalgia suddenly swept over me. We had had too much of it; I was tired and weary of it all. It was mean and miserable after the great anti-climax. It was like coming back to a soiled dungeon.

We picked our way right through where two days before no vehicles could have passed, and I stabled all the animals and carts, and handed them over to where they were needed. Then I ordered that our captured things, our weapons, and my few last belongings should be loaded into one remaining cart, and ordering my men to follow, without a word of explanation I started off again. I had made up my mind.

We passed rapidly enough out and again sped in the blackening night down the long street just as we had returned. Almost too soon we reached that great gate on the corner to find it barred and bolted. Somehow my heart sank within me at this; was it too late?

But there were cries and a confusion of voices. Somebody peered through. Then there was delight. The gate was unbarred by weak women's hands, and the soft Manchu voice which had first begged me to stop was speaking to me again....

Inside I found the courtyards and the lines of rooms which fronted each square were immense and furnished with richly carved woodwork; it was a rich house, and there was a profusion of everything which could be wanted—only no men! We securely bolted and barred the main gate, and for safety loopholed a little, because that is an art in which we had become adepts. Then, with candles murkily shedding their light, I explored every nook and corner to guard against surprise, always with that soft voice explaining to me. It was very quiet and soft with that atmosphere around; it was like a narcotic when a roar of fever still hangs in one's ears. I became more and more content. After all, we had become abnormals; a shade more or less could make no difference.... That night was a pleasant dream....

3

The Sack Continues

August, 1900.

To rediscover the ease and luxury of lying down, not brute-like, but man-like, seemed to me an immense thing. I had had my first night's sleep on a bed for nearly three months, and I wished never to rise again. I wished to be immensely lazy for a long period—not to have to move or think or act. But that could not be. All sorts of marauders were sweeping the city and working their wills in a hundred different ways. Half a dozen times, as soon as daylight had come, shots had been fired through my gateway. European soldiery, who had broken away from their corps, and native vagabonds and disguised Boxers, who had hidden panic-stricken during the first hours after the relief, were now prowling about armed from head to foot. The vast city, which had been given over for weeks to mad disorders and insane Boxerism, was in a receptive condition for this final climax. There was no semblance of authority left; with troops of many rival nationalities always pouring in, and a nominal state of war still existing, with the possibility of a Chinese counter-advance taking place, how could there be?... There was nothing left to restrain anybody....

I thought of these things lying at my ease, and debated how long I could stay in that unconcerned attitude. It was not long. For as I lay, there was a thunder of blows somewhere near, and then a crackle of shots, whose echoes smote so clean that I knew that firearms were pointed in the direction of this house. I jumped up without delay. I was not a minute too soon, for as I seized my rifle, one of my men ran in and shouted to me that foreign cavalrymen had burst in, shooting in the air, and were now driving out all the animals and looting all the carts as well. Nothing could be done unless I lent my leadership.

Hastily I ran out, feeding a cartridge into my rifle-chamber as I rushed. This time I was determined to give a lesson and pay back in the same coin. The marauders were *cossacks* again.

There were only four of them, however, and when they caught sight of me they tried to stampede my mob and bolt ingloriously with them. But we were too quick. I gave the first man's mount my first cartridge in a fast shot, which took the animal well behind the shoulder and brought the rider instantly down in a heap to the ground. That mixed them up so that before they could extricate themselves they were all covered with our rifles and the gates tight shut. Then we calmly dragged the men off their ponies and kept them in suspense for many minutes, debating aloud what to do.

Finally we let them go after some harsh threatening. The man who had lost his mount, nothing abashed, swung himself coolly up behind a comrade, with his saddle and bridle on his arm, without a comment. And as soon as they were in the open street they galloped fast away, as if they feared we would shoot them down from behind. That showed what was going on elsewhere. . . .

I knew now what to expect unless we made very ready, for surely a sharp revenge attack would come as soon as it was dark. So grimly we set to work, with a return of-our old fighting feelings, and rapidly fortified the main gate against all cavalry raids. We dug a broad moat behind the gate, and threw up a respectable barricade with the earth we had gained. Then we brought some timbers and built them in on top with the aid of bricks and stones, so as to have a line of loopholes converging on the entrance. We trained some of the many rifles we had picked up in the same direction, and strapped them into position, just as the Chinese commands had done all along their barricades during the siege. In this way we made it so that in a few seconds a dozen of the enemy could be brought to the ground without the defending force showing a finger. That would be enough for any *cossacks*. . . .

Before midday we had added a couple of lookout posts to the roofs, and then, secure in this new-found strength, I determined to go abroad once more to collect supplies and food. That decision was materially helped by an incident which showed that everyone was acting and that it was the only way. As we cautiously opened our main gate and prepared to sally out, a cart came by, accompanied by several men from the Legations on horseback, who were much excited. Well might they be; they had two of their number inside that cart, both shot and bleeding badly from flesh wounds. They had been right to the east of the city, they reported, where the Russians and Japanese had come in.

It was terrible there, they said. Nothing but dead people and fires and looting. Chinese soldiers had still remained there in hiding and were defending some of the bigger buildings belonging to Manchu princes. Plunderers, also, were everywhere on the road. They advised caution and told us not to trust ourselves in the alleyways. They had been caught like that, and their servants and horse-boys had deserted in a body four miles away immediately fire was opened on them from some fortified house. That made me all the more determined. I would go and be shot, too, if necessary, since it was the order of the day, but I made up my mind that it would be no easy job to catch me sleeping. Already I understood fully the new methods and the new requirements.

We rode away, stirrup to stirrup, I, a single white man, with a dozen doubtful adherents, made savage at the idea of loot, as companions, and held to me only by a questionable community of interests. Yet what did it matter, I thought. One lives only once and dies only once. That is elemental truth. So *tant pis*.

In our joy at being on those open streets again, with never a passer-by or a vehicle to obstruct one's rapid passage, we went ahead in a whirlwind of dust. We passed street after street with always the same silence about us we had noticed the day before. Everything was closed, tight shut; there was not a cat or a dog stirring abroad. Near the Legations and the Palace, where the fear lay the heaviest, it seemed like a city of the dead.

Yet we knew that there were plenty of living men only biding their time and waiting their opportunity. It was only night that these people desired; a good black night so that no one could see them flit about. You felt in the small of your back as you rode along that ugly faces were looking at you from the silent houses, and that at any moment shots might ring out suddenly and bear you to the ground. But that was merely a preliminary feeling. Soon it added zest to the entertainment. What, indeed, did it matter? It only made one more and more reckless.

We sped swiftly along, only twice seeing men of any sort in several miles of streets. Once they were fellows who, on our approach, scuttled so quickly away to hide their identity that we could not be sure whether they were white or yellow. But once, without concealment, a band of mixed European soldiery, in terrible disorder, who first wished to fire on us, and then when they saw me set up a colourless sort of cheer, appeared suddenly, only to disappear. We never paused an instant; we kept straight on.

As we made our way farther and farther to the east and came across rich districts of barricaded shops, signs were clear that pillaging had gone on here already with insane violence, but by whom or at what time it was impossible to say. Sometimes there were battered-in doors and windows, with ugly, swollen corpses stretched nearby; sometimes the contents of a rich emporium had been swept, as if by some strange whirlwind, out on the street to litter the whole driving road many inches deep with the most heterogeneous things. On the ground, too, were dozens of the rude imitation flags which had been so frantically made by the terror-stricken populace in order to disclaim all association with Boxerism and the mad Imperialism being now so summarily swept away. Jeering looters had torn these things down and cast them in the dirt to show, as a reply, that there was to be no quarter if they could help it.

These grim notes limned speakingly on everything, made it plain that a movement was in the air which could hardly be arrested. It made one feel a little insane and intoxicated to see it all; and as one's blood rushed through one's veins, after that long captivity, one had, too, the desire to add a little more destruction, to break down places and to shoot for the amusement of the thing. You could not help it; it was in the air, I say. It was a subtle poison which could not be analysed, but which kept on coursing through one's veins and heating the blood to fever-pitch. The vast open streets needed filling up with noise and rapid movements, one thought; the inhabitants must be galvanised to life again, one felt. . . .

My men needed every kind of wearing apparel, for they had been in rags all through the siege, and as soon as possible they showed that they appreciated the situation, and did not intend to stand on ceremony. They set to work as soon as they saw what they wanted. A huge Chinese boot, gaudily painted on a swinging sign-board, proclaimed a boot-shop, where in ordinary times they could buy every kind of foot-covering. But now it was no good attempting such methods. So they tilted straight at the shop-door without hesitation, and beating a wild *rataplan* of blows on the wooden shutters, demanded an entry in a roar of voices. Otherwise they would shoot, they added. In very few seconds, at this clamour, some shuffling steps were heard and trembling hands unbarred in haste, fearing a worse fate.

We then saw two blanched and trembling shopkeepers, whose

dirtied clothes and dishevelled hair showed that they had had days and nights of the most wretched existence. Shakingly they asked what we wanted, adding that they had not a piece of silver or yet a string of cash left. The Boxers had taken everything weeks before; now honourable foreign soldiery were beating them because they were so poor. My men did not trouble to answer; they went to work. They wanted boots and shoes, and plenty of them, since there were plenty to take, and so they searched and picked and chose.

But presently one man gave vent to an oath, and them, in his surprise, laughed coarsely. He had discovered that there were only boots and shoes for the left foot. There was nothing for the right foot, not a single boot, not a single shoe! Once again they did not trouble to speak, but merely pushing fire-pieces against the luckless shopkeepers' heads waited in silence. Immediately the men broke down anew and began whining more explanations. It was true there were no right feet, they said. The right feet were over there in a neighbour's shop. That shop had all the right feet; they had only left feet.

This seemed strange humour. Yet it was a good, if crude, device which these cunning shopkeepers had hit on even in their distress. For they knew that looters would probably not waste time attempting to match shoes in such confusion, when so much better things were lying near. They hoped at least to save their stock by this device; and it seemed certain that they would. I said not a word; this was a family affair.

In the end a bargain was struck; two pairs of shoes for each man, and the rest to be left untouched. Then the right feet appeared soon enough from hidden places, and the shopmen were saved from further loss. With all the other things the same procedure was adopted along this shopman's street. A bargain was struck in each case, which saved one side from undue loss and gave the other far less trouble. In this new fashion we captured chickens, eggs, sheep, rice, flour, and a dozen other necessaries, only taking a quarter of what we would have seized otherwise, in return for the help given. It was curious shopping, but everybody was curious now. What you did not take, somebody would seize ten minutes later.

These occupations were so peaceful and gave so little difficulty, that it soon seemed to me as if everything was actually settling down quietly in this one corner of the city. Yet it was not so. We were only having momentary luck. For presently soldiers of various nationalities began passing in many directions, some returning from successful forays, and others just starting out to see what they could pick up. And on top of them all came a curious young fellow from one of the Legations, galloping along on a big white horse he must have just looted. He was accompanied by no one. He had been half-mad for weeks during the siege and now seemed quite crazy as he rode.

It was he who had again and again volunteered to play the part of executioner to all the wretched coolies engaged in sapping under our lines who had been captured from time to time, and whose heads had at once paid the last penalty. This man had done it always with a shotgun, and he had seemed to gloat over it; and in the end people had taken a detestation for him, and looked upon him for some strange reason as a little unclean. Now he was madly excited, and as soon as he saw me he called out, in his thick Brussels accent, and made a long broken speech, which I shall never forget.

"Have you seen them?" he said, not pausing for a reply. "It is the sight of all others—the best of all. Hsü Tung, you remember, the Imperial Tutor, who wished to make covers for his sedan chair with our hides, and who was allowed to escape when we had him tight? Well, he is swinging high now from his own rafters, he and his whole household—wives, children, concubines, attendants, everyone. There are sixteen of them in all—sixteen, all swinging from ropes tied on with their own hands, and with the chairs on which they stood kicked from under them. That they did in their death struggles. Everywhere they have acted in the same way. They call it hanging, but it is not that; it is really slow strangulation, which lasts for many minutes, because at the last moment the victims become afraid and try to regain their footholds."

The man paused a minute and licked his dry lips. To me there was something hideous in this story being told on that sacked street. His voice sounded a little like those Chinese trumpets, whose gurgling notes make one think instantly of evil things. Then he went on, more furiously than ever:

"And the wells near the Eastern Gates, have you seen them, where all the women and girls have been jumping in? They are full of women and young girls—quite full, because they were afraid of the troops, especially of the black troops. The black troops become insane, the people say, when they see women. So the women killed themselves wherever they heard the guns. Now they are hauling up the dead bodies so that the wells will not be poisoned. I have seen them take six and seven bodies from the same well, all clinging together, and the men have tried to kill me because I looked. But I was well mounted; I could look as long as I liked, and then gallop away so fast that not even their shots could catch me. The place is full of dead people, nothing but dead people everywhere, and more are dying every minute."

Then he came up to me and whispered how soldiers were behaving after they had outraged women. It was impossible to listen. He said that our own inhuman soldiery had invited him to stay and see. Yet although I swore at the man and told him to go away, I could not drive him from me. He wanted to talk and he had found someone who had to listen. Indeed, he clung to me all the way home, as if he had been at length frightened by his own stories and by his imagination. Steadily he became more and more curious. He watched me eat, he watched me drink, but he would take nothing himself. He wanted to go out again. He must have movement, he said, and he insisted on riding to Monseigneur F——'s Pei-t'ang Cathedral. He had not been there yet, and a curiosity suddenly seized him to see the place where others had suffered in the same way as ourselves.

That reminded me, too, that everybody had almost forgotten about this Roman Catholic cathedral, forgotten completely because they were now at their ease. It had been two whole days before troops were even sent there to see that all was well, and even these only went because a priest had been killed half way between the Legations and the Cathedral. I decided to go, too. It was almost a duty to make this pilgrimage. So we quickly left again.

For a few minutes after leaving the occupied area we threaded streets with men from the relief columns in full view, but soon enough we found ourselves in treacherous roadways, all littered with the ruins and the inexpressible confusion which come of desultory street-fighting spread over long weeks. To me this was a new quarter—one which I had not been near since the month of May, and soon it was equally clear that it was still a very evil place. Only yesterday men who had broken away from the French corps were found here, some dead and some horribly mutilated. Yet in spite of this the same signs of mock friendliness greeted our eyes on every side—those fluttering little flags of all nations, so rudely made from whatever cloth had been handy.

Every building displayed some flag—every single one; but there now were other signs, too—signs which showed that all this quarter had been picked so clean that it was of no more value to marauders. Little notices, some in French, some in English, and a few in other tongues, were scratched on the walls or written on dirty scraps of paper and nailed up. Half in jest and half in earnest, these curious notices said all manner of things. For the wretched people who had been plundered or otherwise ill used had already fallen into the habit of asking from the soldiery for some scrap of writing which would prove that they had contributed their quota, and might, therefore, be exempted from further looting. Scrawled in soldiers' hands were such things as, "*Défense absolue de piller; nous autres avons tout pris*"; or, "No looting permitted. This show is cleaned out." Everywhere these signs were to be seen. Here they must have worked fast and furiously....

Riding quickly, at last we reached the famous cathedral, with great trenches and earthworks surrounding it, and the torn and battered buildings showing how bitter the struggle had been. To our siege-taught eyes a single look explained the nature of the defence, and the lines which had been naturally formed. It was written as plain as on a map. The priests and their allies had now hauled the enemy's abandoned guns to the cathedral entrances and the spires were now crowned with garlands of flags of all nations.

But that was all. There was no one to be seen. Everybody was away, out minding the new business—that of making good the damage done by levying contributions on the city at large. It was all dead quiet, silent like some deserted graveyard. The sailors and the priests and their converts, remembering that Heaven helps those who help themselves, had sallied out and were reprovisioning themselves and making good their losses. Indeed, the only men we could find were some converts engaged in stacking up silver shoes, or *sycee*, in a secluded quadrangle. These had become the property of the mission by the divine right of capture; there seemed at the moment nothing strange about it.

This silent cathedral, with its vast grounds and its deserted quadrangles torn up by the savage conflict, became to us curiously oppressive—almost ghostlike in the bright sunshine. It seemed absurd to imagine that forty or fifty rifle-armed sailors, a band of priests and many thousands of converts had been ringed in here by fire and smoke for weeks, and had lost dozens and hundreds at a time through mine explosions. It seemed, also, equally absurd that the twenty or thirty thousand men who had poured into Peking had already become so quickly lost in the expanses of the city. Where were they all?...

My mad companion had tired, too, of looking, and wanted again to rush off and discover some signs of life. He wanted, above all, to see the place where the first companies of the French infantry had suddenly come on a mixed crowd of Boxers, soldiers and townspeople fleeing in panic all mixed together, and had mown them down with *mitrailleuses*. There was a *cul-de-sac*, which was horrible, it was reported. The machine-guns had played for ten or fifteen minutes in that death-trap without stopping a second until nothing had moved. The incident was only a day or two old, yet everyone had heard of it. People exclaimed that this was going too far in the matter of vengeance. But everything had been allowed to go too far. . . .

We rode out at a canter, and wondered more and more as we rode at the solitude, where so few hours before there had been such a deafening roar. We plunged straight into the maze of narrow streets, and then suddenly, before we were aware of it, our mounts were swerving and snorting in mad terror! For corpses dotted the ground in ugly blotches, the corpses of men who had met death in a dozen different ways. Lying in exhausted attitudes, they covered the roadway as if they had been merely *tired to death*. It was awful, and I began to have a terrible detestation for these Asiatic faces, which, because they are dead, become such a hideous green-yellow-white, and whose bodies seem to shrivel to nothing in their limp blue suitings. Such dead are an insult to the living.

We picked our way on our trembling mounts, trying vainly to push through quickly to escape it all. But it was no good. We had stumbled by chance on the actual route taken by an avenging column, and the men who had been mad with lust to loot the Palace, and had been turned off almost as an afterthought to relieve co-religionists, had vented their wrath on everything. The farther and farther we penetrated the more hideous did the ruins and the corpses become. There was nothing but silence once again—death, ruin, and silence; and at last we came on such a mountain of corpses that our ponies suddenly stampeded and went madly careering away. Frightened more and more by the sound of their galloping hoofs, the animals soon laid their legs to the ground and bolted blindly. Vainly we tugged at our bridles; vainly we tried every device to bring them to a halt. But again it was no good. It had become a sort of mad gallop of death; the animals had to be allowed to rid themselves of their feelings.

Eventually we pulled up far away to the west of where we had started. We were now near the districts which had only the day before been proclaimed highly dangerous to everyone until clearing operations had swept them clean of lurking Boxers or disbanded soldiery. But now attracted by a roar of flames, and indifferent to any dangers which might lurk nearby, we followed up the trail of smoke hanging on the skies to see what was taking place. One's interest never ceased, yet it was only the same thing. French soldiers, some drunk and some merely savage, had found their way here by some strange fate, and being quite-alone had evidently looted and then set fire to a big pile of buildings. They were discharging their rifles, too; for as we approached, bullets whistled overhead, and sobbing townspeople, driven from their hiding-places, began rushing away in every direction. This was strange.

Our arrival was only the signal for a fresh discharge of rifles, and then there was no doubt who was attracting the fire. The men were deliberately aiming at us to drive us away! We halted behind cover, and then with the same callousness as they displayed, we gave them a volley back, as a note of warning. It was my insane companion who drove us to do that; but, forthwith, on the sound of that well-knit discharge, there was more firing on every side, some shots coming from houses quite close to us and some from the open streets. With the growing roar and crackle of the flames these shots made very insignificant popping and attracted but little attention.

Yet I soon saw that this continuous firing could not come from the rifles of European soldiery, unless there were whole companies of them, and that perhaps we had been mistaken for other people. And soon my suspicions were confirmed by a confused shouting in the vernacular, and a rush of men from lanes not a hundred yards away. Then there were some half-suppressed blasts on the hideous Chinese trumpet and—Chinese soldiery.....

They came out with a mad rush and charged straight at the drunken French marauders, firing quickly as they ran after the old manner which we knew so well. As we gazed, the men from the relief columns fell back in disorder without any hesitation—indeed, fled madly to the nearest houses and began pelting their assailants with lead in return. Suppressed trumpet-blasts came again, rallying the attackers; more and more men rushed out from all sorts of places, and as this was no affair of ours, and our retreat would certainly be cut off if we dallied, we retreated at full gallop farther and farther to the west. We were going straight away to where might be our damnation.

I do not remember clearly how far we rode, or why we galloped, but soon we arrived almost at the flanking city walls miles away, and found ourselves among scores and hundreds of the enemy, who were still lurking on the streets, half disguised and mixed with the townspeople. They fired at us as we rode; they fired at us when we stopped;

for many minutes there was nothing to be heard but the hissing of lead and fierce yells. . . .

Conscious that only a big effort would pull us through, we boldly turned bridle and galloped to the south—reached a city gate, went through at a frantic pace, and sought safety in the outer Chinese town. Here it was quieter for a time, but as once more we approached the central streets, down which the Allies had marched, we came across other marauders. This time they were Indian troops going about in bands, with only their side arms with them, but leaving the same destruction behind them. Then we came across Americans, again some French, then some Germans, until it became an endless procession of looting men—conquerors and conquered mixed and indifferent. . . .

It was eight at night before I pulled up on my foundered mount at home. I confess I had had enough. We were dead with fatigue. This was too much after one had those weeks of siege.

4
Chaos

August, 1900.

The refugee columns have gone at last, and have got down safely to the boats at Tungchow, which is fifteen miles away, and in direct water communication with Tientsin. It is good that nearly all the women and children and the sick have been packed off. This is, indeed, no place for them. An Indian regiment sent a band, which played the endless columns of carts, sedan chairs, and stretchers out along the sands under the Tartar Wall, until they were well on their way. That made everyone break down a little and realise what it has been. They say it was like India during the Mutiny, and that it was impossible for anyone to have a dry eye. Even the native troops, rich in traditions and stories of such times, understood the curious significance of it all. They talked a great deal and told their officers that it was the same.

Thus, winding away over the sands and through the dust, the only *raison d'être* of this great relief expedition has passed away. Probably a conviction of this is why the situation in Peking itself shows no signs of improving. Some say that it has become rather worse, in a subtle, secret way. More troops have marched in, masses of German troops and French infantry of the line, and columns of Russians are already moving out, bound for places no one can ascertain. Nothing but moving men on the great roads.

It is the newly arrived who cause the most trouble. Furious to find that those who came with the first columns have all feathered their nests and satisfied every desire, they are trying to make up for lost time by stripping even the meanest streets of the valueless things which remain. They say, too, now, that punitive expeditions are to be organised and pushed all over North China, because these new troops, which have come from so far, must be given something to do, and cannot be allowed to settle down in mere idleness until something turns up, which will alter the present irresolution and confusion....

But for the time being there is little else but quiet looting. Even some of the Ministers have made little fortunes from so-called official seizures, and there is one curious case, which nobody quite understands, of forty thousand *taels* in silver shoes being suddenly deposited in the French Legation, and as suddenly spirited away by someone else to another Legation, while no one dares openly to say who are the culprits, although their names are known. Silver, however, is a drug in the market. Everybody, without exception, has piles of it.

Also, the Japanese, who are supposed to be on their good conduct, have despoiled the whole Board of Revenue and taken over a million pounds sterling in bullion. They have been most cunning. The only currency to be had is the silver shoe. These shoes can be bought at an enormous discount for gold in any form, and even with silver dollars you can make a pretty profit. The new troops, who have arrived too late, are doing their best to find some more of this silver by digging up gardens and breaking down houses. Marchese P——, of the Italians, who always pretends that he has been a mining engineer in some prehistoric period of his existence, calls it "working over the tailings."

In consequence of this glut of silver and curiosities, a regular buying and selling has set up, and all our armies are becoming armies of traders. There are official auctions now being organised, where you will be able to buy legally, and after the approved methods, every kind of loot. The best things, however, are being disposed of privately, for it is the rank and file who have managed to secure the really priceless things. I heard today that an amateur who came up with one of the columns bought from an American soldier the Grand Cross of the Prussian Order of the Black Eagle, set in magnificent diamonds, for the sum of twenty dollars. It seems only the other day that Prince Henry was here for the special purpose of donating this mark of the personal esteem of the *Kaiser* after the Kiaochow affair. Twenty dollars—it is an inglorious end!

The native troops from India, seeing all these strange scenes around them, and quickly contaminated by the force of bad example, are most curious to watch. When they are off duty they now select a good corner along the beaten tracks where people can travel in safety, squat down on their heels, spread a piece of cloth, and display thereon all the lumps of silver, porcelain bowls, vases and other things which they have managed to capture. You can sometimes see whole rows of them thus engaged. The Chinese Mohammedans, of whom there are in normal times many thousands in Peking, have found that they can venture forth in safety in all the districts occupied by Indian troops once they put on turbans to show that they are followers of Islam; and now they may be seen in bands every day, with white and blue cloths swathed round their heads in imitation of those they see on the heads of their fellow-religionists, going to fraternise with all the Mussulmans of the Indian Army.

It is these Chinese Mohammedans who now largely serve as intermediaries between the population and the occupation troops. They are buying back immense quantities of the silver and silks in exchange for foodstuffs and other things. A number of streets are now safe as long as it is light, and along these people are beginning to move with more and more freedom. But as soon as it is dark the uproar begins again. The Chinese have had time now, however, to hide all the valuables that have been left them. Everything is being buried as quickly as possible in deep holes, and search parties now go out armed with spades and picks, and try to purchase informers by promising a goodly share of all finds made. It is really an extraordinary condition. . . .

5

Settling Down

End of August, 1900.

It shows how little is still generally known of what is going on in our very midst, and low disordered things really are, when I say that I only learned today that the whole city—in fact, every part of it—has been duly divided up some time ago by the Allied commanders into districts—one district being assigned to every Power of importance that has brought up troops. They are trying to organise military patrols and a system of police to stop the looting, which shows no signs of abating. Everybody is crazy now to get more loot. Every new man says that he only wants a few trifles, but as soon as he has a few he must, of course, have more, and thus the ball continues rolling indefinitely. . . . Nothing will stop it.

Yesterday, just as a man of the British Legation was telling me that the system was really all right, that it was, in fact, a working system which would soon be productive of results, and that the bad part was over, a huge Russian convoy debouched into the street where we were standing. It was a curious mixture of green-painted Russian army-waggons and captured Chinese country carts, and every vehicle was loaded to its maximum capacity with loot. The convoy had come in from the direction of the Summer Palace, and was accompanied by such a small escort of infantrymen that I should not have cared to insure them against counter-attacks on the road from any marauders who might have seen them in a quiet spot. A dozen mounted men of resolution could have cut them up.

The carts lumbered along, however, indifferent to every danger, in their careless disorder. Their drivers were half asleep, and things kept on dropping to the ground and being smashed to atoms. Just near us the ropes stretched round one cart became loosened by the rocking and bumping occasioned by the vile road, and the contents, no longer held in place, began spilling to the ground. As soon as he had seen this, the Russian soldier-driver became furious. He would have had to do a lot of work to repack his load properly, so he soon thought of a shorter and easier way: he began deliberately throwing overboard his overload!

Three beautiful porcelain vases of enormous size and priceless value suffered this fate; then some bulky pieces of jade carved in the form of curious animals. C—— tried to stop the man, but I only smiled grimly. What did it matter? In Prince Tüan's palace I had seen, a couple of days before, the incredible sight of thousands of pieces of porcelain and baskets full of wonderful *objets de vertu* smashed into ten thousand atoms by the soldiery who had first forced their way there. They only wanted bullion. Porcelain painted in all the colours of the rainbow, and worth anything on the European markets—what did that mean to them!

The convoy at last bumped away, leaving merely a long trail of dust behind it and those fragments on the ground, and C—— became silent and then left me suddenly. Perhaps the idea had finally entered his respectable British head that we had become grotesque and out of date, and that we should retreat and make room for other men. Nobody cares for anybody else. Only a few hours before a reliable story had been going the rounds that some Indian infantry had opened fire on a Russian detachment in the country just beyond the Chinese city, pleading that it was a mistake. How could it have been? There is only one really sensible thing to do, and now it is too late to do that; to set fire to the whole city and then retreat, as Napoleon did from Moscow. The road to the sea is too short and the winter too far off for any harm to come.

The first cables have at length come through in batches from Europe, by way of the field telegraphs, which are now working smoothly and well. Everybody of importance is being transferred, but it is impossible to find out where they are all going. All the ministers now pretend that they had asked for transfers before the siege actually began, and that they will be heartily glad to go away and forget that such a horrible place as Peking exists. Yet from the nervousness of those who have been told to report for orders in Europe, it cannot be all joy.

6

The Forbidden Fruit

August, 1900.

Fortunately my friend K——, of the Russian Legation, rescued me at a moment when I was prepared only to moralise on this infernal situation, and to see nothing but evil in everything both around me and in myself. I like to put it all down to the strange stupor and lack of energy which have settled down on everything like a blight, but I believe, also, that there must be a little bit of remorse at the bottom of my feelings. K—— came in gaily enough, pretending that he was looking for a breakfast and had learned of my retreat by mere chance as he rode by. He had heard, I believe, as a matter of fact, that there were a number of women on the premises, and that I was living *en prince*. Perhaps, he had a number of reasons for coming.

From what he told me, however, it soon appeared that he had known L——, the commander of the Russian columns, for many years, and had just done business with him; and that, in consequence, the Russian commander, who is a pleasant old fellow, risen from the ranks, had said that he could have a private view of the Palace if he swore on his honour that he would not divulge the excursion to anyone. He must, also, not take anything. He did not tell me all at first. It came out bit by bit, after I had been sounded on a number of points. Then he asked me if I would like to come, and if I, too, would swear.

Of course, I duly swore!

Eventually we started on our long ride; for it was necessary for us to go right round the Imperial city, skirting the pink walls so as not to become involved in other people's territory, or to be noticed too much. That was one of the preliminary precautions, K—— said. All the way round, that ride was a beautiful illustration of the way the International Concert (written with capital letters) is now working. At absolutely every entrance into the Imperial city there were troops of one nationality or another: American, British, French, German, Japanese, and others—all looking jealously at every passer-by, and holding so tight to their precious gates, that it appeared as if all the world was conspiring to wrest them from their grasp.

They thought, perhaps, that this palace is the magic wand which touches all China and can produce any results; that both in the immediate and dim future the obtaining of a good foothold here will mean an immense amount to their respective countries. What fatuous, immense foolishness! For a moment, as I looked at these guards, I had the insane desire to charge suddenly forward and call upon the French, in the name of their dear Ally, Czar Nicholas, to hand me their gate, or else take the consequences; to do the same to the others; to mix them up and confuse them; to tell them that a new war had been declared; that they would soon have to fight for their lives against formidable foes—to tell them mad things and to add to the rumours which already fill the air.

These troops, which had been hurled on Peking in frantic haste, had only come because it was a matter of jealousy—that was now clear to me. They themselves did not know why they had come, or with whom they were fighting, or why they were fighting. They knew nothing and cared less. And yet it does not much matter. It is not really they who are to blame, nor even their officers. I know full well how instructions are issued and how little the pawns really count.... The despatches from the Chancelleries of Europe, how grotesque they can be! Everybody is always so afraid of everybody else.

Yet while I was thinking these things, K—— was not. He was secretly worried, as he rode, whether L——'s promise would materialise, or whether there would be another *impasse*. Somehow I felt certain that there would be more difficulties, in spite of all assurances. *Ce n'est pas pour rien qu'on connaît les Russes*, as C——, our old *doyen*, always says. . . .

We passed at length into the Imperial city by the northern entrances, far away from everybody else, and found ourselves in the midst of a big Russian encampment, with rows upon rows of guns ranged in regular formation and lots of tents and horses. All the soldiery here were taking it very easy on this sunny day; had, indeed, stripped themselves, and were now engaged in sluicing themselves over with ice-cold water from a beautiful marble-enclosed canal. These hundreds upon hundreds of clean white men, with their flaxen hair and their blue eyes, seemed so strange and out of place in this semi-barbaric palace and so indifferent. How curious it was to think that only a few days ago the Empress and all her *cortège* had passed here!

We sought out the post commander and told him our purpose. The difficulties began quickly enough then, as I had anticipated. The officer explained to us that our request was out of order and impossible; that no one was allowed inside the inner precincts or had ever been there; and hinted, incidentally, that we must be mad. K—— listened to all this in that insulting silence which is a sure sign of gentility, and then, ransacking his pockets, brought out a letter and handed it to our man. That produced a change which might have been highly amusing at other times. There was the complete *volte-face* which amuses. The officer suddenly saluted, clicked his heels, and said in a silky way, like a cat which has tasted milk, that this order was explicit and made things different; that, indeed, we might go at once if we liked, only we must be discreet—highly discreet. He would accompany us himself. Such trivial details were soon arranged.

We left our ponies and our outriders then and marched forward quickly on foot. The soldiery around us stared and laughed among themselves as soon as they saw where we were going. This made me understand that this excursion had been taken before, probably under the same orders and in exactly the same way. It was only a well-rehearsed comedy. K——, who is really a bit of a coward, did not appear to relish the comments made, and now became suddenly reluctant. He told me afterwards that he had overheard the men saying that we might be killed inside, as there were many people there. So in silence we all marched on.

The first gate we reached was a beautiful example of the art of this Northern country. There were splendid pillars of teak, marble tigers and marble fretwork beneath, with much glittering colouring around. A strong post of Russian infantry was on guard here, and sitting inside the enclosure with the men off duty were a number of palace eunuchs. They all seemed quite intimate together and were chaffing one another—soldiers and eunuchs laughing heartily at some coarse jest.

We wended our way through a marble courtyard, which wore a rather deserted and forlorn look, and which had huge low-lying halls and dwellings for the palace servants ranged on either side. These appeared to be all deserted now, but at regular intervals were Russian sentries standing up on lookout platforms. They were peering over the walls in every direction, and seemed to be keeping a very sharp lookout. The officer said that many guards of other nationalities were well within rifle-shot from here, and that men were continually trying to steal their way right into the inner palace by scaling the walls. He called them robbers!

The next gate was much smaller, and showed from its very appearance that we were nearing the actual palaces—the hidden, mysterious abodes of the Tartar rulers who had so ignominiously fled. Here the sentries had the strictest orders, for, stopping us short with their lowered bayonet points, they looked askance at us, and politely asked the officer who we were and why we had ventured here. In the end, to set their minds at ease, he had to tear a leaf from his pocket-book, write an order, and make us sign our names. Upon this, the non-commissioned officer in charge of this post detached himself and joined our little party. We were not going to be allowed in alone, and imperceptibly the affair assumed a graver and more consequential aspect. Then, quietly advancing, we four were speedily lost in the huge maze of gardens and buildings. The area covered by the palaces was enormous.

Beyond this was a succession of high, picturesque-looking buildings of a curious Persian-Tartar appearance, with little galleries running round them, and drum-shaped gateways of stone pierced in unexpected places. There were also flowering trees and beautiful groves. It was, indeed, charming, and over everything there was a refined coolness which to me was something very new. We came on a last sentry, who, at a word from his sergeant, drew a heavy iron key from a wooden box hanging on the wall and fitted it to a lock. The key turned with a faint screeching, which seemed out of place; the little gate was thrust open and closed behind us, and . . . at last we were within the *sacro-sanct* courtyards of the rulers of the most antique Empire in the world. . . .

Around us there was now a curious and unnatural quiet, as if the world was very old here, and the noises of modern life remained abashed at the thresholds. I knew well from a study of the curious old Chinese maps, which the vendors of Peking *objets d'art* always offer you, where we were, and it was almost with a sense of familiarity that I turned and made my way to the east. There I knew in ordinary times the Empress Dowager herself lodged in a whole Palace to herself. Somewhere not very far from us I caught the soft cooing of the doves, which everyone in Peking, from Emperor to shopkeepers, delights to keep, in order to send sailing aloft on balmy days with a low-singing whistle attached to their wings—a whistle which makes music in the air and calls the other birds. Who has not heard that pleasant sound? Even the Empress Dowager must have loved it. Here, in her private realm, the doves were cooing, cooing, cooing, just like the French word *roucoulement*, spoken strongly with the accent of Marseilles. You could hear these birds of the Marseilles accent saying continually that French word: *Roucoulement, roucoulement, roucoulement*, with never a break....

We ran up some flights of marble steps, following these gentle sounds, and walked along a broad terrace adorned with fantastically curved dwarf-trees, set in rich porcelain pots, and made stately with enormous bronze braziers. The Russian officer, and even the Russian sergeant, were agreeably stroked by the contact with all this quiet and seclusion and this old-world air, and they murmured in sibilant Russian. It pleased them immensely.

We hastened to the end of the terrace, going quickly, because we were anxious to find more delights; and as we turned at the end, without any warning there were a few light screams and a little scuffle of feet which died away rapidly. Women ....

We caught a disappearing vision of brilliantly coloured silks and satins and rouged faces passing away through some doors, and then before we had satisfied our eyes, several flabby-faced men suddenly came out and called imperatively to us to stop and go away. We could not go farther, they said.

The two men of the Russian army, with the instinct of discipline which we lacked, halted as if orders were being disobeyed, and looked at K—— for inspiration. K—— stroked his thin moustaches, and put his head a little on one side, as if he were debating what to say. I—well since I had nothing to lose, and it did not really matter, I went forward without any delay, asking our interlocutors roughly what they meant and what they were doing here, and telling them, too, that we were going on. I knew that they were sexless eunuchs, who would stammer as I had heard them stammer in the old days when I had seen them trafficking things they had been donated by officials desirous of cultivating their friendship, in the mysterious curio shops beyond the great Ch'ien Men Gate. Nor was I wrong. Stammering, they replied by asking how it was that orders had been broken. Stammering, they said that all the great generals had promised that the inner palaces were to be kept immune; now men were forever climbing in, and others were coming openly as we were doing. What did we wish?

I am afraid I was rude, for questions in these times do not sit well on such folk, and I told them more roughly than ever to go quickly away, or else we would hurt them. Perhaps we would even hurt them badly I insinuated, fingering my revolver, for we had a duty to do. We were going to inspect the entire palace and see that all was well. And before these men had recovered from their surprise we had pushed right into the Empress Dowager's own ante-chambers.

I saw, as I walked in, that a long avenue in the distance led directly to a high yellow-walled enclosure. That must be the Imperial *seraglio*, where the hundreds of young Manchu women provided by tradition for the amusement of the Emperor were imprisoned for life. In the haste of the Court's flight, the majority of them had been abandoned, and only the most valuable taken off. Everybody had heard of that.

Gently discoursing to the disturbed eunuchs, we went through room after room, which even on the hot autumn day seemed cool and peaceful. The *objects de vertu* which littered the small tables, and the scrolls which hung from the walls, did little to relieve the sombre effect of those high ceilings and carved wood *frescoes*. Yet there was a little air of distinction and refinement which showed that an immeasurable gulf separated the favoured dwellers of this palace from even the greatest outside. Even here Royalty does more than oblige; it compels. . . .

With the eunuchs protesting more and more vigorously, and seeking to stay our advance by a curious mixture of suggestion and imploring and resistance which is a quality of the East, we slowly passed through apartment after apartment. Some now were furnished with luxurious long divans which eloquently invited graceful repose. What scenes had not this silent furniture witnessed, and how little could the makers have supposed, as they cunningly carved and stained and coloured, that barbarians from Europe would be one day insolently gazing on their handiwork!. . .

I had lagged somewhat behind, when some curses and imprecations dragged my wandering attention to the doors beyond. Two eunuchs had fallen on their knees and were now *kowtowing* and begging with renewed vigour, while a third was standing more resolutely than his fellows with outstretched arms, imperatively forbidding any further advance. The most interesting point had been reached; this must be the greatest thing of all.

But these eunuchs were beginning to fatigue us with their airs of duly authorised custodians who could do as they pleased, and going up, we now told them that unless they went quickly away we would kill them then and there. We all drew our revolvers, stood over them, and waited a minute of two. Then, as if they had acted their parts right up to the end, the men on their knees got up suddenly, shook themselves, bowed to us politely without a trace of feeling, and left. . . . "*Enfin,*" said K——.

At last we were in this dear Empress's bedroom, the abode which shelters for such a considerable number of hours of every twenty-four the most powerful woman in Asia. We looked eagerly. At one side of the room was a large bed, beautifully adorned with embroidered hangings; ranged round there was a profusion of handsome carved-wood furniture, with European chairs upholstered in a style out of keeping with the rest; on a high stand there were jewelled clocks noisily ticking; and hidden modestly in one corner was nothing less than a magnificent silver *pot de chambre*. She was here evidently very much at her ease, the dear old lady. That little detail delighted me. The rest was rather *banal*.

Sans cérémonie, I seated myself on the Imperial bed—it seemed to be the most peaceful act of vandalism I could commit in repayment for certain discomforts occasioned by this old lady's whims during eight weeks of rifle-fire. And as my recollections went back to those terrible days, I came down heavily as I could on this august couch. I must confess that as a bed it was excellent; the old lady must have slept well through it all, while she caused us our ceaseless vigil. . . .

This solitude in the most secluded of spots in the whole Palace made us more and more inquisitive, and soon K—— and myself were hard at work, rummaging every likely hiding-place.

Our escort watched our antics and said nothing. It made an odd enough little scene that, and I liked to think of its incongruity—we two sets of men, who had not known of each other's existence an hour ago, now absolutely alone in this retreat, from whence the siege had been largely directed.

K—— continued rummaging, making an extraordinary amount of noise, and exclaiming to himself now and again as he came across trifles which interested him. Then I discovered a *compote*, or preserve made of rose-leaves, which was so sweet and fragrant that we began promptly eating. There were also Russian cigarettes, *au bonheur des dames*, yet quite fit to smoke, and then just as we were becoming reasonably content, K—— gave a tremendous oath and brought out something in his hand. Then I knew that he was lost—that there would be speedy complications; it was a Louis XV. painted watch—his greatest weakness.

Peking is full of these watches, some genuine enough and many spurious. They were made the vogue centuries ago by the clever Jesuit priests, when the first disciples of Loyola to come to China were playing for kingly stakes in the capital of Cathay, and were not ashamed to use any means which the ingenuity might discover to delight the Manchu rulers of that day. Many of the most beautiful watches in France, with amorous paintings of the most voluptuous kind decorating the inside case, were brought to Peking and distributed among the high and mighty. That set up a fashion for such pretty things; more and more were brought, until Peking became a storehouse, stocked with this specialty. Everyone even today has an example or two of this art, if they can afford it.

I thought of these things as I saw K—— trifle with that watch and scrutinise it more and more closely. He looked at it for a last time longingly, and then, without a word, suddenly placed it in his pocket. That was cool. But at once the Russian officer started forward protesting; we were breaking our words; we had begun looting; he would be forced to arrest us. As he spoke, the man became so red and excited, that K——, who pretended at first merely to smile indulgently, became more and more alarmed, and finally replaced the watch without a word.

But still he continued this curious search, and coming across other things, I noticed vaguely that he seemed to be placing them all together in little collections, so that he could easily get at them again. . . .

Then we wandered away to other great buildings, and we came on a beautiful set of princely rooms, full of ticking clocks and rich tapestries, and with such things as solid gold *bonbonnières*, studded with coarse, uncut stones, lying on the *secrétaires* and small tables. These, I believe, were the Emperor's apartments in normal times. There were lots of beautiful things here—vases, enamels, jade, *cloisonne*, and much wondrous porcelain; and although everyone had been saying that Peking was not as rich as in 1860, when those strings of beautiful black pearls had been brought home for the Empress Eugénie, still it was clear that these palaces contained a wealth undreamed of outside. Indeed, there were magnificent things. . . .

Round the corners, as we walked, we saw the eunuchs looking and lurking, and finally disappearing whenever they thought that they were seen. There were more of them now, too, and, seeing us quite alone, they were beginning to pluck up courage and wished once more to interfere. I thought for an instant as I looked at their evil faces of tearing down some rich embroidery and fashioning from it a sack just as I had seen those Indian troopers do so few days before; then of setting to work and piling everything I fancied into it and making as if I intended to go off.

Yet such a comedy would not be worth the candle; the officer and the sergeant would have to go through the formality of arresting me, and the eunuchs would not even be noticed....

Engrossed with such thoughts, and no longer amused by my surroundings, I must have forgotten myself for a moment in a brown study; for when I came to, I was surprised to find that we four had drifted some distance apart, and that K—— was now whispering rapidly to the Russian officer alone, and that the sergeant was standing far away, with his back turned to them, slyly fingering the things on the tables. Then the sergeant allowed his hand to linger longer than was necessary, and, throwing a sharp look round out of the corners of his eyes, he suddenly thrust some object into his pocket. He, too, had succumbed! I paid not the slightest attention to these curious developments, but pretended to be gazing idly at nothing. Still, I kept my eyes on the alert. K—— was manifestly plotting for those watches; it was not my business—what did it matter to me if he took everything there was?

The officer, whatever the arguments, was obviously not yet very convinced, nor very happy. He shook his head vigorously again and again, and protested in that thick Russian undertone, which always seems to me to explain what Russians really are. Yet those thick tones were becoming gradually monotonous and less emphatic, and presently slower and slower, until they stopped altogether. Then K—— came towards me, and said carelessly that he supposed I wanted to wander around a little more on my own account to see what else there was. It was an invitation to disappear. Very well! I moved off suddenly and sent the eunuchs scurrying back. There was a wish to split up the party for a few minutes so that no one would know what the others were doing. I knew I should immensely annoy the eunuchs by going towards the women's quarters. Well, I would not cavil....

I walked rapidly enough then down that back avenue I had observed before, and looked neither behind me nor to the right or left. I would go straight through to the end, *Dieu voulant*! It would be interesting to have the unique experience of exploring the poor Emperor's most private domains. But then I remembered that the women had screamed and run away when they had caught sight of us in the beginning. Now they would be securely locked in, and it was absurd and dangerous to think of storming a gate by one's self. Farther and farther I walked away until I became doubtful. . . .

I suddenly became aware that I was in front of a small door; that the door was ajar; and that an amused talking and moving was going on very near with many ripples of laughter rising clearly in the still air. It seemed that the fates were helping me for some inscrutable purpose. I must discover that purpose. Without a quiver I boldly walked in.

I came on them without any sense of emotion, although nothing could have been so novel—a number of groups of young Manchu women, some clothed in beautiful robes, some in an undress which was hardly maidenly. They were sitting and standing scattered round a large courtyard, and hidden somewhere above them in the yellow tiled roofs were more of those cooing doves with that strong accent of Marseilles: "*Roucoulement, roucoulement, roucoulement,*" they said very gently this time, yet without ever ceasing. Their soft voices made beautiful music. . . . For some reason none of the harem were surprised. Two or three of the younger women ran back a step or two, and clasped the hands of the others with broken ejaculations.

Then they all sought my eyes, and somehow we began smiling at one another. All women are the same; these knew somehow that I would not hurt them. Yet in spite of this fact I stood there embarrassed, knowing not what to say or do. I had supposed myself inured by now to all the most impossible situations—yet it seemed so absurd that I should be here, alone, absolutely alone, among dozens of young women who were the Emperor's most inviolate property—virgins selected from among the highest and most comely in the land; forbidden fruit, which had not even been tasted because of the Emperor's lack of masculinity. . . . I thought rapidly of the various classes into which these women are divided according to immemorial custom: of the concubines of the first rank, of the second, of the third, and even of the fourth, who are merely favoured hand-maidens of the Biblical type.

Then I wondered whether it was true that when the former Emperor Hsien Feng had suddenly died, and the Empress Dowager had selected the child Kuang-shü to succeed him, she had caused the child to be mutilated, so that the question of the next heir should remain in her own hands. . . . The women would know.

And yet even Imperial concubines must have opportunities which no one suspects, for I was suddenly relieved of the necessity of breaking the ice by their breaking it for me. Without embarrassment they suddenly began plying me with questions, and not waiting for replies, they asked what was going on outside; what was going to happen; who was I; why had I come; why was I not a soldier? . . . The questions came so fast and thick that before I had realised it I had forgotten my surroundings, forgotten the time, forgotten most things, I am afraid, and was deep in the middle of an astonishing conversation, which never flagged and which was continually broken with laughter. Then I was brought to ominously. I heard a door shut with a thump; I saw the women pinch and look at one another and cease talking. What did that door mean?

On purpose I did not turn round; that would have been fatal. I did as I always do now: I gained time to lessen the shock. Some day, when I have much leisure, I shall, doubtless, prepare tables specially adapted to every situation and to every temperament, which will show exactly the number of seconds, minutes, and hours which are necessary on an average to accustom one's self to anything. It is possible to do so; it will be astonishing when it is done. For the time being, I thought of this rather glumly—indeed, without a trace of enthusiasm—and I wished a little that I had not been so foolish in putting my head inside the lion's mouth.

I remembered the story a former Secretary of the British Legation used to tell us of two Englishmen, who, in the unregenerate days in Cairo—or was it Constantinople?—climbed into the harem, and were cruelly mutilated for their audacity before they could be rescued. I became so glum as this flashed through my mind, that my great system of preparation was in imminent danger of breaking down. So I turned suddenly round on my heel, and looked squarely . . . it was as I had thought.

The door I had entered had been quietly locked, and now, inside, were standing, with moving lips and menacing air, those evil-looking eunuchs. This time there were four of them. Two were the two who had knelt and prayed that we should not enter the Empress Dowager's private apartments; one was the man who had stood up and been almost threatening; the last one was so tall that his aspect of strength almost gave the lie to the assumption that he had been mutilated for Palace use. These last two would be difficult; the others I could leave out of my calculations.

Faithful to my theory, and trusting to this strange ally, I merely opened my revolver-pocket; then it was with a sense that I was irretrievably lost that I saw that two of the opponents were armed in the same way. My theories and preparations were all falling to the ground. I would probably follow them in person in a very few minutes. Nobody would be the wiser. . . .

I stood there waiting while these men muttered at me, as if they now hated me bitterly, and yet did not know how to commence, and with the women behind me chattering affrighted. In vain I tried to work out how many eunuchs there really were in this vast palace; whether a great number had gone away with the Court, or whether these four men would summon four more, or perhaps fourteen, and possibly even forty or four hundred. They always say the palace contains three thousand. . . .

It was all no good, however, for it was my turn to play, and without I played we might remain standing there in this manner until it became dark. Then I could be beaten to the ground and thrown down a well without any one being the wiser. No search could be made for me, and if one was made, nothing would be found. Men were continually missing in Peking, and no one knew how they met their fate. . . .

I advanced now with my hands empty and my mind fairly made up. Everything depended on a new theory, which I was about to test, a mere Chinese theory concerning eunuchs—that their mutilation makes them bestial, but also downtrodden and quite spiritless and peculiarly weak. That is why the old Empress could thrash them to death whenever they displeased her, without their daring to raise their hands or make one single struggle. Now, as I walked forward, I could see my old Chinese teacher, who had taught me these strange theories concerning eunuchs, sitting in front of me and slowly waving his fan, and showing by an analysis of things I did not clearly understand, how Nature had laws and decrees which cannot be violated without bringing heavy and immediate punishment in their train. As I walked forward I could not help seeing that old figure of a Chinese teacher in front of me, and prayed that he was correct. If he was not . . . . then I stopped thinking and acted.

I did it neatly, with some brutality, because I had been absolutely surprised, and had not yet recovered, and, also, because I was more than a little afraid. Six paces off I threw myself in two savage bounds against the tall man; caught him with my right hand by the outstretched right arm, hurled him round once by the force of my own impetus and the strength of my grasp; and then, as he swiftly swung with loosened legs, stopped him suddenly short with a mighty up-driven blow of my right knee, which sang so deep and cruelly into his soft flesh, that it grated harshly against his spinal column. Nobody can resist that blow—according to the old man's theory, least of all a eunuch—nobody, nobody. It should be certain as death, once you have the right grip. With a gurgle my man had sunk to the ground a mere shapeless mass, perhaps really dead; and with by breath coming hot through my nostrils at this success I closed fiercely with the second, seized him by the throat, wrenched at him like a madman, and carried him staggering back. The other trick demands the six paces and the impetus; I would have liked to have tried it again, but I had not dared. . . .

But it was finished with dramatic suddenness, for even as I ran the second eunuch, gasping for breath, backwards, the other two rushed to the door, opened it hurriedly, and then stepped aside with loud implorings and supplications. I accepted. I let go my grasp and quickly jumped out. I, too, had had enough. As I went through I caught a last glimpse of that curious scene framed by the red gate-posts and the roofs beyond—the senseless eunuch on the ground, the other standing nearby, coughing and reaching at his throat, the women of the *seraglio* in their gaily flowered coats pressing curiously round. . . . But I had enough. I did not tarry. Rapidly I walked away, with a little prayer in my heart. I felt almost as I had felt once when I was nearly drowning.

I found K——, five minutes later, sitting on the first marble terrace, with his pockets bulging out and an expression of ox-like satisfaction on his face. That was an antidote which speedily sobered me. The officer was farther on, and had also looted by his looks. The sergeant of the guard—well, I knew about him already. K—— smiled when I appeared, and said that I had been very quick and that he did not expect me so soon. I did not take the trouble to answer; explanations are always apologies. If I had told him the truth, he would never have believed me, and certainly never have understood. And if I had lied there would have been the same result. So I merely said I was ready, and that we had seen enough; and then, in silence, each man thinking of what he had done, we covered the way back very quickly and mounted our ponies.

All the way home during that long ride I was amused by watching the heavy posts of soldiery belonging to the other columns, who were so jealously guarding their own entrances. How angry they would have been if they had only known!... That was an extraordinary day.

7
The Few Remains

End of August, 1900.

Imperceptibly, I believe, things are settling down a little and assuming broad outlines which can be more easily understood as the days go by. Most people who went through the siege have now gone away. A few remaining missionaries and their converts have flowed far away and quartered themselves in some of the residences of the minor Manchu princes, and are now selling off what they have found by auction. They have the special permission of the Ministers and Generals to act in this way. Loot-auctions, indeed, are going on everywhere, and the few people who have managed to get through from other places in China with loads of silver dollars are making fortunes. There are enormous masses of silver *sycee* in nearly everybody's hands, and I am certain now that several of our *chefs de mission* are in clover.

My own chief, who pretends to be virtuous because he is something of a *fainéant*, to put it mildly, eyed me very severely the other day and said that everyone reported that I had developed into a species of latter-day robber-chief, and had slain hundreds of people. He said all sorts of other things, too. I let him exhaust his oratory before I replied. Then I inquired regarding the definition of the term treasure-trove, which has become the consecrated phrase for all our many hypocrites. The generals and many of his colleagues had much treasure-trove, I said; I had some, too. Of course, I admitted that if there were investigations, and everyone had to render a strict account, I would do the same; but for the time being I wanted to know that there was going to be only one law for everyone. Those were good replies, for some of the biggest people in the Legations are so mean and so bent on covering up their tracks that they are using their wives to do their dirty work.

I believe my chief thought for a moment that I knew something about an affair in which he was involved, for he only said one word, "*Bien,*" and looked at me in a strange way. I knew I had frightened him, and that he must have thought that if I chose to speak later on there would be trouble. I had no such intention, of course, only I hated being annoyed by a man of little courage. Had he been courageous I should never have answered at all, except perhaps to offer him a share of my private treasure-trove!

Yet with all this settling down it seems to me that people must be becoming suddenly more and more commercial, and that an inspection of their accounts makes them wish for a little more on the profit side. For one morning a young Englishman, who has been living in Peking rather mysteriously for a number of years, marched in on me at a very early hour, accompanied by several Chinese, whom I immediately knew from their appearance to be small officials. The Englishman said that he had a plan and a proposition, and these he unfolded so rapidly that he made me laugh. It appeared that the men he had brought with him were *ku-ping*, or Treasury Guards of the Board of Revenue under the old *régime*; and, according to their accounts, they knew exactly where the secret stores of treasure were hidden in the secret vaults of the government.

They explained that these stores belonged not only to the government, but were also portions of what peculating officials took from day to day and hid away until they could remove their plunder in safety after an inspection had been made. They said, did these informants, that there were millions in both gold and silver. They became very enthusiastic and excited as they talked.

I waited patiently to see how they proposed to solve this problem—did they wish a bold, open, frontal attack or an underground plot? Nothing is very astonishing now, and we have all the resourcefulness of *condottieri*, with a certain modern respectability added. But they were sensible people, and did not dream of the impossible. They supposed, they said, that I knew that the Russians had now full control of the Board of Revenue. Perhaps, if their commander could be approached in the proper way, the matter could be very rapidly attended to. The treasure could be seized in the name of the Russian Government and everyone could get a share. That is what they said.

At first I thought of refusing point-blank, for I was rather tired of these adventures; but the men were so persistent, and I had been so irritated by the pious insincerity of my own chief, that in the end I told them that I would see what could be done, although the matter did not interest me very much. I privately again thought of what our old doyen says, "*Ce n'est pas pour rien qu'on connaît les Russes*," and wondered how long negotiations would last.

Of course it was a wretchedly long business, and before long I regretted bitterly that I had not been more hard-hearted. I managed to communicate with L—— that same day through R——, and explained to him as well as I could the whole affair. I found the Russian commander-in-chief a sly old fox, for his first idea was to thank me for the information and have the whole Treasury searched; if necessary, to dig down to a depth of twenty feet or so with the help of a regiment or two of infantry. That was his idea. In the end we managed to convince him that this was foolish, and that there must be places which his soldiers could not reach even by prodding down with their bayonets and spades to great depths. Secret chambers cannot be easily discovered even in this way, we said. That made L—— very angry, for no reason apparently but that the affair seemed a huge bother and trouble. He said in reply that the Japanese had taken everything in any case, and that this was going to be a fool's quest if he went on with it.

Also, he would not listen to any arrangements being made and put in writing regarding the proportions to be paid to everyone if a find was actually made. Indeed, this last idea irritated him so much that he angrily said that we were deliberately plotting to take away the property of the Russian Government—property which the Russian Government could not afford to lose, and did not intend to lose, either. He even added that this was a city of robbers, and that people would not keep to their own territory, but were always trying to trespass. This made us laugh so much that he suddenly changed his manner, and said that the whole question was a serious one and would have to be referred home by telegraph. Otherwise he could not authorise any payments. K——, who was present, replied sarcastically that perhaps he would like to refer the question direct to the *Czar*, and begged him to be cautious in such a very important affair!

The last thing which could be got out of the Russian commander-in-chief was that he would telegraph at once to Alexieff at Port Arthur and ask his permission to arrange matters. If Alexieff said yes, we would go to work at once; otherwise nothing could be attempted. I knew that probably not a single word would be mentioned to any one out of Peking, and that these were mere manoeuvres. However. . . .

I had almost forgotten the matter when, a few mornings after this interview, I was suddenly awakened at daylight and told that there were several Russian officers in my courtyard who wished to speak to me at once. Their business was urgent. I went out and greeted the men, and they said that L—— would be ready at two o'clock that day to go with his staff to the Board of Revenue and effect the seizure; and that a quarter share on all amounts seized would be given by the Russian Government for the information supplied. These officers added that they would have to go back at once; but in the end they remained with me the whole morning, drinking as hard as they could, and contenting themselves with despatching a Cossack to say that all was arranged.

We started to go to the Russian headquarters at an early hour, but in some mysterious way news must have been conveyed to other people of this latest development, for half a dozen men arrived and appeared immensely surprised to find these Russian officers there with me on their horses. They asked me, each in turn, whether everything had been arranged, and how much everyone was going to get, and where the treasure was to be stored. There was, indeed, no end to their questions, and they said that they estimated that the sum seized would amount to about ten or twelve million *francs*.

Later on, each man took me aside, and explained what he had done to help the thing along, hoping that he would be remembered in the end, as this was a very big affair, and the more people in it the better. I confess I did not clearly understand all this; it was like floating a mining company. But I knew that most of these dear friends had been sitting shivering inside the Legations while the sack was going on, because they had no wish to risk their lives; and now that they thought they could safely earn an honest penny in a legitimate affair, they would stoop to anything!

We were soon such a huge cavalcade that I became nervous about the reception L—— would give us. The Russian officers, too, became more and more drunk in the open air, and kept on saying that they hoped there would be fighting, heavy fighting, for they felt just like it. A charge was what they wanted, they said. No one could find out with whom they proposed to fight, as the place we were going to was only a stone's throw away, with not a Chinaman near and a couple of strong companies of Russian infantry inside. The officers became intensely angry when everyone laughed, and said that although they were drunk, they were not like many people without stomachs about whom there had been so much talk. That was a nasty home-blow for some of them.

We found L—— ready enough; indeed, we had kept him waiting. He had most of his staff with him, and the usual escort of *cossacks* standing by their horses, making it seem very official. Of course, L—— became furious when he saw the big crowd of people, and asked whether it was going to be a picnic. This word tickled one of the drunken officers so much, that suddenly he let his loose legs relapse and clapped his spurs into his animal, which reared horribly, and in the end sent him on the ground. I thought I should die of laughter. Then everybody became more and more fussy, because they were afraid of L——, but, fortunately, the general started off ahead, muttering to himself, and we rode after him like some procession.

It seemed to me very absurd, and at that point I lost all confidence in the success of the expedition. Everyone had become too sanguine, and I fully believe that you cannot have any luck in such affairs with a crowd of idiots. Other people, who had no business to know of the affair, somehow managed to join us on the way, and when we reached the Board of Revenue we numbered dozens of men, not including the escorts.

There were about two companies of Russian infantry in occupation there, as I have already said, and in the first halls we found armed guards superintending hundreds of small Chinese boys at work stringing together copper cash. There must have been millions and hundreds of millions of these worthless coins either piled up in great mountains or scattered on the floors, and it would take months to sort them out and market them. It was the only thing the cunning Japanese had openly left!

L—— now called the officers of the guard, and explained to them that he was about to seize secret treasure which had been so well hidden by the Chinese that the Japanese had not been able to find it. He told them to give their assistance. The new officers, when they heard this, looked so sharply at one another, that everyone began to comment on it, and say that if there was nothing left they knew who was guilty. It was becoming delightful.

We started off in a body with the *ku-ping*, or treasury guards, who were giving the information, leading us. They took us past a good many huge buildings that looked like grimy old warehouses, and then stopped us short at one that appeared to be still barred and bolted. It took some time to open these doors, although the officers of the guard said that they had only been closed after they had taken over the place from the Japanese; and when we got inside it was so dark and dank that we could see nothing and could scarcely breathe. Candles had to be lighted, and as they threw feeble flickers of light across the gloom, hideous bats began flying madly about, and dashing to the ground in their fright great shreds of dusty cobwebs that must have been centuries old. Nobody minded that, however; it seemed just the sort of place where millions could really be found in these prosaic days!

The thing was now interesting, if only from a psychological point of view....

The *ku-ping* advanced, without hesitation, and brought us to a high wooden paling which shut off one half of this immense hall from the other. Inside the paling, as far as we could see, there were just mountains of empty sacks—hundreds of thousands of them, even millions, I should think.

But the paling was impassable. A small gate leading through it was still locked with a heavy Chinese padlock, and there was no key. One of the officers gave a wave of his hand, and a couple of the soldiers went out and reappeared with axes. In a few blows they had cleared a broad opening; the *ku-ping* sprang through, and, like bloodhounds that scent a trail, ran swiftly up the steep slopes of the great masses of empty bags, looking eagerly about them. Then, finally calculating aloud, they marked down a spot. They had located the exact place where they would have to begin to work.

They stripped themselves to the waist with great rapidity, and, feeling that their reputations were at stake, without any warning they were heaving away among those empty sacks like so many madmen. Faster and faster they worked, throwing away the sacks. Choking clouds of dust, now rising as if by magic, filled the whole vast hall and drove us back coughing and gasping for air, until, fairly beaten, we had to stand outside. As if through a thick vapour we could dimly see those men still working more and more rapidly. I wondered how they could breathe.....

In very few minutes, however, they also had had enough, but as they sprang down, and quickly gasping, sought the open air, they brought with them the end of a rope. They had evidently not only located the exact spot they were seeking, but had found the first trace which was necessary to make their search successful. Still, it was impossible to continue work in this way. It would take hours, at such a slow rate, to dig down beneath those mountains of old treasure-sacks.

It would take more hours to excavate or open up chambers beneath. So we held a short consultation.

There was but one thing to do. We must tear down one side of the building, so as to have more light, and to be able to put more men to work. No sooner decided on, than the thing was done, for in this work the Russians are supreme. They called in fatigue parties from the infantry companies in garrison, and telling them in simple language to break down one side of the building, in a few moments a wonderful scene began. I had seen some rapid work at short intervals during the worst agony of the siege, but never have I seen men who could handle the axe and the crowbar like these rude infantrymen. Everything went down under their blows—brickwork, woodwork, stonework, iron stanchions, everything; and with a rapidity which seemed incredible, gaping spaces appeared. Soon, standing outside, from a dozen different points, you could see the Chinese informants inside at work again, in those clouds of choking dust, thrashing up and down, like men possessed.

But energy is not sufficient for some things. Three men were attempting the work of a hundred. We must have more hands.

This time the dozens of small boys stringing cash in the outer courtyards were called in and told to fall to; and forming lines which oddly resembled those made by firemen, they were soon bundling out the empty sacks to the open at the rate of thousands a minute. Faster and faster they worked, as if the same frenzy had spread to them; wider and wider moved the rings of floating dust, until they hung high above everything and made the day seem dull and threatening. Then suddenly the *ku-ping* inside gave a shout. They had got low enough for the time being—they wanted to be able to see. The squads of sweating soldiers and the dozens of grimy little boys desisted and stood openeyed to see what was to follow. They were beginning to appreciate the significance of it all.

We waited patiently and watched the great clouds melt away and settle on our clothes and silt into our eyes; and then finally, when it was clearer, a man inside struck a match, lit a candle and handed it down into a great hole which had been dug through the very centre of these decade-old bullion coverings. How deep the hole was I could not see, but the three men slipped in and were entirely lost to our view.

They seemed a long time down there without giving a single sign or making any noise, and we all became a little nervous. Perhaps the thing was really miscarrying. Soon I felt certain that it had miscarried, and bitterly regretted taking the matter in hand. Then one man came up gruntingly and began cursing and swearing as soon as he saw us. He did that because he was afraid. I feared the worst.

On his shoulders there was one single great lump of silver and nothing else, and as he clambered out to where we stood he tilted it with a dull thud to the ground, and said sullenly that that was the only thing left, and that others had been there before us. He repeated this several times, so that there should be no mistake; there was only this enormous piece of silver and nothing else. The smile's left everybody's face. Never have I seen such a sudden change. However, to me it was *kismet*. . . .

In some trepidation we at length approached L—— and told him what had been said, and then there was another storm. He said that it was impossible—that there must be some mistake—that the men had said that the bullion was there, and there it must be. As he spoke his anger rose again, and coming up and kicking the massive silver ingot, he asked again and again in a few words of French, which I believe he had learned especially for the occasion, "*Mais où est l'or? mais où est l'or?*" It was almost pitiful to hear him repeat these words again and again like a child. He believed we were cheating him. . . .

The position had now become suddenly ridiculous, and I did not know what to do. Everyone soon took up L——'s attitude, and felt that they had been cheated by someone. Indeed, they acted as if they had lost valued possessions. They all clambered around me, and said that it was disgraceful, and that something should be done to punish the men who had brought the false information. They became so excited that it was necessary to create a diversion by going down into that hole ourselves to see exactly what it meant. That proved the last straw.

It was the dirtiest and most uncomfortable descent I have ever made. Sliding down through those piles of sacks led one to a false floor, some planks of which had been forced up by the Chinese informants. Beneath this was a short ladder, and, stepping down, one found one's self in an immense underground chamber. The air was so thick and dank here that it was almost impossible to breathe, and in the flickering light of the candles we could just see a confused mass of chests and boxes ranged round. Everyone of these had been battered open. The cunning Japanese must have been there first and taken everything. Alone that big lump of silver had been left because of its weight.

But there was something I missed. These *ku-ping* had been emphatic about the valuable weights we would find hidden—the standard weights of China in pure gold, which were centuries old, they said, and were the same as had been used during the Ming dynasty hundreds of years before. I asked for them—where were they kept? Perhaps we might at least have these.

Alas! they led me to a smaller chamber, with a curious little door formed of a single slab of stone, and pointed once again disconsolately to more rifled boxes. These outer chests covered smaller boxes, which were of the size of the weights themselves. I had always heard that the biggest weight of all was a square block of gold equal to the weight of a full-grown man. I would like to have seen that, but everything was gone. It was useless wasting any more time.

We came up again carrying some of those silk-lined boxes as explanations and souvenirs. But our friends were now all standing round some soldiers, who had accidentally knocked aside some flags of stone, and had found a deep hole underneath. They were now jerking away violently at some last obstruction, and finally they swept aside everything and bared some steep steps. As we stood wondering what had been discovered, and our hopes were almost revived, far down below appeared a grimy face, and a man at last ran up, rapidly exclaiming from surprise, as he mounted to the surface. It was one of our Chinese informants!

Then suddenly we saw the point, and in spite of our discomfiture began laughing. The soldiers of the fatigue parties, slower than us to understand, at length followed our example; then the hundreds of small Chinese boys; then everyone else, until we were all laughing. For we had been fooled and well fooled by those clever little Japanese. When they had seized the Treasury, they had not only discovered the general stores of silver, but had managed to find this hidden entrance or some other nearby. Without any trouble they had gone down and taken everything, swept the place clean, and left, probably as a supreme sarcasm, that one enormous lump of blackened silver. . . . We were indeed well sold. It was immense.

At that particular moment I do not think anyone was very bitter at this absurd anti-climax after those great expectations. That is, excepting the old general. Somehow, he became convinced by our preparations that there would be much gold found as a just reward. Now once again he accused us all of making a fool of him, of knowing from the beginning that it was a wild-goose chase. I thought sarcastically about his telegram and the desire he had had in the first place to haggle about the terms; and I let him mutter on. It is always the one who laughs last who laughs best. I made a little plan.

We retired from the Chinese Treasury with rather indecent haste. L—— did not even look at the guard which turned out as we passed the entrance. When we had entered they had hurrahed him, and hoped that his health was good, in a chorus after their custom; and he had made a little speech in return, trusting that his children were also well! It was amusing if you happened to be able to appreciate that kind of wit. Most of my companions, however, did not. And yet with the clouds of dust which had settled on us and covered us from head to food with dirt it was impossible to look even dignified with success. And all my friends, who had been so cordial and admiring in the morning, how cold and distant they had become! They had not made anything—was not that a sufficient excuse for any behaviour?

Somehow news of this expedition must have leaked out everywhere through the indiscretion of confident busybodies, until everybody knew about it, for we kept on meeting men riding across our road as if by chance, and asking what luck we had had. This made the companions I had gathered more furious than ever, and at the last moment, as we parted, I could not restrain myself. I rode up to one of the staff officers who had been the most officious and the most offensive, and begged him not to forget to remind the general that he had a duty to perform. An account must be telegraphed at once to Alexieff! That was the last word—the very last.

8

The Palsy Remains

September, 1900.

I have now ridden to every point of the compass in the city, and even beyond, and I have inspected everything with a critical eye. It is wonderful how things shape themselves. There are now some portions of the city that are reasonably peaceful even at night, and where even women can come forth and walk openly about; others that are quiet on the surface and yet throw up mad things at all hours; and lastly, there are those where riot and disorder still reign supreme. Some people estimate that half or even three quarters of the native population have fled, and that this accounts for the curious silence which now reigns, only to be broken by the noise of marauders or marching troops.

Yet I do not believe that so many of the population have really fled; many people remain half hidden in quiet spots, where, packed dozens and dozens in a single house, they tremulously await the return to happier days. The Chinese, I sometimes think, of all peoples of this earth must have their historic sense enormously developed. Thousands of years of civil wars and countless endless sieges have placed them in the dilemma of today more often than it is possible to say. Only fifty years ago the Taipings made whole provinces suffer the way Peking has now suffered. . . . Such things must live in the blood of a people and never be quite forgotten. . . .

You muse like this very often when you ride out and meet lumbering military trains going back to Tientsin, laden with countless chests of loot. What immense quantities of things have been taken! Every place of importance, indeed, has been picked as clean as a bone. Now that the road is well open, dozens of amateurs, too, from the ends of the earth have been pouring in to buy up everything they can. The armies have thus become mere bands of traders eternally selling or exchanging, comparing or pricing, transporting or shipping.

Every man of them wishes to know whether there is a fortune in a collection of old porcelain or merely a competence, and whether it is true that a long robe of Amur River sables, when the furs are perfect and undyed, fetch so many hundreds of pounds on the London market. There are official military auctions going on everywhere, where huge quantities of furs and silks and other things come under the hammer. Yet it is noticed that the very best things always disappear before they can be publicly sold. A phrase has been invented to meet the case. "*Cherchez le général*," people say.

Even with these sales the stocks never seem to sink lower. There are always fresh finds being made—seizures made officially by an officer or two with a few files of men so that there may be some reasonable excuse to offer to those who persist in remaining mulishly prudish. These new finds are, of course, called treasures-trove. They are good words. Looting has officially ceased; is, indeed, forbidden under the most severe penalties. That is why it is being systematised and made open and respectable. It is in the blood. You cannot escape it; it still follows you everywhere, no matter how far away you go.

Listen to this. I rode some days ago into the Imperial city in order to climb the famous Mei Shan, or Coal Hill, built, according to ancient tradition, so that when some immense disaster overwhelmed the ruling dynasty, it might be lighted and consume in its flames the whole Imperial family. That is the tradition—that the hill is an immense funeral pyre. (Nowadays, however, ruling dynasties are so human that they merely run away.)

All the way up that historic hill I was followed by the whining voices of disappointed looters. A battalion of the French troops, which came straight from Europe a week or so too late for the relief, was in garrison at the base of this eminence, and French soldiers escorted me to the top, probably under orders to see that I did not try and chip off the gold-leaf which is reputed to line the roofs of the pavilions. You can never be quite certain for what reason you are watched by rival nationalities now.

It was a long climb to the top, up winding steps that never ceased and through little pavilions which looked out on the scene below. A final flight of stairs at last introduced you into a structure which crowned the whole. From here the view was magnificent. Right below you could see far into the Palace and inspect the marble bridges, the lotus-covered sheets of water and all the other things of the Imperial *plaisaunce*. Farther on, the city of Peking spread out in huge expanses hemmed in only miles away by the grey tracing of the city walls and the high-standing towers. Farther again were waving fields with uncut crops rotting as they stood, because all the country people had fled to escape the vengeance. On the very horizon line were dark hills. The view was indeed immense and wonderful.

I stood lost a little in this contemplation, and forgot the attendants who had so persistently followed me, until suddenly their voices rose in a dispute which was purposely loud so that it should engage my attention. At last, as the *stratagem* had failed, and I did not turn, a soldier bolder than his comrades pushed up to me, and saluting politely enough, said that they had a few things to sell, although they had had hard luck and had found Peking almost empty. Indeed, before showing me anything, they complained bitterly of the men from Tonkin, who were no better than disciplinary battalions and who got everything because they had come with the first columns. This they called cruelly unjust. Then from their pockets and tunics these men began producing their little *articles de vertu*. They made me laugh at first, for they had systematised so much that each man's possession had a ticket attached, with the price in francs clearly marked. That was good commercialism brought straight from France.

They were, however, only the usual things—watches, rings, snuff-boxes, hair-ornaments, curios of minor value, and a few stones of bad colour. But the men crowded round me and extolled their wares like the hucksters of Europe, and beseeched me to buy in a most anxious manner. They would sell cheap, very cheap, they confessed, at the present moment, because they had just learned that an order had been issued to search all their kits and to turn over the finds to a common fund. Rumours had spread to Europe, they said—it was the first I had heard of it—of the dark things which had been going on, and the generals were becoming alarmed....

Fortunately I had with me some gold coin, and for a mere song I purchased everything. I did not want to do so, but already experience has taught us that it is best to buy when you are alone and no help nearby, otherwise your pockets may be turned out and everything taken without an excuse. That happened to a man in the German Legation.

I climbed down from the famous Coal Hill, thinking very little of the renowned view. I wondered merely when it was all going to end, and how normal conditions were going to come. I wandered, thinking in this manner, over the famous marble bridge, that delicate, delightful tracing of stone which so charmingly crosses an artificial lake thick with swaying lotus. I turned this way and that, not thinking very much where I was going; and presently, on my way back, walked past the Little Detached Palace, where, they say, the Emperor was imprisoned after the 1898 *coup d'état*.

Here there was a curious sight, which brought back my wandering attention. French and English soldiers divided the honour of guarding this palace entrance. Rival sentries stood only ten or fifteen feet away from one another and jealously watched to see that this prize was not secretly seized. The British regiment had the actual gates; it seemed that the French had posted themselves so close merely to watch. I passed these lines of sentries and wandered along, only to be accosted once more as soon as I was in a quiet alley. I soon found that this man and his mates were more cunning than those with whom I had had previously to deal and that some time must elapse before a bargain could be struck. They wasted time ascertaining who I was, and only hinted at good things—not the usual watches and rings, they said, but really things worth their weight in pure gold.

Then one man tempted me deliberately with an abrupt movement which reminded me of the way the sellers of obscene playing-cards in Paris disclose to the unsuspecting stranger their wares. He drew from his tunic a little wooden box, opened it quickly, and laid bare a most exquisite Louis XV. gold belt-buckle, set in diamonds and rubies, and beautifully painted. I, who knew a little of Manchu history, understood that belt-buckle. It must have been one of the countless presents made during the early days of the Jesuits in Peking, when they almost controlled the destinies of the Empire. It was a priceless relic.

Of course I succumbed. Such things have an international value, and were not merely the sordid pickings from deserted private dwellings. Who would not rob a fleeing Emperor of his possessions?

After this we went into the English camp unostentatiously, and by some means men came forward from nowhere, and without greeting or superfluous words showed me what they had. The English are good traders; they never waste their words; and as I looked I thought of the anguish which the patrons of the Hôtel Drouot or Christie's would have felt could they have seen this marvellous collection. For these common men had made one of such taste and value that there could be no doubt where the things had been obtained. Every piece was good and a century or two old. There were enamels and miniatures which must have lain undisturbed for countless years watching the Manchu Emperors come and go. There were beautiful stones and snuff-boxes, and many other things. There might be none of the black pearls of General Monttauban, Comte de Palikao, that had delighted the Empress Eugénie half a century ago, but there were *objets de vertu* such as duchesses love.

In the end, I, too, became commercial and arranged that some men should come and find me that same evening, bringing as much as they could carry of the spoils they had amassed. They were to be paid in gold coin or in gold bars just as I pleased, weight for weight, and a quarter in my favour. That was soon settled. In the evening the men duly came, not the few I had supposed, but so many that they filled my courtyards, yet managing to remain curiously, silent. For them an important turning-point had been reached; they would make small fortunes if the thing went through successfully. With scales in front of me and gold alongside, we weighed and calculated unendingly—weight for weight, with that one quarter in my favour.

It took two hours and more, for these common men were very careful, and everything had to be written down and recorded with strange marks and numbers, denoting the private division of profits which would afterwards follow. In the end everything was finished with and bought. Then the men stood up and shook themselves as if they had been bathed in a perspiration of anxiety, and the spokesman, a dark man with a quick tongue, which showed that he had not always been a soldier, thanked me curtly. When they had drunk, at my request, he explained to me how it was done.

There was something dramatic in the way he described. It was so simple. I recorded what he said so as not to forget. "When it's dark" he said, in a low voice, with no introduction, "there's only the picquets. They have everything to themselves excepting that the Frenchies are just alongside. The Frenchies watch us close, but we watch them closer, and there's always a way. Rounds are not kept up the whole night, for everything is slack now, and when they are finished the fun begins. The reliefs, lying on the ground, strip off everything so that they can crawl like snakes and that no one can get hold of them. They crawl in through holes, over walls, with never a match or a light to show them how. In the end they get inside." The man laughed a little hoarsely, spat, and again went on.

"The palace they call the Little Detached Palace will soon be picked clean—clean as any dog's bone, with the Frenchies only fifteen feet off, and you'll get nothing more from there. Sometimes the Frenchies suspect and want to march right in on us, but our corporals are waiting, and are ready for them, and our bayonets stop them short. Twice it's happened that their officers march a guard right up to the gates of the Little Detached, and want to stay there all night with our fellows crawling about inside. They suspected. But we bluffed them away every time, and now that all the good things are gone we are carrying away the big ones—vases, small tables, carvings, jars, bowls—everything. We wrap them up in a bundle of great-coats and feed-bags in the morning, and carry them away; no one's ever the wiser. All round the palace they are doing the same. The Yankees, the Russians, and all of them are in the same boat. All night they climb the walls to get the swag. Give them another six months and there will be nothing left."

Thus spoke the spokesman of the party. It was organised plundering, and everybody winked at it. After they had gone I sat long and reflected. This was the retribution and the vengeance. We were all tarred with the same brush; we were returning to primitive methods. Yet, what could be done—what steps could be taken? It was rather a hopeless tangle, and once more I gave it up.

9

Drifting

September, 1900.

There is not a single scrap of news worth recording, although telegrams are now coming through more and more freely by the field telegraphs from Europe. Still, no one knows what is going to happen. As an appreciation of the astute action of the Court in fleeing at the last second of the eleventh hour becomes more and more general, people begin to see how absurd we have become with our avenging armies which were going to do so much, and are now merely traders collecting and valuing and slowly taking away the best loot of the capital. The troops effected the relief, it is true; but there should have been other steps. If these are now taken it is too late. Some, indeed, say that punitive expeditions are going to be sent into the country as soon as a transport service can be organised.

Even now nests of Boxers and disbanded soldiers are reported in great numbers only a few miles beyond Peking. These men seem to understand that they are quite safe even so close as this to the European corps, and that ample warning will be conveyed to them directly there is any movement, so as to allow them to escape. They, too, are now pillaging and setting fire far and wide. Cossacks and other cavalry are supposed to be out many miles beyond Peking, sweeping the country, and blowing up or setting fire to temples and rich country-seats as a warning to others of the fate which may overtake all for harbouring evil-doers. Yet even this is done on no system. It is irresolute, foolish.

A day or two ago, from the top of the Tartar Wall, where I was idly sitting, I saw a huge pillar of smoke roll up on the horizon ten or fifteen miles away, and gradually spread farther and farther. The air was very still, for the heat can still be baking in the midday of this autumn month, and that smoke hung on the skies like some funeral pall. Into the hearts of a whole country-side it must have struck a blind terror, for the peasants still believe that they are all to die as soon as the troops move out. The panic is thus only being added to; and a sort of blind scourging of people who may not be in the least guilty can never be of use. There is also still the same palsy on everyone and everything in Peking.

No one really knows what is going to happen. No one very much cares. They say that this is being debated in Europe, and that there are divided counsels which may bring about a split and really turn the various corps now nominally allied to one another into active enemies, as I dream when I see those jealous guards at the palace entrances . . . .

Yesterday some Chinese whom I had known in the old days came stealthily to see me, and as soon as they were alone with me, without excuse or warning, they fell on their knees and began bitterly weeping. How sad, indeed, they were, these respectable people of the Chinese *bourgeoisie*—so sad that for a long time I could not persuade them to speak. Yet even as they wept they were dignified in a curious way, and you felt that you were in the presence of men who had only been cruelly wronged. At length they began speaking. They had lost everything, absolutely everything, they said, what with the Boxers and the sack, all this long, unending Reign of Terror. But that they did not mind. They were bitter and beyond consolation because they had lost the intangible—their honour. Each one had had women of their households violated. One, with many hideous details, told me how . . . soldiers came in and violated all his womankind, young and old. That account, muttered to me with trembling lips, was no invention. Their blanched and haggard faces showed that it was only the truth they were speaking. About such elemental tragedies no one lies.

I tried to comfort these poor men as best I could. I told them old sayings which had once been familiar to me; it was hard to know really what to do. Yet they at length became more philosophic, and said they understood that this was a visitation which the nation had deserved. China had been utterly wrong; it had been madness. Then they remained silent, and that silence was like a sermon straight from Heaven, both for them and for me. I saw dimly for a few seconds many things, and understood that it was useless saying more. But as they were wretchedly poor, I gave them silver from the rich men's houses, which seemed very Biblical—each man as much as he could carry—and told them that they could always come for more. I asked them also to tell all the people I had known to come, too; I would do as much as I could for all of them. So all today they have been coming, and I have showered largesse. A few households have thus some relief, but the last man who came told me that a Hanlin scholar, who was his neighbour—a learned man, who in the times of peace was courted by all—is now selling wretched little cakes down the side alleys so as to save himself and his few remaining relations from slow starvation. Such things are the dregs. It is too much. . . . .

10

Picking Up Threads

September, 1900.

I suppose in some subtle way the conviction is being gradually forced home that something must really be done to try and ameliorate the general situation. It could obviously not go on forever in this way, with the commanders of the rival columns almost fighting among themselves, and with everybody quietly looting, and our Ministers, who have lost so much, just twiddling their thumbs and delaying their departure because they are afraid of worse things happening. So somebody has been getting into communication with whoever represents the last vestiges of Chinese authority in this ruined capital, and diligent search has discovered that there are actually a few high officials left and a great number of smaller ones. These have all shown a trembling haste to oblige; and after some *pourparlers*, there is now a faint possibility of a *modus vivendi* being arranged during the next few weeks.

For it soon transpired, after the confidence of these remaining officials had been gained, that Prince Ching had been discreetly dropped by the fleeing Court only about fifty miles to the southwest of Peking—dropped just behind the first mountain barriers, so that he was at once safe and yet within easy call. He had been in waiting there for weeks, it appears. Sage old man! Those conciliatory despatches, coming from the officers of the defunct Tsung-li Yamen, have made of this old Manchu prince the natural person to bridge over the ever-widening gulf the Court has dug by its insanity. People remember now that this procedure of leaving behind a Prince to begin the first *pourparlers* is only the precedent of 1860. Then Prince Kung played exactly the same *rôle* when the Court had fled to Jehol.

Prince Ching fenced a long time before he would move forward, or even disclose his safe hiding-place; but in the end he was prevailed upon by someone. And yesterday he actually entered Peking through the same Northern Gates which witnessed the mad flight of the Court a month ago.

Many rode out to see this entry, half expecting something spectacular, which would give them a change of thought. But they were grievously disappointed. Prince Ching merely appeared in a sedan chair, looking very old and very white, and with his *cortège* closely surrounded by Japanese cavalry, whose drawn swords gave the great man the appearance of a prisoner rather than that of an envoy. Every Chinese official, large and small, in the city came out on this occasion for the first time since the troops burst in; and sitting in what carts they could find, and clothed in the remains of their official clothes, they paid their Manchu dignitary their trembling respects. What terror these wretched men exhibited until they actually met the prince, and saw that there was going to be no treachery of shooting down by ignorant soldiery!

For a whole month everyone of them had been living disguised in the most humble clothes, escaping over back walls directly news was brought that marauders were at their front doors; offering their very women up so as to escape themselves; living in all truth the most wretched lives. Hourly they had expected to be denounced by enemies to the European commanders as ex-Boxer chiefs, and then to be summarily shot. That is what had happened for miles round Monseigneur F——'s cathedral, it is being whispered. The native Catholics, having died in hundreds, and lost whole families of relatives, had revenged themselves as cruelly as only men who have been between life and death for many weeks do. They had led French soldiers into every suspected household, and pointing out the man on whom rumour had fixed some small blame, they had exacted vengeance. Even on this day of Prince Ching's entry this search and revenge was still going on; there were so many scores to pay. . . .

It was plain to me that every official was thinking of these things, for the little convoys that I watched all day wending their way to the north of the city represented petrified fear in forms that I hope I may never see again. I stopped one cart, all bedecked with flags—German flags, English flags, Russian flags, French flags, Japanese flags, every kind of flag, to help to protect from all possible injury—merely to inquire at what hour precisely Prince Ching would arrive and where he was going to live. What a result these questions had! Instantly he heard my voice, the official inside the cart crawled half out with a deathly green pallor on his face, and with his whole body trembling so violently that I thought he would collapse for good.

As it was, he remained in a sort of stricken attitude, like a man who has been stunned. He was quite speechless. I called to him several times that all was well, that he would not be hurt, to calm himself. . In vain. Every word I spoke only added to his terror and remained unintelligible because of his panic. He was a lost soul—forever. The iron had entered too deeply. He was so smitten that he never could be cured.

His outriders, who had swung themselves from their saddles, at last bowed to me. They were a little pale, but quite collected. "Excellency," they said, "forgive him; it is not his fault. He has been frightened into semi-insanity." "*Hsia hu-tu-lo,*" they said. Yes, that is the phrase, frightened into semi-lunacy. They are employing this for everyone. The tragedy has been so immense, the strain has been endured for so many months, there has been so much of it, that all minds excepting those of the common people have become a little unhinged. Half the time you speak to men you are not understood; they look at you with staring eyes, wondering whether the rifle or the bayonet is to follow the question. It is past curing for the time being.

Meanwhile Prince Ching has got in safely, and has been given a big residence, which is closely guarded by the Japanese. Perhaps the *modus vivendi* will after all be arranged.

11

The Impossible

30th September, 1900.

Prince Ching has been here a number of days now—I have not even taken the trouble to note how many—but still nothing has been done. They say that half the Powers refuse to treat with him until things are better arranged, and that the Russians have already raised insuperable difficulties because they say the Japanese have the big Manchu in their pocket. Others argue that expeditions must really be launched against a number of cities in Northern China, where hideous atrocities have been committed, and where missionaries and converts were butchered in countless numbers during the Boxer reign. Until these expeditions have marched and had their revenge, there can be no treating. There must be more killing, more blood. That is what people say.

The fleeing Court has reached Taiyuanfu, it is reliably reported. This is three hundred miles away, but the Court does not yet feel safe; it is going farther west, straight on to Hsianfu, the capital of Shensi province, which is seven hundred miles away. That is a big gulf to bridge; yet if there is any advance of European corps in that direction, already Chinese say that the Empress will flee into the terribly distant Kansu province—perhaps to Langchou, which is another four hundred miles inland; perhaps even to Kanchau or Suchau, which are five hundred miles nearer Central Asia. These cities, lying at the very southwestern extremity of the Great Wall of China, look out over the vast steppes of Mongolia, where there are nothing but Mongols belonging to many hordes, who live in the saddle and drive their flocks of sheep and their herds of ponies in front of them, forever moving. It is nearly two thousand miles in all; no European armies could ever follow, not in five years. They would slowly melt away on that long, interminable road. With such a line of retreat open the Court is absolutely safe, and knows it. It can act as it pleases.

Prince Ching is so miserably poor, they say, and has so little of the things he most needs, that he has been forced to borrow looted *sycee* from corps commanders and to give orders on the Southern Treaty ports in payment. It is an extraordinary situation.

A number of little expeditions have already been pushed out forty, fifty and even sixty miles into the country, feeling for any remnants of the Chinese armies which may remain. I went with one of these *faute-de mieux*, as Peking has become so gloomy, and there is so little to do that it fills one with an immense nostalgia to remain and continually to contemplate the ruins and devastation, from which there can be no escape.

Never shall I regret that little expedition into the rude hills and mountains, where climbs in wonderful manner the Great Wall of China. It was divine. There was a sense of freedom and of openness which no one who has not been a prisoner in a siege can ever experience. In the morning sweet-throated cavalry trumpets sounded a *réveillé*, which floated over hill and dale so chastely and calmly that one wished they might never stop. How those notes floated and trembled in the air, as grey daylight was gently stealing up, and how good the brown earth smelt! I almost forget the other kind of trumpet—that cruel Chinese trumpet which only shrieks and roars.

Each day we rode farther and farther away, and higher and higher, beating the ground and examining the villages, from which whole populations had fled, to see that no enemy was secretly lurking. Travelling in this wise, and presently climbing ever higher and higher, we came at last to little mountain burgs, with great thick outer walls and tall watch-towers, where in olden days the marauders from the Mongolian plains were held in check until help could be summoned from the country below. It was a wonderful experience to travel along unaccustomed paths and to come on endless ruined bastions and ivy-clad gates, which closed every ingress from Mongolia. Once these defences must have been of enormous strength.

One night, after journeying for a long time, we camped in one of these little mountain burgs, taking full possession, so that there should be no treachery while it was dark. The night passed quietly, for even fifty miles beyond Peking the terror lies heavy on the land, and in the morning we wandered to the massive iron-clad gates and the tall watch-towers which stood sentinel on either side to see if there was anything to be had.

How old these were, how very old! For, mounting the staircase leading to the towers, we found that, although the rude rooms beneath showed signs of having been recently occupied, the stone steps which led to the roof-chambers were covered with enormous cobwebs and great layers of dust, showing that nothing had been disturbed for very many years. That was as it should be. At the very top of one tower we discovered a locked door, and beating it in amid showers of dust, we penetrated a room such as a witch of mediaeval Europe would dearly have loved. Nothing but cobwebs, dust, flapping, grey-yellow paper and decay. It was immensely old.

And yet we found something. For there were some chests hidden away, and prizing these open, we discovered great books of yellow parchment, so old and so sodden that they fell to pieces as soon as one touched them. They were in some Mongol or Manchu script. They, too, were centuries old. But there was something else—a great discovery. Beneath the books we found helmets, inlaid with silver and gold and embellished with black velvet trappings studded with little iron knobs. There were also complete suits of chain armour.

It seemed to us in that early morning that we were suddenly discovering the Middle Ages, perhaps even the Dark Ages. For these things were not even early Manchu; they were Mongol; Mogul—the war-dress of conquerors whose bodies had been rotting in the dust for five, six, seven, eight, or even nine centuries. These relics had lain there undisturbed for all this time because China has been merely tilling the fields and neglecting everything else. In a curious mood we donned these suits and went down below clad as the conquerors of old.

There were some Indian troopers waiting, and when they saw these things they exclaimed and muttered excitedly to one another, casting half-startled looks. These were the same trappings and war-dresses as in the days of the Great Moguls at Delhi. The very same. The conquerors who had swept across high Asia had worn such things, and every man from Northern India must have understood their meaning and message.

As they looked the Indian troopers chattered and talked to one another in a growing excitement. It seemed as if we had suddenly dug up some links of the half-forgotten past which showed how the chain of armed men had been tightly bound by Genghis Khan and Batu Khan, and all the other great Khans, from the Great Wall of China all round Northern and Central Asia, until it had reached down over the

Himalayas into India. It was very curious.

When we had finished this reconnaissance, which carried us in every direction under the shadow of the Great Wall, we turned bridle and made back towards Peking by another route. A day's march away from the capital, word was brought us that there were still numbers of disbanded soldiery and suspected Boxers hiding in the Nan-Hai-tsu—a great Imperial Hunting Park, which had fallen into decay during the present century. We would have to sweep this park, which was dozens of miles broad and quite wild, and scatter any bands we might find. So starting after midnight, we marched hard in the gloom for several hours with native guides leading us, and daylight found us under the encircling wall of the ancient hunting-ground. We halted there a bit and refreshed ourselves quickly, and then galloped in through a breach.

There were miles upon miles of beautiful grass stretches, and we and our mounts were fairly pumped before we saw or heard anything. But towards midday we came on some tiny hills and a few low buildings, which seemed suspicious, and no sooner had we approached than a whole nest of men rushed out on us, firing and shouting as they ran. Some had only huge lances made of bamboo, fifteen feet and more long, and tipped with iron and with little red pennons fluttering; yet these were the most effective of all. Waving these lances violently, and holding them in such a manner that it was impossible to get near, these men scattered our charge before it got home and unhorsed a number of troopers. Then it became a general *mêlée*, which ended in the killing or capture of a few of the enemy and the rapid escape of the remainder.

Very late in the evening we rode into Peking with our helmets and our coats of mail and our long lances as trophies. The capital seemed terribly listless and oppressed after the country beyond, and I was bitterly sorry that expedition had not lasted for weeks and months.

12

Suspense

October, 1900.

Another month has come and there has been practically no change. They say now Prince Ching has no power to treat, and that he is a mere Japanese prisoner. Li Hung Chang is in Tientsin, too, it appears. He is to be the other plenipotentiary when negotiations really commence, but for the time being he is the Russian captive. The Russians have him surrounded with their troops, and no one but a favoured few may even see him.

Already there has been trouble with the British on this score at Tientsin, and some people say that some pretext will be seized to bring about an international crisis among the expeditionary corps. They are fighting about the destroyed railway up to Peking already. Various people are claiming the right to rebuild the line, and refuse to give up the sections they have garrisoned. Everywhere there are pretty complications in the air.

Meanwhile, in Peking itself things have become more and more quiet, and as the policing is slowly improving, confidence is a little restored. But still new troops are being marched in all the time—notably German troops—and as soon as night closes down all these men fall to looting and outraging in any way they can. They say that the Kaiser, in his farewell speech to his first contingent, before Peking had been heard of for weeks, told the men to act in this way. They are strictly obeying orders.

Even the officers of the new troops take a hand in this looting in a modified way. They force their way into the remains of the curio shops, take the few pieces which are left, place a dollar or so on the counter and then walk out. This makes a legitimate purchase.

In the Japanese district, which is now the best policed and the most tranquil, shops are being reopened, but are now being panic-stricken by this new procedure. It is the refinement of the game, and there is no redress possible. Beyond this I know not of a thing worth the mentioning.

13

Still Drifting

October, 1900.

There is, after all, to be no immediate peace—that seems now quite certain. We hear that the Russians have invaded all Manchuria and are strengthening their hold there by bringing in more and more troops from the Amur districts. They say, too, that the French have crossed the Tonkin frontier. But really accurately we know nothing very much of what is being done. With sixty or seventy thousand soldiery suddenly flung down on the ruined stretch of country between Peking and the sea, everything has been put in the most horrible confusion.

You can get nothing, nor hear anything. Telegrams are the only things which are coming through with any regularity, and even these are cut to pieces by the field telegraphs or continually getting lost. The mails, it is true, have at last arrived, but they are all mixed in such a way, and there is such old correspondence heaped on top of the new, that general instructions and the proposals made read in this way seem to be the ravings of madmen. There are hundreds of despatches of April, May and June, showing the calibre of some Foreign Offices in an unmistakable way. I sometimes wonder if only the fools are left in the home offices.

Still, after a good many headaches, one can begin to appreciate the general plan which was finally settled on by the various *Chancelleries*, and to understand what delayed the relief so much. Most of all it has been the South African war. Also, is seems to me, they wanted Waldersee, the German field marshal, to have time to take over the supreme command for the sake of peace in Asia, and so that there should be an enormous massed advance on Peking, which would capture all North China to Christendom and enslave the cunning old Empress Dowager, and do everything as arranged in Europe. It was, above all, necessary not to cause an imbroglio in Europe.

Of course, the very opposite has happened, and everybody is now as discontented and jealous as before the siege. Waldersee is in Tientsin and has been there for weeks for some new decision to be made. The grand advance is finished and done with, but now some column commanders wish to push down into the south of the province and isolate the Court, if possible. Meetings are being held the whole time, but as Waldersee is coming up, nothing is to be done until his arrival. By one ingenious stroke—the sudden flight of the Court—the Chinese have turned the tables on allied Europe and made us all ridiculous. Any one might have anticipated something of this—there is a precedent in the histories. Yet history is only made to be immediately forgotten.

14

Punitive Expeditions

October, 1900.

At length Waldersee has arrived. He made a sort of entry which seemed to me farcical. I only noticed that he was very old, and that the hats that have been served out to the special German expeditionary corps are absurd. They are made of straw and are shaped after the manner of the Colonial hats used in South Africa. They have also a cockade of the German colours sewn to the turned-up edge. This must be some Berlin tailor's idea of an appropriate head-dress for a summer and autumn campaign in the East. The hat is quite useless, and had it been a month earlier all the men would certainly have died of sunstroke.

Of course, now with Waldersee in Peking, something more has to be done, and the rumour is today that the Court has begun fleeing yet farther to the West. The rulers of China are being kept accurately informed of every move by someone, and any indication of a pursuit will see them penetrate farther and farther towards the vast regions of Central Asia. It seems to me that it would be almost amusing (would not the consequences be so tragic) to begin this pursuit and really to attempt to push the Court so far away that it finally lost touch with all the rest of China. Then something beneficial to everyone might come.

An ultimatum, to which attention would be paid, might be served, and guarantees exacted which would do service for a number of years. At present the flight has done no harm whatever to China. The Court is not even ridiculous in the eyes of the populace. It is merely terribly unfortunate—a really luckless Court, which deserves to be commiserated with and wept over rather than upbraided. For it is plain to everyone that the first and last reason for all this is the foreigner and no one else. Everything the foreigner does is always a source of trouble.

Even the machinery of government has not been disturbed by the fact that vast Peking, the vaunted capital, is in the hands of ruthless invaders. At first everyone thought that with the palace empty, and all the great Boards and offices made mere camping-places for thousands of hostile soldiery, the government of the whole empire would be paralysed—sterilised. Yet that has not happened. The government goes on much the same as ever. We know that now. For as the Court flees it issues edicts, receives reports and accounts, is met with tribute from provincial governors and viceroys, is clothed and banqueted, makes fresh appointments, does its day's work while it runs.

I cannot understand, therefore, how this is to end. It is beyond the keenest intellects in Peking, and people are now simply waiting for things to happen and to accept facts as they may be dealt out by the Fates. It is an inevitable policy. For you must always accept facts when you cannot mould them.

15

The Climax

October, 1900.

I am becoming tired of it all once again—inexpressibly tired. It seems to me at times now as if those of us who remain had been very sick, and then, when we had become convalescent, had been ordered by some cruel fate to remain sitting in our sick-rooms forever. A siege is always a hospital—a hospital where mad thoughts abound and where mad things are done; where, under the stimulus of an unnatural excitement, new beings are evolved, beings who, while having the outward shape of their former selves, and, indeed, most of the old outward characteristics, are yet reborn in some subtle way and are no longer the same.

For you can never be exactly the same; about that there is no doubt. You have been made sick, as it were, by tasting a dangerous poison. Great soldiers have often told their men after great battles have been fought and great wars won that they have tasted the salt of life. The salt of life! Is it true, or is it merely a mistake, such as life-loving man most naturally makes? For it can be nothing but the salt of death which has lain for a brief instant on the tongue of every soldier—a revolting salt which the soldier refuses to swallow and only is compelled to with strange cries and demon-like mutterings. Sometimes, poor mortal, all his struggles and his oaths are in vain. The dread salt is forced down his throat and he dies. The very fortunate have only an acrid taste which defies analysis left them.

Of these more fortunate there are, however, many classes. Some, because they are neurotic or have some hereditary taint, the existence of which they have never suspected, in the end succumb; others do not entirely succumb, but carry traces to their graves; yet others do not appear to mind at all. It is a very subtle poison, which may lie hidden in the blood for many months and many years. I believe it is a terrible thing.

Nobody should have been allowed to stay behind after hearing for so many weeks that ceaseless roar, sustaining that endless strain, enduring so much. They should have been made to forget—by force.

And yet even this nobody understands or cares to speak of, although a number of men are still half mad. The newcomers, soldiers and civilians alike, who never cease streaming in now to gaze and gape and inquire how it was all done, are quite indifferent. Some say that it must have been an immense farce—that there was really nothing worth speaking about. Others wish to know curious details which have no general importance. The Englishmen are proud, and want to know whether you were inside the British Legation, their Legation, and when they have heard yes or no their interest ceases. They little know what the Legation stood for. The Americans march up to the Tartar Wall, talk about "Uncle Sam's boys," and exclaim that it requires no guessing to tell who saved the Legations. The French are the same, so are the Germans, so even the Italians. Only the Japanese and the Russians say nothing.

At first I was at some pains to explain to each separate man what really occurred. I pulled out my rough map, all thumb-marked and dirtied with brick chips and the soil of the trenches, and showed stage by stage how the drama unrolled. It was no good. Poor me! nobody quite understood. Some thought possibly that I was a glib liar; others did not even trouble to think anything. How much they understood! They had not the background, the atmosphere, the long weeks which were necessary to teach even us ourselves. They had not tasted the poison and did not yet suspect its existence. So I gradually desisted. Now I say nothing, never a word. I listen and understand how history is made. It is best never to explain or argue if you thoroughly understand. Rhetoric is only the amplification of something long understood in one's heart of hearts.

I am, therefore, tired of it all, inexpressibly tired. I wish to escape from my hospital, to go away to some clean land where they understand so little of such things that their indifference will in the end, perhaps, convince me and make me forget.

Yet can one ever forget?

16

The End

November, 1900.

Another month, and I have made up my mind quite suddenly. I have finished with it—at least, in outward form. After waiting a couple of weeks and wondering what I should do, a last argument brought it about—an argument with a German which ended by enraging me to an impossible point and making me challenge him to anything he liked. That showed me that my last safe moment had arrived.

He was a youngish officer sent from the field-marshal's staff to discuss some diplomatic-military details with my chief. The business part was soon over, for there was really little to decide, and then the man fell to talking about what should be done. He said that were there not so much rivalry and jealousy, and could Waldersee only act as he wished, they would have proper punitive expeditions which would shoot all the headmen of every village for hundreds of miles, and make such an example of everybody that the memory would endure for generations in every district where there had been Boxers. The officer was eloquent because he had only just arrived, and understood nothing—absolutely nothing. For some reason our stars crossed and I hated him immediately. So I waited until he had finished so that I could begin. Then I began.

I cannot even remember all I said, for I was greatly enraged by the brutality of the man's ideas, but I treated him as he had never been treated before. As I poured out my lava stream and he slowly understood what I meant, he first became very red, and then very pale, and finally he stood up. I took advantage of that action, and since we all still are armed, I told him he could have satisfaction, at once if he wished, and at any number of paces he chose to name.

My chief then suddenly intervened, and, trembling violently, said that it could not go on—that it was a mistake. He took the blame on his shoulders, he said, and would apologise himself later on. For many minutes he harangued, and in the end the officer went away with his eyes glittering, but not too reluctantly. He knew that I could have killed him with my second chamber unless his first shot hit my vitals.

After that there was a second scene—but one which was much more brief. My chief attempted to deal with me, and to him I spoke my mind. I am afraid I said many things which were so brusque that modern society would have reproved me. I told him that it was well known that he and every other man of position had been tremulously fearing death at every turn for weeks, and had been unwilling to do anything when they might have really saved the situation; merely because they were so afraid; that everything had been misstated in the reports, and that although the full truth might not be known for years, eventually it would be known and people would understand.

I said that this petty life created by men without stomachs had ended by disgusting me, and that I had finished with it for good and forever. Then I went out in silence, slamming the door behind me with all the strength of my arms. It was a most enormous slam. It had to be so; it was my last word. In my commandeered residence I found that the breath of misfortune had also come. The rightful owners had managed to steal into Peking in the train of some big official who had had an escort of foreign soldiery provided him, and now smilingly and cringingly greeted me, and thanked me for my guardianship during their unavoidable absence. The Manchu women were grouped round in great excitement. They did not relish the change—they did not want it. The tall and stately one who had first touched my knee on that dark night during the sack was not there.

The rightful owners irritated me intensely with their obsequiousness. I was irritated because they lived: they should have ceased to exist long ago. They were still very much afraid, although they had reached Peking in safety, for they half thought that I would hand them over to some provost-marshal as Boxer partisans in order to get rid of them. They were very afraid. The Manchu women were all talking and praising me, and telling wonderful stories of all I had done. But the most important one of them was absent. I became vaguely conscious that this also meant something, that perhaps there was to be another tragedy. I found her later wishing to kill herself, to commit suicide, so that she, too, need never return to her other life.... That was more terrible than the other scenes. I could do nothing, yet my responsibility had been great. In the end something was arranged. I hardly remember what.

I was soon ready to go; on the same afternoon I had completed all my preparations. I had so little to prepare. Then I rode out for the last time with all my men behind me, and not a single other person. We passed down the streets out from the Tartar City, through the ruins of the great Ch'ien Men Gate, and then followed straight along the vast main street, still covered with *débris* and dirt, and skulls and broken weapons, as if the weeks and months which had gone by since the fighting had been quite unheeded. Near the outer gates of the city I met my three cavalrymen of the Indian regiment waiting to bid goodbye. They joined me with some attempt at gaiety, but that soon fizzled out. I had so plainly collapsed.

We passed into the country with the tall crops still rotting as they stood, because everyone had fled and no one dared to return. We went on faster and faster as the roads broadened, and as we galloped we met new troops marching in on Peking. They were Germans driving captives of many kinds in front of them. "Damned Germans," said the smaller officer, who was the senior, and who had been quite silent for some time. "Damned Germans," repeated the two others mechanically, as if this was a new creed, and I, approving, faintly smiled. That stirred them to talk again, and they told me that the expeditions had been settled on, and that they would have to go, too. Orders had come from home that they must not fall out with Waldersee.

It was highly important to placate the Germans because of South Africa. But the Americans would not go, neither would the Russians, nor yet the Japanese. It was to be a new arrangement. They went on talking in this wise for a long time, and I heard these scraps of conversation vaguely as in a dream. Cynically I thought that, although I was leaving it all behind me in company of men who were strangers to Peking, the last words would still be concerned with our tortuous diplomacy. Yet my gallant friends were only trying to console me—to make me forget. Such things they understood far better than others. They were from India, where men think a good deal, and sometimes act. They were treating me as best they could.

Then when we came to a sharp rise over which the road curled and crawled, they halted suddenly, stretched out their hands, and bade me goodbye. They meant it to be a sharp wrench—to be over quickly. Just on the rim of the horizon stretched the grey of the fading Tartar Walls with their high-pitched towers. The sun sinking behind the western hills threw some last flames of golden fire, but the air remained chill. It was becoming cold, and even the dust no longer rose in clouds. Everything was pinned to the soil—tired—finished....

I rode on abruptly. Then, for the last time, my cavalrymen turned round and shouted faintly back to me. It was a word which carried well. "*Chubb, Chubb, Chubb,*" they were shouting, to give my thoughts a turn. They knew what I must be thinking. They knew; they had been in India. I quickened my horse into a gallop, rode faster and faster, and before night had fallen I had gained the river-boats. It was over....

ALSO FROM LEONAUR
AVAILABLE IN SOFTCOVER OR HARDCOVER WITH DUST JACKET

THE 9TH—THE KING'S (LIVERPOOL REGIMENT) IN THE GREAT WAR 1914 - 1918 *by Enos H. G. Roberts*—Mersey to mud—war and Liverpool men.

THE GAMBARDIER *by Mark Severn*—The experiences of a battery of Heavy artillery on the Western Front during the First World War.

FROM MESSINES TO THIRD YPRES *by Thomas Floyd*—A personal account of the First World War on the Western front by a 2/5th Lancashire Fusilier.

THE IRISH GUARDS IN THE GREAT WAR - VOLUME 1 *by Rudyard Kipling*—Edited and Compiled from Their Diaries and Papers—The First Battalion.

THE IRISH GUARDS IN THE GREAT WAR - VOLUME 1 *by Rudyard Kipling*—Edited and Compiled from Their Diaries and Papers—The Second Battalion.

ARMOURED CARS IN EDEN *by K. Roosevelt*—An American President's son serving in Rolls Royce armoured cars with the British in Mesopatamia & with the American Artillery in France during the First World War.

CHASSEUR OF 1914 *by Marcel Dupont*—Experiences of the twilight of the French Light Cavalry by a young officer during the early battles of the great war in Europe.

TROOP HORSE & TRENCH *by R.A. Lloyd*—The experiences of a British Lifeguardsman of the household cavalry fighting on the western front during the First World War 1914-18.

THE EAST AFRICAN MOUNTED RIFLES *by C.J. Wilson*—Experiences of the campaign in the East African bush during the First World War.

THE LONG PATROL *by George Berrie*—A Novel of Light Horsemen from Gallipoli to the Palestine campaign of the First World War.

THE FIGHTING CAMELIERS *by Frank Reid*—The exploits of the Imperial Camel Corps in the desert and Palestine campaigns of the First World War.

STEEL CHARIOTS IN THE DESERT *by S. C. Rolls*—The first world war experiences of a Rolls Royce armoured car driver with the Duke of Westminster in Libya and in Arabia with T.E. Lawrence.

WITH THE IMPERIAL CAMEL CORPS IN THE GREAT WAR *by Geoffrey Inchbald*—The story of a serving officer with the British 2nd battalion against the Senussi and during the Palestine campaign.

AVAILABLE ONLINE AT **www.leonaur.com**
AND FROM ALL GOOD BOOK STORES

www.ingramcontent.com/pod-product-compliance
Lightning Source LLC
Chambersburg PA
CBHW030229170426
43201CB00006B/158